Alabama
Canoe Rides and
Float Trips

Alabama
Canoe Rides and
Float Trips

*A Detailed Guide to the Cahaba and Other Creeks
and Rivers of Alabama Plus Put-Ins, Take-Outs, and
General Information about Numerous Other Streams of
the State.*

John H. Foshee

A Strode Book

Published by

The University of Alabama Press
Tuscaloosa

Published in 1986 by
The University of Alabama Press
Tuscaloosa, Alabama 35487–0380

Library of Congress Cataloging-in-Publication Data

Foshee, John H.
  Alabama canoe rides and float trips.

  ''A Strode book.''
  1. Canoes and canoeing—Alabama—Guide-books.
2. Rivers—Alabama.   3. Alabama—Descriptions and travel—
1981   —Guide-books. I. Title.
GV776.A2F67   1986   917.61   86-19192
ISBN 0-8173-0334-0   (alk. paper)

Contents

Foreword   7
Introduction   9
Some General Comments on Alabama Streams   11
How to Use This Book   12

PART ONE: THE FLOATER

Safety   17
Equipment   23
Camping, Permissions, and Litter, Transporting Your Boat   30
Winter Canoeing   35
Rivers and Lakes—The Big Difference   41
Books to Read and Study   45

PART TWO: THE RIVERS

About the Maps and Symbols   49
The Cahaba River   55
Little Cahaba River (Purdy)   103
Little Cahaba River   104
Six-Mile Creek   112

The Locust Fork of the Warrior   117
Blackburn Fork   137
The Mulberry Fork of the Warrior   146
West Fork of Sipsey   153
Blackwater Creek   159
Tallapoosa River   168
Hatchet and Weogufka Creeks   183
Little River   195

PART THREE: APPENDIX

But John—What Happened to the Rest of the Rivers?   206
A Small Explanation of the Appendix   207
Explanation of River Charts   208
West Fork of the Choctawhatchee River   211
East Fork of the Choctawhatchee River   213
Choctawhatchee River   214
Big Creek   218
Whitewater Creek   219
Pea River   221
Conecuh River   230
Patsuliga Creek   242
Sepulga River   245
Big Escambia Creek   248
Perdido River   251
Styx River   253
Yellow River   255
Little River   257
Escatawpa River   259
Why I Didn't Include Some Rivers!   261
Fishing   262

Foreword

Eleven years have passed since the first edition of this book was published. In that time there have been great strides forward in the development and availability of boats and equipment, a tremendous increase in both the popularity of canoeing and, logically enough, the use of the state's canoeing waterways. The rivers, however, have remained essentially the same and, as a result, so has this book.

I said "essentially" for there have been some changes here and there. South of Birmingham, for example, a new freeway bypass and general expansion and development have resulted in some new bridges and some construction on the river bank. Most of this occurs in my Section 4 of the Cahaba. You're paddling through more yards now, but the river itself still winds along in its same old course. Farther down the Cahaba, the take-out for Section 11 is no longer at the bar just below the County 27 bridge, but at the bridge itself—steeper and rougher—but not on private property as is the access to the bar.

The Little Cahaba River—the one near Montevallo—has a few changes. Parking is no longer allowed at the Cahaba Valley Church put-in (the beginning of Section 1) and you can't go ashore at the Mile 3 Fall on this river without trespassing—so—don't go ashore there or just upstream or just downstream from it.

The often-used Six-Mile Creek take-out on the Little Cahaba (Section 2) is also now barred from public use because it is now private property. This, of course, also proscribes it as a take-out for the Six-Mile Creek Run described in the book, so you'll have to paddle on down to the Cahaba River take-out for Section 11—a long total trip.

On Six-Mile Creek itself, the "Sinks" are still there but not in their former glory. Apparently some internal collapse took place—some water still flows through the hill but most of it now flows back in its normal bed—at least at "normal" water levels.

The Locust Fork (Sections 3 and 4) and the Mulberry Fork (Section 2) have evolved in the last few years into favorite white water runs, heavily used in seasons of "good" water. As a result of this popularity, many of the rapids now have more distinct and colorful names than "R" and "S."

Farther south, the long-delayed dam on Section 2 of the Tallapoosa has been completed so the part of the run described in Section 1 and the first two miles of Section 2 are now under a lake.

Not too far away, there is a good run on Hatchet Creek—upstream of my Section 1 and ending at my Section 1 put-in. When this book was first published that section was inaccessible so wasn't included. Thanks to a new highway below Sylacauga, there's now a convenient, public-access bridge for these miles of river.

Water level indications? Don't ask! They're long obliterated—at least mine are—so use your judgment or ask someone who recently went down wherever it is you intend to go. You will find some "official" gauges on more of the rivers now—at least until they're washed away or vanish from other causes. It could be a lifetime job just painting on water levels!

Those are the major changes I know of *on* the rivers. Were we actually *redoing* this book as opposed to simply *reprinting* it, I would make some changes over in the front too. For example, there is a much better system of water and paddler classification now available, although the one shown in the book is also still in use. For paddles I now recommend the Mohawk Paddle as the best-for-the-money beginning paddle. Mad River, Perception, Illiad, and a host of others surpass the Old Town and Grumman paddles—at least in my estimation. Finally, canoes of ABS foam core construction are *the* material now (and have been for a number of years), so I would like to replace a lot of the photos that have aluminum canoes in them with photos of boats made from these newer materials, but again, we're *reprinting* not *redoing*. Other than that I can't think of much else I would change.

However, be reassured that the accuracy of the river maps and descriptions in this reprint are still close to 100%. Should you not find it so—well—write and let me know where the error lurks. After all, we may *redo* one day—who knows?

Until then, enjoy the rivers and do what *you* can to see they change as little in the coming years as they have in the past ones. *And, of course— happy floating!*

Introduction

Most of the trips in this book could fall under what are generally called "float" trips—the progressing from one place on a river to another by river current or with very leisurely paddling. This leisurely floating is only possible in times of "normal" water, however. In Alabama the summer's usually low water levels frequently force the leisurely paddling to become more energetic and to be aided by some wading, shoving, lifting, and dragging. Then, too, I have included a few "whitewater" trips where, again with good water levels, the exertion required quickly obliterates the "easy" aspects of the trip.

Strictly speaking then, a more apt title for this book might have been "A Hodgepodge of Miscellaneous Paddle Boat Trips," but that didn't sound as nice. So let's compromise and say that these trips are on small or relatively small streams, on the upper portions of rivers or stretches that are generally free of power boat traffic of any size, or on small or shallow or obstructed creeks and waterways where the paddle boater can enjoy peace and quiet and the chance to be pretty much as alone as he wishes, but for which benefits he will have to put forth a little effort here and possibly a little more there!

Obviously there is a lot of water in the State that's missing in this book. Some rivers are just too big to enjoy in a paddle boat. Some have too much commercial or private power boat traffic. Some are so dirty or so populated along their shores or so full of dams that their inclusion would have been a waste of effort to the person likely to read this. But even these remnants of waterways sometimes have parts that could be enjoyable to the floater, and a few of them are included too. Then, too, there are a lot of interesting streams in the state that I just haven't covered so if I've left out your favorite, forgive me, or better yet, write me and tell me about it, and I'll try to add it in the future.

The selection of floats was mostly personal taste. I've been on every ride described here except those in the appendix. Some of them appealed to me, and some didn't, and, as everyone looks for something different on their trips, I'm sure the selection will strike you the same way. I don't expect everybody to like all of them. If everybody did, we would all find ourselves on the same river at once!

And—I've probably made a mistake here and there. I have been known to do that. I'd appreciate it if you'd let me know when you find one (or two or three).

The book is written from a canoeist's viewpoint, but it's not just for canoe or kayak or foldboat, although these will prove to be the most practical on many of the rides. Rafts or inner tubes can be used very successfully on some and "john" boats or pirogues or similar type boats, on others, although there are a few on which these boats may be more of a hazard than a help.

This is not an instruction book on canoeing or any other kind of boating. It's just a guide to places to go with some practical pointers tossed in to help you enjoy a safe trip and perhaps avoid some of the mistakes many novice floaters seem to fall heir to.

Finally, upon advice of counsel, I hereby state that I accept no responsibility for any loss of equipment or injury or death to anyone making the trips described in this book. Kind of grim, isn't it?

SOME GENERAL COMMENTS ON ALABAMA STREAMS

Alabama is abundantly blessed with water. Within its boundaries are four river systems that are so prominent that almost every stream and creek in the State ultimately flows into one of them. The only major exception to this is the southeast one-fifth of the State which drains into the Gulf. Across the north of the State flows the Tennessee, and across the south central parts is the Alabama. On the west and upper central parts is the Warrior with its three big tributaries, and on the east is the Coosa-Tallapoosa system. Draining the center of this "box" of water is the Cahaba.

Despite the propensity of various businesses, utilities, and individuals to make "recreational" impoundments and pools out of the State's streams, creeks, and rivers, many sections of these rivers, their tributaries or feeder streams are still natural appearing and open to use by the individual who wants more for his time than the broad expanses of lakes, the roar of a motor, and the dodging of water skiers.

In Alabama you can find just about any kind of water you care to float. The State has cold, tumbling mountain streams and warm, flat, peaceful, slow moving, pastoral creeks. You can enjoy the thrill of superlative whitewater or the different beauty of a semitropical float. Alabama has big streams and tiny ones, many of which are still relatively free-flowing. There is an enjoyable, floatable stream within a short distance of almost everyone. In fact, many of these close-to-home floats are excellent choices quite apart from any other consideration, because they can be enjoyed when you only have a few hours to spare.

Some of the best streams are passed by or driven across everyday; some of the most beautiful stretches are spanned by bridges, and access is usually no problem at all. For the history buff—Alabama's early development, like that of many states, was centered on its rivers and streams, and some of them remain almost as they were in the early days of the State's history.

Unfortunately there is a dark side to this story too. Alabama has only one official canoe trail, and I have already mentioned the tendency to dam every piece of water that moves. There is also a serious problem with pollution due to inadequate and weak water pollution control laws. As a result, poorly treated sewage is often dumped into our streams, and strip mines and industrial spillage frequently cause fish kills and destroy vegetation. As an adjunct to this, the strip mines are allowed to encroach on the river's banks and often even push spoil into the river itself, thereby destroying the beauty of the river. Almost as bad, to my way of thinking, is the sharply increasing trend to *build* directly on river banks. A simple 100 yard or even 50 yard buffer zone of natural growth would help here, but these buffer zones are nonexistent. To me, there is little pleasure, beauty, or sense of isolation in floating through a shopping center or apartment complex.

Alabama's contribution to and encouragement of the Scenic and Wild Rivers Act is negligible. As a result, each passing day finds another section of river built up, contaminated, or dammed.

Alabama has much to offer the floater now, but it's going fast. The destruction of our streams can only be halted by legislation, and the legislators only prompted to action by the people. *You* are reading this book, so you must be interested— won't you help do something about it?

A little pre-run training.

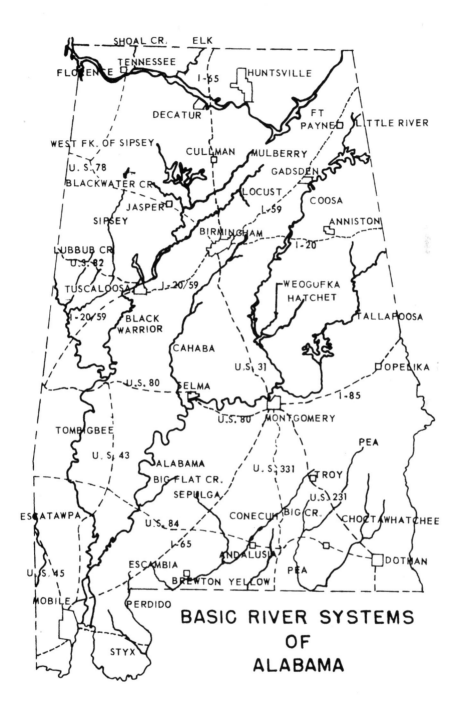

BASIC RIVER SYSTEMS
OF
ALABAMA

HOW TO USE THIS BOOK

This book is divided into three parts. Part I, as you can see by a glance at the contents page, covers general paddle boating practices, recommendations on equipment, suggestions for safety, and various random tips and hints to help make your float trips more enjoyable.

Part II covers actual trips—52 of them—enough for one a week for a year. This section is divided into groups of short trips on a particular river. Most of these trips can easily be made in one day, although there are some that take less than a day and a few that will push you to cover in one day. On each river group the trips start up the river and work progressively down it. Any canoeable streams entering this river will be found at the end of the section. Where necessary I have added maps to aid you in finding an area.

Although a good road map and the detail map on the streams should provide enough information between them to guide you unerringly to your chosen stretch of water, remember that roads do change. You might have to resort to a small amount of assistance from topo, county, or state road maps, or possibly a little judicious inquiring in the vicinity of the river.

Part III is an appendix containing brief descriptions of rides and their put-ins and take-outs. It follows the general format of Part II but omits the maps.

The maps of the streams show falls, shoals, and drops and other obstructions, hazards, or places of interest (for one reason or another) to the canoeist. Bear in mind that water level determines the presence of these items—the shoals may disappear completely in higher water, and the falls and rapids get more hazardous. Most of these maps were made in seasons of low water for the simple reason that the shoals showed then—although you can usually spot them in higher water by the surface turbulence. Do be sure that they *are* there, however. As a canoeist I know how disconcerting it is to be assured that there is nothing but clear floating for the next 3 mile stretch—then wade and tow your canoe the whole distance!

PART ONE
The Floater

A valuable and enlightening (though slim) section of tips, general information, and various esoteric things to smooth the waters on which you may paddle.

Rest stop on one of our southern rivers.

CHAPTER 1
SAFETY

The whole idea of a recreational float down a river is just that—recreation. You're out to enjoy yourself, but you won't enjoy the loss of equipment, damage (or loss) of boat, and hazard to life that could result from ignoring the basic aspects of safety on the river.

Safety covers a wide field—from technical skill in handling your boat—to proper clothing for the weather—to not being overconfident of your ability. It's impossible to cover every little thing that might happen, and if a floater *did* go prepared for, and fearful of, every eventuality, he wouldn't have much fun. *But* there are fundamental rules that will help to ensure that your fun day won't end in tragedy, and these rules should be observed. In the following pages are a few discussions of some of the safety measures and sometimes overlooked hazards that you should know about—and better yet, believe in.

PERSONAL FLOTATION

ALWAYS CARRY A LIFE JACKET—one for every person in the boat. You may not wear it in a shallow creek in the summer, but it's there if you think you need it, and if you do need it, it doesn't do you much good stuffed under a seat at the other end of the boat, so keep it handy. Remember that you can fall out or be thrown out of your boat and be knocked unconscious, so put the jacket *on* if you have the faintest idea that you might need it. *Always wear* it if you're not a good swimmer.

Here are the various personal flotation devices as rated by the Coast Guard:

TYPE I—Has more than 20 pounds of buoyancy and will turn an unconscious wearer face up in the water (jacket).

Type II—Same as Type I except a minimum of 15.5 pounds of buoyancy (jacket or "horsecollar" type).

Type III—Same as II except will *not* turn an unconscious wearer face up in the water.

Type IV—These are throwable flotation devices. Now the only use that I can think of for a ski-belt is as a pillow if

17

you're camping. Seat cushions can be used for pillows or to sit on at lunch. As life-safety devices, neither of them has the slightest use at all for the person likely to read this book. Life jackets of type I or II are the only type of flotation device worthy of mention to the canoeist or kayaker.

BOAT FLOTATION

Although the average floater probably will never need it, the occasion may arise when he thinks of adding more flotation to his boat. Large inner tubes wedged under thwarts or seats are good. The tighter they're inflated, the more likely they are to be punctured, so use some judgment here. Foam blocks are also good but a little harder to attach securely. In a decked boat you can use factory-made airbags such as those used in kayaks. Even rubber balls stuffed under a deck will work if you use enough of them. Whatever you elect to use, be sure it's in firmly—extra flotation is only useful to you if it's floating your boat. It doesn't help much floating down the river by itself.

EQUIPMENT SAFETY

First refer to the section on waterproofing items that can be damaged by water. Remember that waterproofing alone is not enough for an item such as a camera that is likely to be damaged by impact. Pad your ammo boxes or whatever you use to carry relatively fragile equipment.

Tie everything in the boat. Use a strong cord and a bow knot at the boat end for things you won't be needing in a hurry. Leave enough slack to get to the item. This way a spill or a swamping may *float* everything in the boat, but unless the cord breaks, the equipment won't float off downstream by itself to be lost.

Oh yes—if you wear glasses, secure them to your head some way. As nails or screws are hard on the skull, I suggest either the elastic type of holder sold for athletic use or drilling a hole in the earpieces of your glasses for a string that ties behind your head.

Take an extra paddle for each person. Many people scoff at this until they suddenly find themselves holding one piece of a paddle while the other piece floats away. Believe me—paddles break at peculiar times. I know of one instance in which a paddler hung onto his paddle as he spilled but somehow broke his tied-in *spare* paddle as he went over!

Tie this extra paddle in at a place that's out of your way and yet easily reached from your normal paddling position. Use a lighter string, so in case your bow knot jams, you can break the string by hitting the end of the paddle. Take heed of this; as I said, paddles do break when you're least expecting it.

RAPIDS RUNNING WITHOUT YOUR BOAT

Occasionally you may find yourself running a rapid or swift stretch of river without benefit of your boat. This happens sometimes. There is a safer way to do this than merely trusting to fate.

First off, let's hope that you had your life jacket on. This helps, but even if you don't, the following is what you should try to do:

Float face up with your feet downstream, near the surface, and together. Keep your knees flexed slightly. This way your outstretched legs and feet will protect your torso and also absorb part of the shock if you hit something. Paddle with your hands to keep your body near the surface. Try to work your way into an eddy, and if you can't make it from there to shore, climb out on whatever is making the eddy. At least rest in it.

Although your boat is an excellent giant life preserver, never fail to abandon it if you see that it's pulling you into danger and you're safer without it. If the water and weather are cold—*never struggle* with the boat—just get yourself out while you still can. If you do hang onto the boat, stay on the upstream end only. The boat can easily crush you if it's full of water and catches you between it and an obstruction. Try to work your boat into an eddy if you do hold onto it.

In connection with staying upstream of the boat—if you hang up on a rock or obstruction and have to step out of the boat to get it free—always step out on the upstream side for the same reasons outlined above. Even if your boat is not swamped, the removal of your weight may get it loose, and it's not fun to be run over by even an empty boat.

19

DAMS, LEDGES, HYDRAULICS, AND SOUSE HOLES

If you've ever watched a log caught in the turbulence at the foot of a dam, you've noticed how it rolls and tumbles, submerges and rises—but stays right there. What you are seeing is a hydraulic jump, and it can hold you and your boat just like it does the log.

This is what sometimes makes dams and ledges dangerous to run. Even a small fall of water can create enough force to pull your boat back under the overflow and swamp you. While not dangerous in this particular case, it is wet and disconcerting.

With larger volumes of water this backflow can be deadly. First off—if you scout a ledge and see "standing" waves below it, waves that are a constant height but don't flow on down the river or "break" like ocean waves, then you're safe in running it because even if you spill, you'll be washed downstream. BUT—if you see a trough (or "souse hole," as it is called) and signs of an *upstream* current, then beware—if you swamp you could be swept into the trough and held there. You might be able to swim out the *end* of the trough or remove your life jacket and swim down to the bottom and then underwater downstream—but then again, you might not.

Hydraulics are very dangerous, and many river drownings can be attributed to them. They are particularly prevalent when the water is high in volume—just another reason to stay off flooded rivers.

A hydraulic with a strong back flow.

COLD WEATHER—COLD WATER

These present their own hazards and are discussed more fully under the heading of Winter Canoeing.

CONFIDENCE

Confidence is a fine thing—overconfidence on the river can get you in trouble. After this section you'll find a couple of charts on water and paddler classifications. Mismatches of the two classifications can be very dangerous. So don't *underestimate* the power of the water, and don't *overestimate* your ability. Never boat alone on high water rivers or in rough water; stay off flooded rivers completely; go with trained, experienced people if you *do* want to try the rougher stuff; and first off, get technical training on river canoeing—it really is different from lake canoeing.

GUIDELINE TO WATER CLASSIFICATION

As recreational and competitive canoeing and kayaking grew in popularity, it became obvious that some type of classification of water difficulty was necessary. So through the years the following rating system was developed and is generally accepted throughout the eastern United States:

Class 1. **Very Easy.** Waves small and regular. Passages clear. Sandbanks, artificial difficulties like bridge piers. Riffles.

Class 2. **Easy.** Rapids of medium difficulty, with passages clear and wide. Low ledges.

Class 3. **Medium.** Waves numerous, high, irregular. Rocks, eddies. Rapids with passages that are clear though narrow, requiring expertise in maneuver. Inspection usually needed.

Class 4. **Difficult.** Long rapids. Waves powerful, irregular. Dangerous rocks. Boiling eddies. Passages difficult to reconnoiter. Inspection mandatory first time. Powerful and precise maneuvering required.

Class 5. **Very Difficult.** Extremely difficult. Long and very violent rapids, following each other almost without interruption. River bed extremely obstructed. Big drops, violent current, very steep gradient. Reconnoitering essential but difficult.

Class 6. **Extraordinarily Difficult.** Difficulties of Class 5 carried to extremes of navigability. Nearly impossible and very dangerous. For teams of experts only, at favorable water levels and after close study with all precautions.

Of course the classifications are all a matter of water level, volume, and individual opinion, but maybe these accepted standards will help you form your own educated opinion. In the western United States the ratings of the rapids are graduated over a ten level system instead of stopping at Class 6.

GUIDELINE TO PADDLER CLASSIFICATION

Ratings for the comparative ability of paddlers were developed along with the water ratings. Here they are as outlined by the American Whitewater Association:

Grade 1. **A Beginner.** Knows all basic strokes and can handle the boat competently in smooth water.

Grade 2. **A Novice.** Can use effectively all basic whitewater strokes in the kayak or in both bow and stern of the canoe. Can read water and negotiate rapids with assurance.

Grade 3. **An Intermediate.** Can negotiate rapids requiring complex sequential maneuvering. Can use eddy turns and basic bow-upstream techniques, is skillful in both bow and stern of double canoe, and single in canoe or kayak, in intermediate rapids.

Grade 4. **An Expert.** Has proven ability to run difficult rapids in both bow and stern of double canoe, and single in canoe or kayak. Has skill in heavy water and complex rapids.

Grade 5. **A Senior Leader.** In addition to expert canoeing skills, has wide experience and good judgment for leading trips on any river.

CHAPTER II
EQUIPMENT

PADDLES

Many canoe books go into great detail on types of paddles and get all carried away with methods for determining the correct paddle length for you. This is all fine, but good paddles are expensive, and if you are a novice, you won't have the foggiest idea what length you really want until you get out and paddle awhile. So don't sink a lot of money into paddles at first. You're going to break them anyway, and while you're determining *your* preferred length (through experience), buy the cheaper wooden ones. Start with a paddle that is about chin high with the tip resting on the ground, and work from there. After you've paddled enough to know what you want, then invest in a good, sturdy paddle that exactly suits *you*.

Paddles are made of wood, plastic, fiberglass, aluminum, and combinations of these. Some can be shortened easily by sawing off the shaft. They come in various widths and blade shapes, too. Look at other people's paddles to see what's being used. Aluminum shafts and fiberglass blades are very strong, light, and efficient—but expensive. Plastic blades and grips lower the cost and the quality. Wood is not always cheap, but a wider variety of price and patterns is available.

Oldtown, Grumman, and Norse are three good brands in plastic-fiberglass-aluminum. A good cheap learner's paddle is "Featherbrand," sold in many discount stores. The better quality, higher-priced paddle can be bought pretty well tailored to your requirements—but you pay for it.

BAILER AND SPONGE

A very useful combination—good for the removal of rain, splash, and those last few quarts when you've spilled or swamped. A good bailer can be made from a gallon size plastic jug with a built-in handle. Leave the cap on the neck, and cut the bottom of the jug off. Most canoeists tie this and the sponge together with about two feet of cord and wrap the cord over a thwart once to keep the combination in the boat.

*Life jacket, bailer and sponge, knee pads, canteen—
all essential equipment—and don't forget the boat!*

WATERPROOF CONTAINERS

There are rubber, vinyl, plastic, and fiberglass containers on the market. Most of them are either too small, too expensive, or waterproof only in a rain—not if they are out floating the river on their own.

For one day trips where you carry only a little gear or for such expensive items as cameras, the best, sturdiest, and cheapest container is an army ammunition box. These are commonly available in any army surplus store in two sizes. They are usually absolutely watertight if the gasket around the cover is good, but it's still best to check them by submersion in water overnight before you put anything valuable in them.

For larger items such as sleeping bags there is a heavy plastic bag with a special "locking bar" top that is good. Voyageur is one trade name. They come in several large sizes and can be bought with an outer cloth cover to protect the plastic from cuts. I have seen the bar top pull loose under the pressure of moving water but this doesn't happen often.

For light loads two plastic garbage bags are good. Put one bag inside the other, and tie each one closed individually. These bags are not too sturdy, but they are good for things like extra clothes and sleeping bags—items with bulk but not weight.

24

CLOTHING

Clothing may seem a funny thing to put under equipment, but after all, it's pretty necessary and pretty important. Clothes keep you dry, warm (or cool), comfortable, and from being arrested. They also help protect your skin from the sun and from the cuts, nicks, and abrasions that can easily result from a spill or an accident.

A good all-around outfit for summer is long pants, a long-sleeved shirt, and tennis shoes. Reinforce the knees of the pants for kneeling and the seat for sitting. This may sound a little hot for the dead of summer and probably will be. Obviously there are trips where a spill means nothing but a cooling dip in the water—you have to weigh each trip on its own and dress accordingly.

Do wear shoes. The rocks in shoals and rapids are frequently very sharp and unpleasant to step on when you have to climb out of your boat. Too, when swimming in a rapid in the accepted manner of face up, feet first, the shoes give you better protection than the bare skin of your feet.

For rain a rainsuit is best, a raincoat next, a poncho not desirable at all. For one, a poncho won't keep you dry when you're paddling, but, more important, it is more likely to catch on the boat or on an obstruction in the water if you spill.

The wearing of hats and sunglasses is a matter of personal taste, although both are nice at times. I've heard remarks about broad-brimmed hats getting in your way when paddling, but I've never found it so. If you wear glasses, as I do, nobody has to tell you that you can't see much when they're covered with rain drops. Wearing a hat will help you see those elusive downstream "v's" under such bad weather conditions.

Sunglasses help take some of the glare off the water—especially helpful in the afternoons of trips when you find yourself paddling through a rock garden and facing into a declining sun. Some swear by polaroid glasses; some say they're no better than standard lenses. I don't know—but do tie them on your head, whatever you wear.

In the winter extra clothes are essential safety equipment; in cooler weather they're nice to have to put on when rain or an unexpected spill wets you through. Needless to say, if your extra dry clothes are to remain dry, they need to be packed in something waterproof.

KNEE PADS

Knee pads are used by canoeists when they're kneeling in the bottom of the canoe either because of rough water or because they prefer to paddle that way. Most canoeists put them on at the beginning of a trip if they think they're going to need them, rather than take them on and off during the trip. The two most common types are sold for gardening or miners' use. Both strap to your leg above and below your knee. One is a stuffed pad, and the other is a formed rubber shape with a thin foam pad in it. The leather pad is uncomfortable once it gets wet, because it stays soggy for hours. I much prefer the black rubber one which is just as comfortable and dries quickly. The foam pads usually fall out the first time you use them, but I haven't found that they make much difference in comfort, anyway.

CANTEENS

Just a word—get the plastic kind; besides not bending, they are so much quieter than the metal ones. On hot summer trips you might try freezing your full canteen the night before—then you'll have ice water for awhile the next day. If you do freeze it though, leave the cap off while you're doing it or you'll burst the canteen.

Greig Foshee at the "Falls of the Cahaba," a shoal with a forbidding name.

SUGGESTED INDIVIDUAL ONE DAY TRIP LIST

Summer

Rainsuit or raincoat (poncho not recommended)
Lunch
Knee Pads
Life Jacket
Extra Paddle
Canteen
8' x 8' plastic for rain tarp at lunch
Garbage bag with ties
Matches (waterproof or in waterproof container)
Camera, cigarettes, etc., as desired

Add a bailer and sponge per boat to the above.

Winter

All of the above plus a complete change of clothes and a towel in something absolutely waterproof. If you want a hot lunch, you might add a small stove (with fuel) and cooking and eating utensils.

Group Items

Throwing rope (50-60 feet)
Duct tape
First aid kit

SYNOPSIS OF TRIP TIPS

1. If it can be hurt by water, put it in something waterproof:

    a. Ammo boxes.
    b. Rubber or heavy plastic special purpose bags made for the purpose.
    c. Double plastic bags such as garbage bags with both bags folded and tied.

*Two ways of going through the same place—
Bill Carney braced, Pearl Hawkins didn't.*

2. Tie everything in the boat.

   a. Use slip knots that can be undone with one pull but won't come loose accidentally.
   b. Don't have long strings, ropes, etc. lying in the bottom of the boat to entangle your feet and gear.

3. Use your gear to help trim the boat. Normally the canoe should ride level in the water with the paddlers in their normal positions.

4. If you wear glasses, tie them on your head.

5. Carry a spare paddle for *each* paddler:

   a. Put blade on bottom of the boat, tie grip to underside of thwart with slip knot. Grip facing paddler.
   b. Use light enough string so that if the knot jams, you can break the string by hitting the paddle.

6. In winter always carry spare clothes—a complete change and a towel in something waterproof. Also carry matches in a waterproof container. Another good cold weather idea is to take along a flask of magic fire fluid like Coleman fuel or kerosene to help start a fire quickly. A wet suit is recommended.

7. Don't trail your painters in the water. Do have 10 foot painters on bow and stern.

8. Put your name on everything. A black "Marx-a-lot" is good for this. A lot of people have identical equipment, and this way there's no question of what belongs to whom. If "Marx-a-lot" writing won't show up on the equipment (such as knee pads), stick a strip of adhesive tape on it, then write on the tape.

CHAPTER III
CAMPING, PERMISSIONS, AND LITTER
TRANSPORTING YOUR BOAT

CAMPING

Camping is the other half of the fun of canoeing to me, and many of the one day trips listed in this book can be combined into two day or more floats with overnight camping.

Everybody's camping style is different, and this isn't a camping book, but, as a floater, canoeist, fisherman or whatever capacity or interest takes you to the river, you should know some important points relating to camping that will affect you and others that travel the river after you.

Places to camp are becoming more scarce. Land owners are cutting off access to the rivers and stopping camping on their river banks. In most cases this is because thoughtless persons or groups have irritated the owner by a complete lack of respect for his property or for him.

So—the first thing to remember is to get permission to camp if you're on private property. If the permission is denied, then don't get belligerent. After all, he may have very bitter memories of other campers. Just thank him and go elsewhere. Also remember that if you do get permission and have camped, then leave the camp site as clean and preferably cleaner than it was when you arrived. It's not a bad idea to thank the owner either if he is handy or write him if he is not.

Don't bury your garbage. Do burn anything that will burn and carry the rest with you in a garbage bag that you take for this purpose. Littering probably irritates people faster than anything else. Lunch stops are not really different from camping, and you should be just as respectful of the property on these.

Be extremely careful with fires, and when you leave, drown them completely and hide the traces. An old trick that serves the possibly useful purpose of showing that your fire didn't start a forest burning is to lay two dry, crossed sticks over the grave of your fire before you leave.

Don't cut trees, bushes, or anything else. Firewood can usually be found on the ground or on dead trees, and tent poles and pegs should be carried with you.

RELATIONS WITH THE LOCAL FOLK

The local people with whom you come in contact should be treated as courteously as anyone else. Some people don't do this and engender bad feeling between the local population and any person who didn't grow up in the vicinity. Try to behave toward them as you would anyone else. Remember you're the outsider, and *you* may be the one to bear the brunt of the ill will created by the last guy to canoe through this particular place.

Occasionally, as in any society, you may run across drunks or hard cases who are determined to make trouble. All I can tell you is to back out of it as gracefully as you can, if you can, and go on down the river.

You will also find occasions when someone is shooting into or across a river. A few loud yells will let them know you're coming. I've never run across anyone who wouldn't stop shooting until you have passed. There are also a few total idiots who delight in shooting *up* or *down* a river, apparently receiving great delight from the ricocheting of the bullet. This is serious business because they may be out of hearing range of a shout. Pull over behind a bank or something and shout or get out and walk upstream on the bank (this isn't too safe either). All you can do is attract their attention some way without getting shot in the process.

CARRYING YOUR BOAT ON YOUR CAR

Some states have laws prohibiting this. These laws were brought on by canoes and other small car-topped craft coming loose and flying down the road. The results can be sticky—a torn-up boat, somebody else's car to pay for, possible law suits, and injuries or fatalities in the car your boat struck.

Car-topping is the easiest way to transport a small boat, so do your part to keep such restrictive laws from being introduced in Alabama. You don't have to *overdo* it, however. I've seen people secure their boats so firmly and with so many knots and layers of rope that I, personally, would rather have stayed home than have to struggle with getting them on and off the car. It doesn't take a lot of complicated yardage to be sure the boat is firmly held on–just a little attention to the *way* it's held on.

First, get a good rack. You can get them at most canoe dealers. The best ones are very sturdy, *clamp* to the rain gutters on your car, and don't touch the car top at all. If you have a car with no rain gutters, there is a good, sturdy variety of rack that has pads that rest on your roof but still securely *clamp* to the trim along the roof edge. These heavy-duty racks cost more, but

One high–the usual way to carry a canoe.

they are more reliable and, in the long run, less trouble than racks held on by woven straps and suction cups. The straps rot and stretch, and the suction cups deteriorate from the sun and from strain, and they all have to be replaced about every year or less. These types of racks are usually thin gauge metal and are basically a waste of money.

Racks can be bought to carry either one or two canoes (usually 60 inches or 75 inches long) or the single canoe racks can have removable extensions added. The two canoe size is far more useful on a shuttle, and I recommend that you buy it.

There are several secure ways to hold the boat to the racks. Nylon or heavy woven strap-type tie downs are sold by some canoe dealers, or you can make your own. Ropes will hold it down but are more trouble to tie. I like rubber straps such as are used on trucks to hold down tarps. They have "S" hooks on each end, and the 36-inch length is about right for the average canoe. The carrying racks, even the clamp-down type, should not be relied on to actually hold the boat down to the car. Neither should the woven rubber straps or the ropes if they attach only to the racks. All the racks are for, basically, is to provide a platform that won't move around, and all the straps do is to prevent the boat from shifting and rattling around on the platform. *Always* tie the boat down front and back to the bumpers or, better, to eye bolts in the bumpers. With eye bolts there is less likelihood of the ropes being sawed in two by a sharp edge.

Three up—a common way to carry a third boat.

The easiest, quickest, knot to tie and untie either wet or dry is the "truckers hitch." It will hold securely yet can be undone with one *intentional* pull. It can also be pulled as tight as you want it. Here's how to tie it:

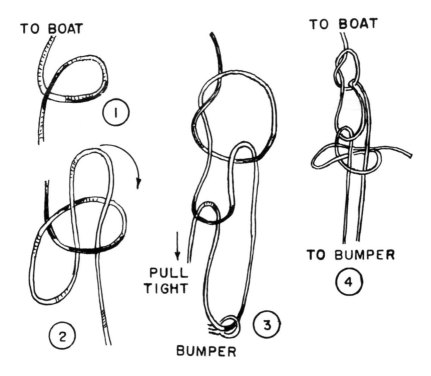

I'm a bit embarrassed to mention it, but I have seen a few canoes loaded up the wrong way on a car. You *do* carry a canoe bottom side up!

One final word: Keep the river and shoreline clean!

CHAPTER IV
WINTER CANOEING

For some reason many canoeists store their paddles and leave their boats to gather dust from the time the first cold wind sweeps across the river until the first warm breeze of spring blows away the icicles. Yet winter canoeing certainly has its rewards. It demands a little more in the way of fortitude and equipment, but these "extras" are frequently well worth their price.

First, let me say that I'm no hero—a raw, wet, windy, winter day is my idea of a good day to sit inside and *read* about the rivers. The best part of any trip made in such weather is talking about it the next day when, under the influence of warmth and dryness, I have decided that I was a hero after all.

But not all winter days are so bleak and uninviting. Here in the south we are blessed with many times when a low temperature is more than offset by a lack of wind and a clear sunshine-filled sky. These are the days when you can really enjoy the river.

First of all—the river will probably be pretty well deserted. Secondly, the underbrush and the trees will be bare, and you can see cliffs and rocks and details of the ground back from the riverbank that you would miss in the summer. If you decide to go ashore to investigate something, then walking is easier.

The river will usually be higher than in the summer, too, which means an easier trip—faster if you want it. Of course on a rapid stream section the higher level adds to the excitement of the shoals and rapids. I'm assuming, of course, that you are canoeing safely at *moderate* water levels and not flooded ones.

Perhaps the greatest reward is the silence and the peace of the deserted river. It's a world that you can drift through with the satisfying knowledge that it's a pretty private thing, that the quite different face that winter puts on the world is, for the length of the trip, exclusively yours and your companions'. More, it's a view that you share only with a few others. For, as the percentage of canoeists in the world is low, the percentage of winter canoeists is even smaller.

The face of the world that you see may be bare with browns and grays and blacks, or it may be covered with the white of snow or frost and garnished with icicles. Some of the prettiest ice formations form where small streams trickle off a cliff, splash, and freeze. The variety of glittering shapes is beyond imagination, and the filigree of ice forms a special lace available only to you.

Of course there is one other reward, briefly mentioned before. You may have been warm and comfortable on the river and thoroughly enjoyed yourself—or you may have been cold, wet, miserable, and longing for home. Either way your non-canoeing acquaintances will usually picture the details of your trip merely as a function of temperature, a wet river, some damp woods, and constant misery. So your reward is that you've done it and they haven't, which can give you a smug air of satisfaction even though down deep you know that it wasn't really nearly as tough as *they* think it was!

Of course not all winter canoeing
is done on *the river.*

WET SUITS AND WOOLIES

Warmth and dryness are the two requirements for enjoyment of the river in the winter. They are completely interlocked for, with the exception of wearing a wet suit, it is almost impossible to be warm when wet. Wet suits and wool are basic protection. Let's look at both of them.

36

WET SUITS

Wet suits are ingenious devices and well worth their cost if you anticipate any cold weather canoeing or, like me, are very sensitive to cold water. In a wet suit you are wet but warm. A full wet suit is a close-fitting (like a second skin is best), two piece neoprene suit that usually has an inner lining that makes it easier to get on and off. The better ones will have five zippers—one on each arm and leg and one on the coat. If you ever try to get in or out of a wet suit that has no zippers, you'll quickly see their advantage.

Wet suit coats have (or should have) a tail piece that comes up between your legs in the front and snaps to the front bottom of the coat—thus ensuring that no icy-cold gap opens up between the trousers and coat. Most wet suits are black, but they can be bought in various colors, patterns, and thicknesses. For general use here in Alabama, a 3/16 or 1/4 inch thick suit is adequate.

Wet suits come in short and long sleeves and with full-length and short legs. Usually the jacket part costs almost as much as the whole suit, so you might as well get the complete outfit, although you may want to wear only the jacket part at times. Wet suit boots and gloves are also available and make welcome additions to the rest of the suit. Women's suits are made with obviously different cuts on the coat portion. Hoods provide a lot of warmth but interfere with your sense of direction in a shoal or rapid because you can't hear the water.

A wet suit is just that—wet. A thin layer of water trapped between your body and the suit is quickly warmed by your body heat. The suit by virture of being close-fitting keeps this warm layer from being replaced by cold water in such quantities or so rapidly that you feel it.

The advantage of a wet suit is two-fold. First, it insulates you from the general cold of the water, and secondly, it helps reduce that heart-stopping initial shock when you first hit the water. I say "reduce" and not "stop" because human beings just don't come in standard sizes. Because of this, most "off-the-shelf" wet suits will not fit a person absolutely perfectly, and there will usually be a few loose spaces which a pool of cold water will immediately find. These pools warm up rather quickly, but you still feel them at first.

There is one other factor about a wet suit—it needs something lightweight worn over it to protect the neoprene material from being torn. Most of my canoeing friends also wear oversize tennis shoes over their wet suit booties. One other note—wet suits are buoyant, but you should still wear a life jacket—don't rely on the suit alone.

WOOLIES

Wool underwear, I have heard it said, helps keep you warm simply by scratching your skin. I have also heard that it keeps you warm by making you scratch. It all depends on your affin-

Wet suit and woolies—recommended
wear for a winter day.

ity for wool, I suppose.

Nevertheless, for cooler but not cold water (or for some not unduly affected by cold water), wool outer clothes are very good, especially with an inner layer of wool "long johns" as a foundation. Wool is pretty warm even when wet. Unfortunately long wool underwear is a little hard to find, and all wool clothes are expensive. In fact, wool underwear, pants, and shirt will run you pretty close to the cost of a wet suit. I will admit that I admire the wool clothes tremendously—they're really more comfortable than a wet suit and have that rugged, outdoor look about them. Too, you can wear them at non-canoeing times in places where a wet suit would look ridiculous. One other advantage is they're adjustable for comfort. In a wet suit you may well stew in your own juices even on a winter day if the sun shines and the day warms up a bit. About all you can do is unzip the zippers a little. A wool shirt, on the other hand, can be removed or the sleeves rolled up or something done quickly and easily to keep from being uncomfortably hot.

HYPOTHERMIA

Wet suits are not cheap, but they are well worth the investment. Cold water quickly saps your strength, leaving you helpless to extricate yourself from the water or, if you reach the shore, to help yourself further. It is perfectly possible to get out of the water and die on the bank. Consider the following table of exposure times:

Water Temperature:	"Safe" exposure time:
40° or under	*Less* than 10 minutes
40°–50°	5–20 minutes
50°–60°	15–40 minutes
60° or above	1 hour or more

Remember that this table does *not* reflect the fact that you will be weak long before these times are up.

What actually kills you is hypothermia—a condition caused by exposure to cold that results in a steady lessening of your body temperature until you lapse into a coma and die. Actual hypothermia begins when the body temperature drops to a point where it can no longer generate heat to offset the cooling process—usually about 92°. At this temperature you are shivering uncontrollably. Being unable to generate heat, the body's temperature keeps on falling. Around 82°–81° you become rigid, and at about 80° you lapse into unconsciousness. From there it is a short road to oblivion. The problem with hypothermia is that by the time the symptoms of staggering, uncoordinated motion, slurred speech, and inability to think are present (about 87°–86°), it's too late for you to even realize it, much less do anything to help yourself.

As the body cannot help itself, it must be warmed with some other heat—a fire, immersion in warm water (impossible on a river bank), hot drinks, or even sandwiching the victim between naked bodies. Obviously you must get him out of his wet clothes first and into some relatively protected location—at least out of the wind. The obvious answer to hypothermia is don't canoe alone in the winter and be sure your partners can both recognize the symptoms and know what to do about it.

OTHER POINTERS

Chill factor accounts for a great loss of heat. This is simply the apparent lowering of the temperature caused by the wind blowing across your body. For example, if you dress for 20° weather, a ten-mile-an-hour wind gives the effect of a temperature of 2°, and that is cold!

Hands, face, and head are great heat losers, so wear gloves, a watch-cap (toque), or at least a hat and maybe a ski mask if the day shows promise of wind. A windproof outer jacket or "jump suit," even over a wet suit, helps a lot.

Remember, several thin layers are warmer than one thick one and also give you a method of remaining comfortable if the day warms up. Wool socks or thick wet suit booties will help that "frozen to the bottom of the boat" feeling in your feet, and a cushion to sit on will help reduce chill on other parts. A fire and something hot to drink at lunch will serve to sustain you through the afternoon. Well—maybe it will. It won't do any harm.

CHAPTER V
RIVERS AND LAKES—THE BIG DIFFERENCE

Almost every new canoeist wants to dash out immediately and find the nearest "whitewater." To the novice, the word conjures up visions of frothing, churning water with a kayak or tandem canoe expertly snaking its way through a gauntlet of rocks and waves. When seen on TV or in the movies, it looks like a lot of fun—and very, very easy. What the novice doesn't think about is the other side of the picture—the canoe's keel mashed up to the thwarts, a few ragged, foot-long rips in the hull, and a dozen husky guys chest deep in cold water struggling to get the hulk disentangled from one of those froth-covered rocks. Still another thing that seems to never enter his mind is that he doesn't have to be in "whitewater" for this to happen.

So let's eliminate the classic "whitewater" picture from our minds and substitute just plain, old *moving* water, without the froth and waves and roar. The twelve guys could still be out there struggling—maybe not quite as hard—but struggling nonetheless.

And there lies the *big* danger to novice river canoeists and the single point that seems to be missing from most writing on canoeing. This point is simply that there is *no* difference in the effect of whitewater, wild water, rapids, or whatever you choose to call the froth and roar, and just plain moving water except one of degree. The important difference lies in the two words "moving" and "still," for a canoe reacts completely differently and requires different techniques to control it when the water is moving.

Unfortunately, most budding river canoeists have received whatever training they have on still waters, usually lakes. When they try to use their lake (or still water) methods on a river, they find that many just don't work, and others do not apply. They have just distinguished the important point of difference. The smaller and swifter the river, the more quickly the point is brought home.

The reason for this basic difference is that in a lake (disregarding wind), the only force acting on the hull is the result of the paddle strokes. In moving water you still have the effect of the paddle (which you control), but you also have the very powerful force of the water flow which may be pushing your boat sideways, diagonally, downstream, or even upstream (which you do *not* control).

While the subject is too complex to explain in this brief discussion, there are basic practical effects that result from the application of these forces to a canoe hull, effects that you just don't have in still water. In connection with these effects are fundamental behavior rules for the moving water itself, which must be known and considered. There are also basic river canoeing maneuvers and techniques designed to either offset these forces or to use them to the canoeist's advantage—but they are *river* techniques—moving water techniques—and few of them can be learned by trial and error. They need to be taught.

Probably one of the most common situations that typifies all three of these basics (and sinks many boats) is a bend in a narrow stream. On the outside curve of the bend some obstruction (a tree, for example) has fallen into the river. The water is still flowing through the tree branches, but there's no hole big enough for a canoe to go through.

Normally the main river flow, the deepest part of the river, and, therefore, the main force of the water will not follow the center line of the river around this curve. Instead it will swing to the *outside* edge of the bend, then back to the middle of the river as the bend straightens. This is your fundamental water behavior.

The canoe is in this current, and when the bend is reached, it is swept toward the outside of the bend and straight toward the tree in the water. The novice canoeist usually tries to turn and power his way out of trouble by paddling *forward* and away from the tree. This is exactly the *wrong* thing to do. He now has two forces working—the current is pushing him to the outside of the bend, and, as he turns, he becomes slightly sideways to both the tree and the current. As he tries to paddle out toward the center of the river, he is moving forward all right, but at the same time the river is still pushing him sideways toward the tree. Will he clear it? Maybe yes, maybe no—but probably not. It's a risky way to try.

If he doesn't clear, then he'll broadside on the tree. The water pressure will force the upstream gunwale below the surface until the canoe sinks and rolls into the branches under-

John Foshee at the first fall on the Little Cahaba.

water. Quite possibly the canoeist goes with it and equally possibly also gets entangled in them underwater.

The basic maneuver used to avoid this situation is called a "back ferry." It's a river canoeing technique used to avoid any kind of obstruction. It's simple and effective and probably the most used river canoeing maneuver, but it's just not taught to lake canoeists because there's no necessity for it.

Other basic river maneuvers are the "forward ferry," the "eddy turn," and the "peel-off"—none of which apply or even *work* in still water, yet are essential in moving water. The basic forward or "J" stroke is usually the first lake canoeing paddle stroke taught. In river canoeing instruction the *back* stroke usually takes precedence in the teaching order. Prys, push-aways, draws, high and low braces, and combinations of these paddle techniques are other strokes taught—they're all essential in current.

If all this sounds complicated, it's not. Canoeists do need to have basic lake canoeing skills, but if they're going to canoe on rivers, then they need the specialized river canoeing skills also. It's something like learning to drive a car. Learn on a straight shift, and you can drive an automatic, but it doesn't work the other way. Similarly, river canoeing techniques are much more adaptable to lakes than are the lake techniques to the rivers.

Possibly an even more important point to novice river canoeists is that they realize that river techniques training is essential from a safety standpoint. *Trial* and error on the river—especially alone—can cost them a canoe and possibly a life.

The time to learn is when there is no penalty for the errors they are sure to make—and this means in the company of experienced canoeists and with instruction.

CHAPTER VI
BOOKS TO READ AND STUDY

Here are a few books that might be of interest to the floater. There are many more, of course, but I know from personal experience that these are pretty good in their own field.

CANOEING, KAYAKING, "HOW-TO" BOOKS

Basic River Canoeing by Bob McNair
American Camping Association, Inc.
Bradford Woods
Martinsville, Indiana 46151

As of this writing, this is one of the best technique books you can get on river canoeing.

Canoeing and *Basic Canoeing*
American National Red Cross
Washington, D. C.

The above are basically lake canoeing books. *Canoeing* covers almost everything in this field and is very interesting. *Basic Canoeing* is a synopsis of the lake techniques only.

White Water Sport by Peter Dwight Whitney
Ronald Press Company
New York

White Water Handbook For Canoe And Kayak by John T. Urban
Appalachian Mountain Club
5 Joy Street
Boston, Massachusetts 02108

CANOE CAMPING BOOKS

Wilderness Canoeing by John W. Malo
The Macmillan Company
New York

Malo's Complete Guide To Canoeing And Canoe Camping by
John W. Malo
Quadrangle Books Inc.
12 East Delaware Place
Chicago, Illinois 60611

CAMPING

The Complete Walker by Colin Fletcher
Alfred A. Knopf
New York

This is a book that I consider one of the best for pure camping skills and equipment discussions.

Camping by the side of the river. This site was a little crowded.

PART TWO
The Rivers

Then I dreamed I saw a river running swift
into the hills
And it pulled me and it called me 'till I couldn't
stand its goad,
So I dusted off my duffle and I packed the
old canoe
And I paddled down that luring, silver road.
Oh, the freedom that engulfed me as the miles
were left behind
Rejoiced my heart and soothed it 'till I
felt I most could weep,
As the riffles in the water and each pull of
paddle blade
Caressed my soul and woke it from its sleep.

On the Cahaba—probably the most floated stream in Alabama.

48

ABOUT THE MAPS AND SYMBOLS

GENERAL

I have tried to make each map as useful as possible without cluttering it with extra details of little interest to the floater. Sections of streams that have a lot of shoals, rapids, or other obstacles or hazards are shown to a larger scale and are more detailed than those that are relatively unimpeded.

No attempt has been made to show every little road or town in the area—only those features are included that may be necessary for you to find the section or help you identify your location on the section. For details of the area I suggest that you consult the appropriate topographic maps which are referenced for each section.

The usual or more convenient put-in and take-out points are shown. These are nearly all public access locations such as bridges, fords, or boat ramps, so you won't have any trespassing problems. The few private access points are so shown on the map, but this usually means that it is a campground or fishing camp which you can use by asking permission or possibly paying a small fee for parking. Sometimes there are intermediate access points that can be used to shorten or lengthen a trip, but these should always be checked to be sure they are open to the public.

If a town or city lies within the range of the river map, then I've shown it as a block. This block in no way reflects the size of the town—just that it's there. After all, you are fleeing the streets for a day or so; details are just not relevant.

The roads leading to this nearest town or city are also shown. These are generally at the access points. Remember, however, that there may be numerous twists and turns before you reach that town or city; these windings may not be shown on my map. A county road map might come in handy in some cases.

I have not always shown the shuttle roads because of the simple physical inability to squeeze them into the confines of the page size. Where they are shown, however, they represent what I consider to be the best route. There may be others. Junctions in roads can be awfully confusing. I have tried to eliminate

49

this by showing these junctions where they occur on the map. Lest you think there are a lot of short roads around, let me point out that at these junctions only the main route is continued. If a road is marked "dirt" and you find it hard-surface, don't be surprised. County road departments are always out paving roads. Also they are constantly cutting out *new* roads and obliterating or changing old ones, so you may find some difference between my map and the real world. However, my maps were up-to-date as of the time of publication, so I did try. Do bear in mind however that access points get built on or blocked or by-passed sometimes and bear with me if you find this has happened here and there.

These river maps are accurate in all respects except for the width of the river. This is drawn out of scale for the sake of clarity.

Each map has a scale which applies only to that map. It also has a north arrow which has been included for two reasons. One, it will help you decide which leg of the river you're on in case you lose track of your location and provided you have a compass and know how to use it. The second reason is that it just seems to me that all maps should have north arrows. Each map also has the river miles marked on it. At the end of a trip you may swear that the distance is twice that shown, but it really isn't.

The final bit of information is the direction of river flow. I don't really think you'll get confused and paddle *upstream*, although that's feasible in some places, but it seemed like a good idea to show it. That takes us through the comments on the maps, so let's turn to the various impediments shown *in* the rivers.

OBSTACLES

First off, I have shown no more or less temporary obstructions such as log jams. Some streams seem to be dedicated to catching every stray stick that comes along and to piling these up into non-boatable masses. Other streams never seem to have a jam. High water may sweep them away or add to them, depending on the whims of water and the nuances of landscape. No matter—they are temporary when compared to the stones on the shore, for example, so I haven't shown them. They *are* dangerous, however—extremely dangerous—so keep your eyes open for them.

The symbols I have used are as follows:

Shoal	(S ⊠)	(S)	Mile Marker	o2	
Rapid	(R ⊠)	(R)	Road	– – – –	
Drop		(D)	Bridge	⊐ ⊏	
Fall		(F)	Town	⌐ ¬	
Shallows			Power Line	–P·—·P–	
Bar	(B)		Telephone Line	–T·—·T–	
Island or Bar	(o)		Railroad	⊦⊦⊦ ⊦⊦⊦ ⊦⊦⊦	
Rocks or Boulders			County Line	– – · –	
Prominent Rock Formations, Bluffs or Cliffs			North	➤N➤	
Creek or Stream			Flow	➤F➤	
Small Road	⟍ ⟍⟍⟍⟍		Foundations	**FDNS.**	

The fall usually occurs at the end of the shoal or rapid but not always. As you can see, I have broken the obstructions down into various classes. Obviously *my* definitions of a class may well differ from yours. Equally obvious, a "shoal" at one level may be only a little surface turbulence at another, while a drop at low water may turn into a bump with a big standing wave when more water volume flows over it. Shallows will vanish as the water rises. There are numerous possibilities. You will ultimately have to rate them yourself by running the sections at various water levels.

MY DEFINITIONS

Shallows are places that even in moderate water may be completely covered and not apparent. They have few or no obstructions to dodge and are fairly uniform in drop and level.

Shoals (S) are places that in moderate water will usually require some maneuvering and will generally be noticeable even in higher water by surface roughness. They are more irregular in drop, have larger and more frequent obstructions than shallows, and may have small ledges and drops.

Rapids (R) are locations where standing waves, frequent drops, natural obstructions, and/or water volume and force or combinations of these at normal water levels create a necessity for caution.

Drops (D) are abrupt changes in elevation to about two feet in height taking place over a small horizontal distance. They may be angled anywhere from straight down to about 45°. I have shown the height of some of these drops on the maps, but this varies greatly with water flow.

Falls (F) are vertical or almost vertical drops over two feet in height. The height is usually noted on the maps, but this is at one runnable point only. The height may vary from side to side of the river or stream.

TWO GENERAL NOTES

1. **"Right"** and **"left"** when referring to any river direction is always facing downstream.
2. **"Drop"** is average feet per mile for that particular section.

DIFFICULTY RATING

0. No shoals or rapids, few or no shallows or obstructions that cannot be easily negotiated. Current not normally

swift, wide river with no sharp bends or narrow stretches. Inexperienced canoeist could handle in normal water levels.

1. Some shallows, shoals, or very mild rapids that may require minor maneuvering. Narrow river or sections that are narrow, swifter current, sharper bends, some low drops. Canoeist should have basic river canoeing training.

2. Some rapids of Class I or Class II. Swift current, narrow river, sharp bends, areas where natural obstructions will require more precise maneuvering, some drops. Canoeist should have river canoeing training and be practiced in ferrying.

3. Numerous Class I and II rapids, some Class III rapids, strong current, sharp bends and changes in elevation combined, drops, and runnable waterfalls. Canoeist should be an experienced river canoeist and be practiced at ferrying, eddy turns, and braces.

4. Numerous Class III or higher rapids. Do not run unless an experienced river canoeist and then only in company with at least two other canoes—preferably more.

Narrow and rocky—a good place for caution.

WARNING–CAUTION
OR WHATEVER YOU WANT TO CALL IT
BUT READ THIS!

Any river, stream, or creek can and does become danger-ous in high water—and the higher it gets, the more extreme the danger. *Flood time is not the time to go canoeing*, and you'll rarely find an *experienced* canoeist out on a flooded river. The volume and speed of the water combine to create a sheer, brute force that can demolish your boat and drown you. Bends in small rivers are one of the worst dangers because no one ever thinks of them as such. There are specific whitewater tech-niques to handle such situations as bends. If you don't know them and are not practiced at them, then stay off any narrow river or creek that's even slightly high and *off all* of them that are flooded. Remember—your lake canoeing skills won't help you in a fast-moving river. You can rarely power your way out of trouble in a strong current, and still water techniques just don't work.

Bill and Sue Carney nearly vanish beneath the waves.

THE CAHABA RIVER

The Cahaba is an interesting and unique river. It is one of two river systems in Alabama that flows entirely within the state, and except for one short stretch of about three miles near Birmingham, it is entirely free flowing. In addition its shores are surprisingly undeveloped despite its proximity to several large towns and cities. This is particularly amazing when you consider that approximately 60 percent of Alabama's population lives within a 100 mile radius of some part of the river.

The river flows through or borders eight counties and, like most of the State's streams, has a general southwesterly trend. Cutting through four geological zones as it does, it has a great variety of scenic and floral interest.

Several portions of the river are noted for their seasonal display of water lilies, and one species of this plant is unique to the river. Being undeveloped, the shores and waters have quite a bit of animal and bird life.

The river contains 123 of the 148 species of fish found in Alabama, including some that are unique to the river itself or are found only in a few other locations in the State. It also has one—the goldline darter—that is found in only two locations in the United States—Georgia and the Cahaba between Helena and Centerville.

Access to the river is simple, convenient, and frequent. In fact it is completely broken up into segments of seven to twelve miles by bridges or fords. This makes it one of the easiest rivers to float for a one day trip.

For purposes of floating the Cahaba may be divided into two major sections. From Trussville to Centerville the river has bluffs, rapids, and shoals and is in and through a generally rocky area. At Centerville it flows into the coastal plain area of the State and immediately becomes a slow-moving, winding, pastoral stream with gravel bars replacing the rocks of its upper reaches.

The Cahaba is very sensitive to rainfall. Its upper parts (basically from Trussville to County 52 bridge) get very low in the summer—so much so that until you become adept at reading the river, your "floats" may be more like walks. As you progress downstream and the river widens and drains more area, this situation improves, although in a normal summer you will still have difficulty in places. Below Centerville there is always enough water to float even in the driest parts of the year.

On the other hand, the river also rises very rapidly. A hard rain can swiftly turn the narrow upper parts into a dangerous torrent and create a lot of swift and powerful current in the wider, lower sections.

Possibly because it is such a convenient and well-known river, the Cahaba is often viewed as a "training ground"—a simple, easy river suitable for the rankest novice. In general it is just this, but its closeness and familiarity should never breed contempt for its power.

Of the eleven official tributaries of the Cahaba, only two are included in these rides. Short stretches on the others are often quite feasible, however, and undoubtedly have much to offer the floater.

An unorthodox paddling position but effective in fighting a windy day.

SECTION 1

CAHABA RIVER 7 MILES

U. S. 11 to County 10
Drop: 16   Difficulty: 1-2
Topos: Leeds, Argo   Hazards: Three rapids (one Class 2)

CAUTION: UNDER NO CIRCUMSTANCES STOP FOR
            LUNCH OR ANY OTHER REASONS ON
            CAMP COLEMAN PROPERTY!

Put-in parking is in the Trussville city park just upstream
from the bridge. Don't drive out across the grass or leave your
vehicle parked so that it blocks the road.

This is a scenic run on the very upper stretches of the
Cahaba and one that is often overlooked because of the shallowness of the water at the put-in. The river stays just about the
width you see at the put-in except in places where it is necked
down by boulders, ledges, islands, or bluffs. There are numerous
"blind" bends on this stretch, so be cautious. The current is
swift, and you could find yourself pinned (or sunk) on a logjam
or fallen tree.

For the first mile the river is flat and shallow, and you'll
have to zigzag your way along following the main current. Just
after you turn south around the end of the mountain parallel to
U. S. 11, you'll encounter your first shoal. From this point on
for the next 4¼ miles you'll have numerous bends and shoals,
most of the shoals with a marked drop in elevation and well
spiked with sharp rocks. After you turn south, you'll pass
through sections with rock bluffs on one or both sides of the
river. You may go to either side of the island just before the
first big bend back to the west, but if you go to the right, be
prepared for some narrow slots and sharp turns.

About a mile further on you'll see some boulders in and
along the river, then a farm on your left. You are now on Camp
Coleman property. Pass through a five foot slot between the
bluff on your right and some boulders. Just past the Camp Coleman footbridge you'll pass through two Class 1 rapids, over a 12
inch drop, and past a beautiful waterfall coming in over a bluff

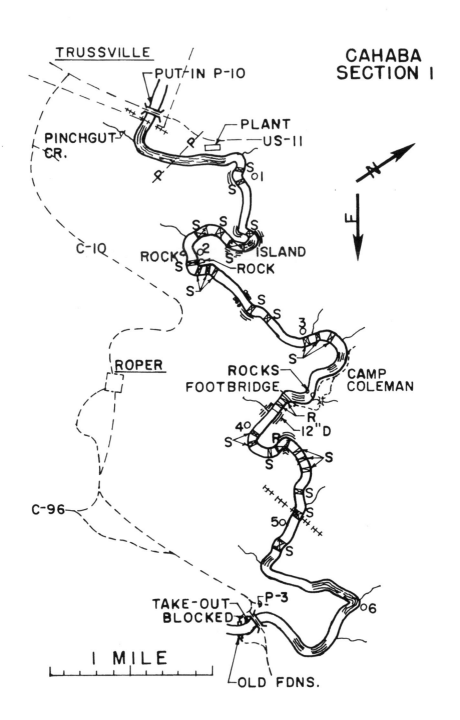

TRUSSVILLE

CAHABA
SECTION I

PUT-IN P-10

PLANT
US-11

PINCHGUT
CR.

C-IQ

ROCK

ISLAND
ROCK

ROPER

ROCKS
FOOTBRIDGE

CAMP
COLEMAN

R
12"D

C-96

TAKE-OUT
BLOCKED

P-3

OLD FDNS.

1 MILE

on your right.

About ¾ of a mile past the footbridge you'll come to a good Class 2 rapid complicated by a bend to the right, a bluff on the outside of the bend, and a blind approach around a left-hand bend. Approach it from the **RIGHT** with caution, and scout it if you've never run it before. There's a rock ledge on the right to stop on, but be careful, or you'll be swept over before you can stop.

Run this rapid by skirting the left-hand end of the ledge as closely as possible, then immediately turning downstream, staying on the right-hand side of the chute. There are usually four big standing waves in this rapid. You may have to ferry to avoid being swept into the bluff on your left. For the next ½ mile you'll have some more sharp shoals, but after you pass under the railroad bridge, it's mostly just shallows to the take-out.

Take-out parking is very limited; in fact there is only one place. The other obvious places are either posted, blocked, unsafe to leave your vehicle because of the danger of theft or stripping, or you will be blocking a road. Do **not** park on County 10 except to unload because the shoulder is too narrow, and you can't get your vehicle completely off the road. The **only** relatively safe place to park is about 200 yards north of the bridge. There is a dirt road going up to a house and a small dirt road turning off this one down into a field. You can park here **if you get permission from the people in the house.** Your vehicle will be pretty safe and also out of the way.

The take-out is easy—just on the downstream, right-hand side of the bridge. You'll have a short but steep haul up to the road.

SECTION 2

CAHABA RIVER 8.4 MILES

County 10 to Lovick Bridge
Drop: 5.3   Difficulty: 0–1
Topos: Leeds   Hazards: None

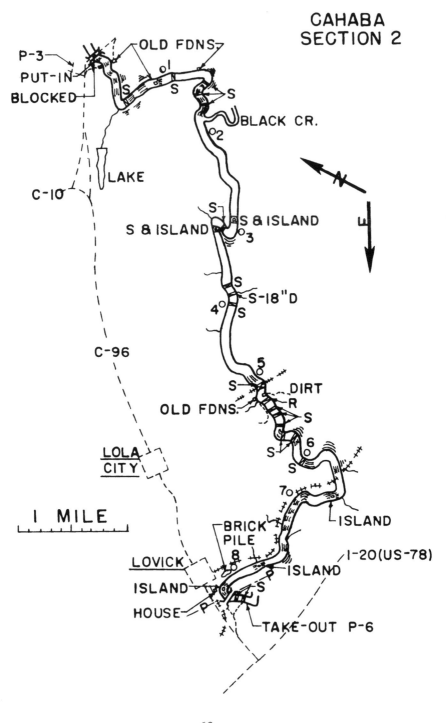

CAHABA
SECTION 2

OLD FDNS

P-3
PUT-IN
BLOCKED

1

S

N

S

S

BLACK CR.

2

LAKE

C-10

S

S & ISLAND

S & ISLAND

3

S & ISLAND

S

S-18"D

4

S

C-96

5

S

DIRT

OLD FDNS.

R

S

6

S

LOLA
CITY

S

7

1 MILE

ISLAND

BRICK
PILE

8

I-20(US-78)

LOVICK

ISLAND

ISLAND

HOUSE

P

S

TAKE-OUT P-6

This section is a real delight for the floaters who just want a pretty and easy float. There's nothing magnificent in this section—nearly all of it is bounded by low rolling hills and/or banks of five or six foot height that lead back to flat areas adjoining the river. There are very few signs of habitation and these only in the last 1½ miles. It's just a nice, pleasant float. Although I show many shoals, these are usually ledges or one single line of low rocks across the river. They are actually more like shallows than shoals but will require a little picking and selection at lower levels of water.

See the take-out information for Section 1 for a description of this put-in.

The river is about 30 feet wide at its beginning and gradually widens to about 50 feet at the take-out. Water level for Section 2 can be read off the orange painted gauge on the downstream side of the western bridge pier on I-20, just below the take-out. At the lowest mark you will have some bottom dragging in places but should be able to find a floatable path almost everywhere; at plus four inches you will have no problems at all.

For the first two miles (to the confluence of Black Creek) the river is pretty shallow, and it's here that you'll have difficulty at low water levels. You'll see some rock formations on your right at about mile ½ and some bluffs back from the river along this same section on both the right and left. If you run Section 1 and 3 of this river, you'll find that there is a distinct difference in the appearance of the land surrounding each section. Section 1 is precipitous, sharp, and rocky. This section (2) is low, gentle, rounded hills, and in Section 3 you'll see sharper, steeper, higher hills much closer to the river.

About mile 1 you'll see a chunky piece of formed concrete about eight feet high and twelve feet square right in the middle of the river. This is a good place for logjams and has a little shoal around it too. Just downstream you'll see a high foundation on your left and some lower ones back in the woods. This was probably for an old railroad line.

After Black Creek comes in, the river deepens considerably, and for almost a mile you'll have a long pool flowing through low banks. At the end of this pool is a picturesque rock island best run by on the right.

The little stream at the eight inch drop just before mile 4 is too small to paddle up but has some pretty, tumbling little drops of its own if you care to look. At mile 4 are some boulder formations on your left on the shore and down in the water. The little stream on your right just below mile 4 has a natural rock dam about 12 inches high that is so perfect it looks man-made.

At mile 5 after passing under the railroad bridge, you'll see high old foundations of large stone blocks which were probably the old location of these tracks. Just past these you'll enter a sort of valley with higher, steeper hills on your left, and you'll come to the only rapid on this stretch. It's a little turbulent, has a 12 inch drop, then a short run and another drop. There are large rocks on the shore and a big one on your left near the end of the run. This is a very simple clear-cut Class 1 rapid and should be no trouble at all. The hills will be steeper for the next mile, and at about 5¾ miles you'll see some of the few bluffs in this section that are actually in the river. These are on your left and about 20 feet high. The next ones are about 50 feet high, preceded by some pretty rock formations, and are on your left just before the next railroad bridge. An interesting note on this crossing—as you come down the river, look at the tracks. You'll see they are **not** sitting on the right-hand pier in the river. This is an old stone pier exactly like those you saw back up river, and as you float by it, you'll see that a new concrete pier just behind it has replaced it. Still it's sort of startling at first glance.

At about mile 7½ there are some long, low bluffs on your left (and a railroad track on your right). Just below mile 8 you'll come to a strange looking pile of stuff on your right—like strip pit tailings. These are thousands of old and broken bricks on the hillside from the brick kiln on top of the hill. Around the curve there is a heavy shoal just below the concrete bridge, and just below it is the take-out on your right.

The take-out is an easy slope up to a dirt field. At present, there is plenty of parking and turn-around space and an easy carry to your vehicle.

SECTION 3

CAHABA RIVER 5.9 MILES

Lovick Bridge to County 143 (Grants Mill)   **Difficulty: 2**
Drop: 8   **Hazards: One Class 1 rapid,**
Topos: Leeds, Irondale   **one 2½ foot drop**

This is a very pleasant short ride. See the take-out information for Section 2 for a description of this put-in. Water level for Section 3 can be read off the orange painted gauge on the downstream side of the west bridge pier at the I-20 bridge. This is a series of orange marks in two inch increments. At the lowest mark you should be able to float this stretch. Two inches below this mark you may have to lift over a place or two or at least step out. You will definitely have to get out at the last shoal just above the take-out. The river is about 50-60 feet wide at the put-in and averages this width all the way.

The first mile of this run is mostly shallows, and the second mile has quite a few houses on the right shore. Below the I-20 bridge is a pretty area with low rocks all along both banks. The small shoals are easy; however, there are some big rocks in the river at the beginning and end of the shoal near mile 1.6, and these plus the bend in the river should be watched out for at higher water levels. The left bank turns into a high steep hill just past this shoal followed by some 10-20 feet high rock formations that go directly into the water.

Just around the next bend the river is necked down by a lot of low rocks out from the left shore. You can run this rapid on the right by following the main current, for even at low water there is a nice chute. This is about a two foot drop in elevation. Watch this place if the water is up about one foot.

Note the scenic rocky hillsides on your right just before this rapid. At about mile 2¾ just past the second house, is a shoal with an overall drop of about three feet. In low water it is a long shallow with a lot of little rocks and very low drops. In higher water you can run right through it.

With the exception of a few shallows and low drops (six to eight inches), the next two miles are essentially taken up by a pool with scenic hillsides alternating along both shores.

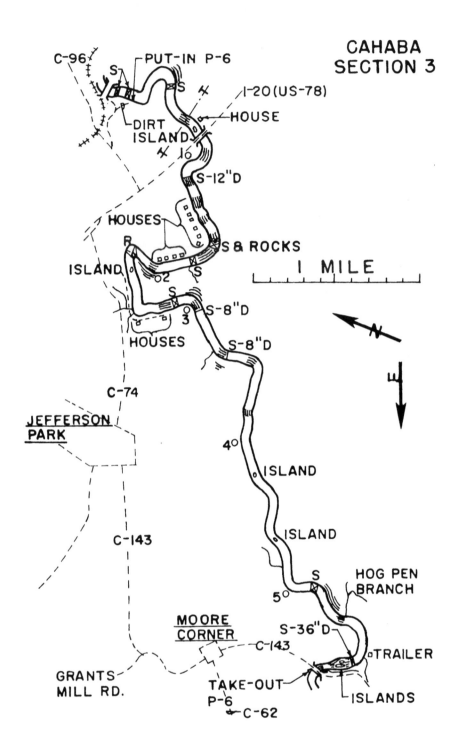

CAHABA
SECTION 3

C-96
PUT-IN P-6
S
S
I-20 (US-78)
HOUSE
DIRT
ISLAND
S-12"D
HOUSES
S & ROCKS
ISLAND
2
S
1 MILE
N
S
S-8"D
3
S-8"D
HOUSES
E
C-74
JEFFERSON
PARK
4
ISLAND
C-143
ISLAND
HOG PEN
BRANCH
S
5
MOORE
CORNER
S-36"D
C-143
TRAILER
GRANTS
MILL RD.
TAKE-OUT
P-6
ISLANDS
C-62

At mile 5 is a harder shoal—a stairstep affair with a total drop of about three feet and preceded by a long shallow. The last drop in this shoal is very ragged and rocky. Down the middle is about the best path (the only one in low water).

Just after you pass a trailer on your left is the last drop—about 2½ feet in the middle, less on the ends. In low water (zero or less) you will probably have to lift over or just slide down the rocks. The drop is ragged and inclined with rocks scattered about at the bottom. In higher water be cautious in the paths around the island immediately below this drop as they are good logjam creators.

The take-out is steep and gets slippery when wet. It's on the downstream, right of the bridge. When you park here, it's best to park on the east side of the highway as you can get farther off the road.

Lifting over a logjam, a place where it helps to have friends!

SECTION 4

CAHABA RIVER 13.2 MILES

County 143 (Grants Mill) to U. S. 280
Drop: 2.5 Except 20 from Mile 8-9.7   Difficulty: 1
Topos: Irondale, Cahaba Heights   Hazards: U. S. 280 Dam

This map and description covers two rides—County 143 to River Run Bridge (7½ miles) and River Run Bridge to U. S. 280 (5¾ miles). All this section is relatively flat, about 50 feet wide, and with only two really noticeable changes in elevation. One of these is just before mile 5 in the first ride and is a wide, easy chute. The second is at mile 9 on the second ride and is a long shallow that slopes down. In low water you will find very few channels to follow at the mile 9 shallow and will possibly have to walk. In high water, however, exercise caution, as the bend at the end of this drop is pretty abrupt.

See the take-out information for Section 3 for a description of the County 143 put-in.

This entire section down to mile 9½ is very shallow in the summer. I haven't made an attempt to show all of these shallows on the map because a few inches of water means "float"; a few inches less means "drag." Below the last shallow (mile 9½) you enter the upper parts of the pool behind the 280 dam, and, except for the possibility of a few trees fallen in the river, it's clear sailing from here to the take-out at the dam.

This pool requires a little paddling as it gradually gets wider and slower, but it's a cool, pretty float on a hot summer day down to the last half-mile. At this point the river widens to about 150 feet, and, unless you stick to the trees and bushes, you'll be out in the sun.

The Little Cahaba River comes in on your left above the 280 take-out. You can paddle part of the way up this narrow, winding little river without much trouble. Coming down it is a ride of its own, and this is shown on another map.

The take-out is under the **new** 280 bridge. There is a well-beaten-out parking spot by the **old** 280 bridge on the right. Unfortunately this is now blocked to traffic but you can walk to it. On the left is a gradual slope up to old 280 that you might

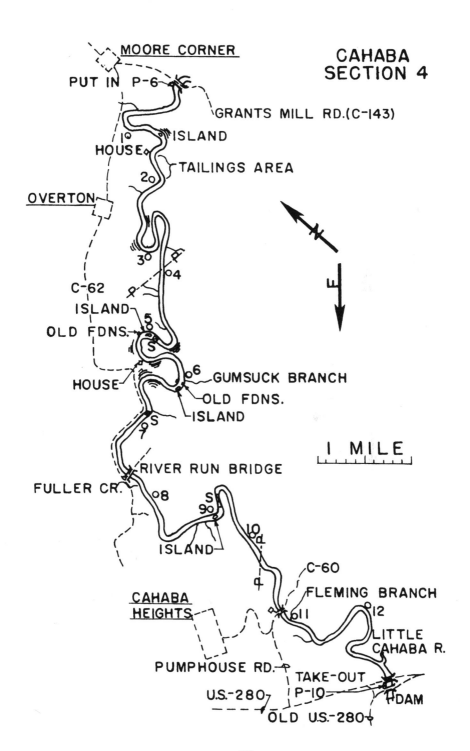

MOORE CORNER

PUT IN P-6

GRANTS MILL RD.(C-143)

ISLAND

HOUSE

TAILINGS AREA

OVERTON

CAHABA
SECTION 4

E

C-62

ISLAND

OLD FDNS.

S

HOUSE

GUMSUCK BRANCH

OLD FDNS.

ISLAND

S

1 MILE

RIVER RUN BRIDGE

FULLER CR.

S

ISLAND

C-60

FLEMING BRANCH

CAHABA
HEIGHTS

LITTLE
CAHABA R.

PUMPHOUSE RD.

TAKE-OUT
P-10

U.S.-280

DAM

OLD U.S.-280

The U. S. 280 dam in flood.

prefer. Both put-ins are good as they are low and with gentle slopes into the water.

The pool above highway 280 is one of the few places on the Cahaba where an easy round-trip ride can be made. The 4 2/3-mile round-trip paddle from 280 to County 60 (the pumping station) and return or from 280 up to mile 9½ on my map (about 6½ miles round trip) are two favorites. Another variation is floating from County 60 down to U. S. 280.

In the summer when the river is practically stagnant, the 280 pool is often covered with scum and moss—not too inviting-looking. The only hazard on this ride is the 280 dam. This is about 50 yards downstream from the take-out and is no danger unless water is actually running over it and you paddle right up to the edge.

CAHABA RIVER 3.1 MILES

U. S. 280 to County 29 (Caldwell Mill)
Hazards: Likelihood of Arrest!

This section of the Cahaba is the only part that should not be floated. There are a number of privately owned dams on this stretch, and the property owners of the houses adjacent to these dams tend to get irate if you portage on their property. Some puff up enough to threaten you with arrest for trespassing.

Now, whether they own the river or the dam or can legally prevent you from bypassing the dam is a moot point which could best be tested by numerous court cases. As court cases are expensive to both parties, however—as well as time-consuming and temper-raising—it's probably easiest to just skip the Cahaba from U. S. 280 to the County 29 (Caldwell Mill) Bridge.

To be fair, however, I feel that most of the property owners probably have a basis for their attitude. There are possibly a few who suffer from inherent irascibility, but, more likely, blatant disregard for their property or rights coupled with littering and insults by irresponsible floaters has contributed greatly to this feeling of enmity. And, as much as I hate it, there **are** a lot of irresponsible floaters.

SECTION 5

CAHABA RIVER 8.2 MILES

County 29 (Caldwell Mill) to Lorna Road
Drop: 3   **Difficulty: 0**
Topos: Cahaba Heights, B'ham. South, Helena   Hazards: None

This is an extremely easy float but does have numerous shallows in it that will give you problems in low water. To my mind this section is not as scenic or interesting as some on the Cahaba. The river is about 40 feet wide at the put-in and widens to about 50 feet at the take-out. It is bordered much of the way by six to eight foot high earth banks that are topped with wide,

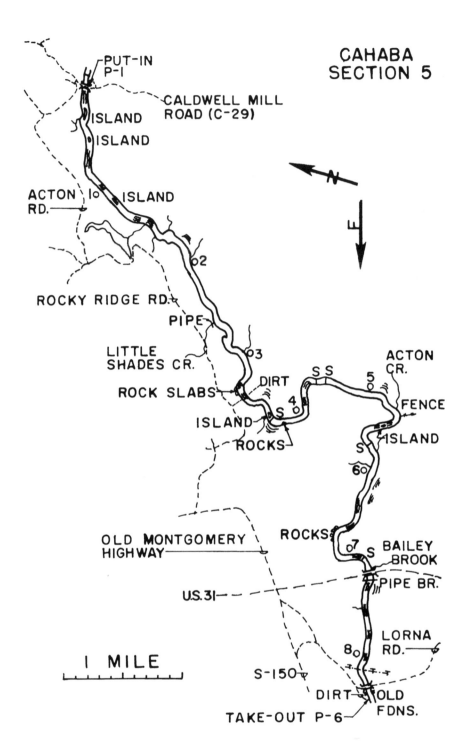

CAHABA
SECTION 5

PUT-IN
P-1

CALDWELL MILL
ROAD (C-29)

ISLAND

ISLAND

N

E

ACTON
RD.

1o

ISLAND

o2

ROCKY RIDGE RD.

PIPE

LITTLE
SHADES CR.

o3

ACTON
CR.

ROCK SLABS

DIRT

S S

5
o

FENCE

S
4
o

ISLAND

S

ISLAND

ROCKS

S
6o

ROCKS

OLD MONTGOMERY
HIGHWAY

7
o

S

BAILEY
BROOK

U.S. 31

PIPE BR.

LORNA
RD.

1 MILE

8
o

S-150

DIRT

OLD
FDNS.

TAKE-OUT P-6

70

flat areas. A few low hills reach the area, and occasionally a steeper one will present itself in the sharp bends. There are only a few rock formations and bluffs, but for the golf addict, you do pass by two golf courses.

The put-in only has parking room for one or two cars on the shoulder of the road. There is a small private road on the left, upstream from the bridge, that leads to a low dam just above the bridge. This offers parking space for eight to ten vehicles and a little better put-in. This is private, however, so seek permission before you use it. There is no water level indicator for this stretch.

The flat area on your right for the first ¾ of a mile is a golf course. The islands and shallows in the first three miles offer no problems, and the ford at about mile 3½ is just another shallow with a dirt road leading into the river on both sides. Just before the ford are some big rock slabs along the shore that offer a break in the usual dirt banks. In the sharper bends past mile 3½ you can see a few low rock bluffs on the right leading into a rocky hillside at about mile 4.

The shoals at mile 4½ and those on down this stretch are single low lines of rocks in the river with clear paths through them. After mile 5 you will see slightly higher hills in places, with some rock formations and a few low bluffs back off the river.

After you pass under the U. S. 31 bridge, there is another golf course on your right which extends down to mile 8. The take-out is about 50 yards downstream from Bains Bridge (Lorna Road) on your right. It is a dirt road leading to within about 50 feet of the river and has limited parking (about six cars). After a rain this road is slippery and so is the carry from the river up to the road. The U. S. 31 bridge offers a very poor take-out due to high, steep, overgrown, and rough banks.

71

SECTION 6

CAHABA RIVER 9.8 MILES

Lorna Road to County 52
Drop: 4   Difficulty: 0
Topos: Helena, Greenwood   Hazards: None

This is a peaceful, easy float in generally shallow water. The river is about 50 feet wide, gradually changing to about 75 at the take-out. There is a painted gauge on the west bridge foundation at the Nash Bridge (County 52). At the 0 mark you can float through everything in Section 6, and the most shallow places will be about six inches deep. The only possible hazards in this stretch are fallen trees in the river. This map was made at mark 0.

Parking is rather limited at the put-in, and the path to the river is slippery when wet. See the take-out description for Section 5 for more details.

Most of the ride is through low, dirt banks or low hills. There are quite a few small rock formations along the river's edge, some bluffs and larger formations back from the river, and a few medium bluffs on the river. The rocks and bluffs become more frequent as you progress down the river, and at about mile 5¾ the gravel bar shallows become less frequent and begin to change to small shoals, usually consisting of a single line of rocks across the river.

There are some very pretty pools in the last 4½ miles of this section. Except for a few houses set back from the river, the section has few signs of civilization, and the banks are generally heavily wooded. Some of the prettier bluffs and rock formations are at the bend at mile 3, at the mile 4.5 power line crossing, at the shoal just before mile 6, and at the bend about mile 7 1/3—all on your left. Because of the wooded shores and the lack of nearby roads, the entire section is very quiet and hushed. If you drift through the pools, the only sounds you will hear will be the calls of birds and the rustlings of the forest.

Most of the islands shown are real islands, but a few of them are only grass hummocks which would be covered at water levels of about plus 12 inches.

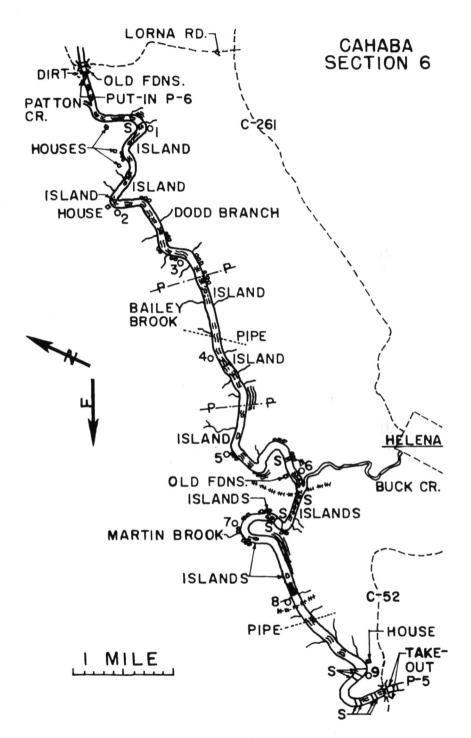

CAHABA
SECTION 6

LORNA RD.

C-261

DIRT

OLD FDNS.
PUT-IN P-6

PATTON
CR.

S 1

HOUSES ISLAND

ISLAND

ISLAND
HOUSE 2

DODD BRANCH

3

P
P

ISLAND

BAILEY
BROOK

PIPE

4 ISLAND

P P

ISLAND

HELENA

5

S 6

OLD FDNS.

BUCK CR.

ISLANDS

S

S ISLANDS

7

S

MARTIN BROOK

ISLANDS

C-52

8

PIPE

HOUSE

TAKE-
OUT
P-5

S 9

S

N

E

1 MILE

73

The take-out is fairly overgrown, and you'll have about a 50 yard carry up a path to the road if you take-out downstream of the bridge on the left. Parking at the take-out is on the shoulder of the road, but it's wide enough so there's no hazard. There is a shorter and clearer, but steeper, take-out on the right by the west bridge foundation that you might prefer.

SECTIONS 7–8–9

CAHABA RIVER 6.3, 7.1, AND 6 MILES

County 52 to Booths Ford   Difficulty: 0
Drop: 3.1, 2.8, 3.3   Hazards: None
Topos: Greenwood (7½ minute), Montevallo, Blocton (15 minute)

This description covers three sections as this entire 19.4 mile part of the river is alike from section to section, only varying in width as you progress downstream. It is also the longest single run on the Cahaba that is almost totally wilderness. One cabin, a few footpaths and fire roads, two gas line crossings, and a railroad trestle are the only reminders that you are not far in the forest. A number of miles of Section 7 flow by a clear-cut area on the right, but a buffer zone of vegetation has been left along the bank that effectively masks the cleared area from the river.

Water level indication for all three sections is on a painted gauge on the right-hand bridge pier at County 52. The bottom mark is "0," and you can float through all of Section 7, 8, and 9 at this level with no problems. At four inches below 0, you can still float everywhere but will have to pick your way and begin to watch for the slabs under the water; at eight inches below 0, you will have to get out of the boat at about ten places—the first two being immediately below County 52. You will also have to be very selective of your path at a lot of other spots, most of which are concentrated in the last few miles of Section 9.

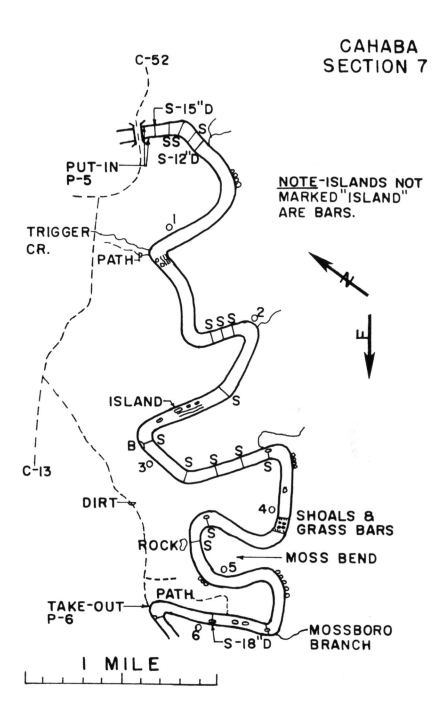

CAHABA
SECTION 7

C-52

S-15"D

S

SS
S-12"D

PUT-IN
P-5

NOTE-ISLANDS NOT
MARKED "ISLAND"
ARE BARS.

TRIGGER
CR.

PATH

o1

N

E

SSS

o2

ISLAND

S

B S

3o

S   S   S

S

C-13

DIRT

4o

SHOALS &
GRASS BARS

ROCK

S
S

MOSS BEND

o5

PATH

TAKE-OUT
P-6

6

S-18"D

MOSSBORO
BRANCH

1 MILE

75

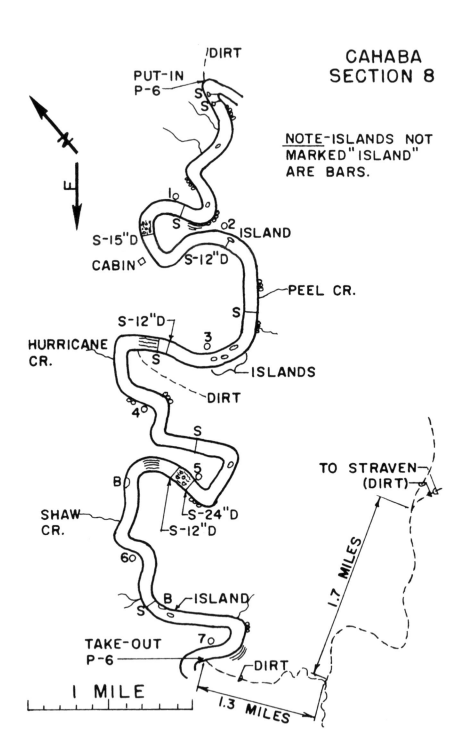

CAHABA
SECTION 8

PUT-IN P-6

DIRT

NOTE-ISLANDS NOT MARKED "ISLAND" ARE BARS.

S-15"D

CABIN

S-12"D

2 ISLAND

PEEL CR.

HURRICANE CR.

S-12"D

3

ISLANDS

DIRT

4

5

S-24"D

SHAW CR.

S-12"D

6

B ISLAND

TO STRAVEN (DIRT)

1.7 MILES

TAKE-OUT P-6

7

DIRT

1 MILE

1.3 MILES

76

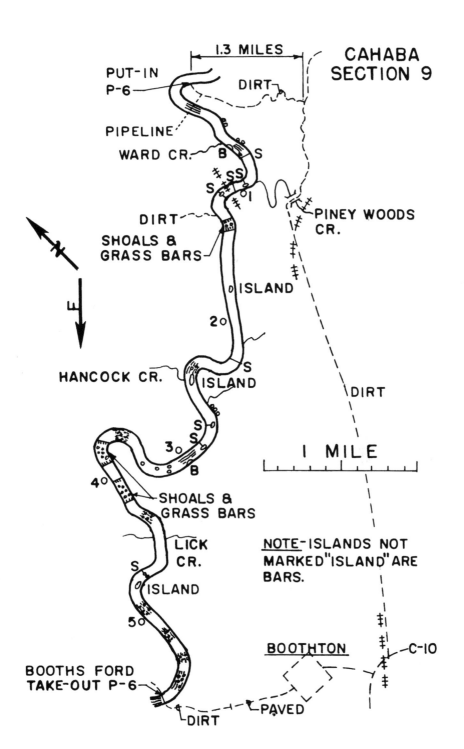

CAHABA
SECTION 9

1.3 MILES

PUT-IN
P-6

DIRT

PIPELINE
WARD CR.

B S

S SS
S I

DIRT
SHOALS &
GRASS BARS

PINEY WOODS
CR.

ISLAND

2

HANCOCK CR.

S
ISLAND

S
S

DIRT

3

B

1 MILE

4

SHOALS &
GRASS BARS

LICK
CR.

NOTE-ISLANDS NOT
MARKED "ISLAND" ARE
BARS.

S
ISLAND

5

BOOTHTON

C-10

BOOTHS FORD
TAKE-OUT P-6

PAVED

DIRT

N

E

77

You can also judge the level for Section 9 by the water over the slab at the Booths Ford (Section 9) take-out. About two inches of water over the ford roughly corresponds to the eight inches below 0 level. This map was made at eight inches below 0.

All of the shoals are very mild, usually only a short line of rock shelves across the river. At several locations there are low, single lines of rocks across the river that are not shoals. There are also numerous islands or bars of grass on gravel. Many of these would be covered at a "0" level, and others would create shallows. Many of the shoals would also virtually disappear at the "0" level, and, of course, the grass is not there in the winter. There are a lot of slabs of rocks under the water, but none of these will give you any problems except at very low water.

All of Section 1 is very winding. In Sections 2 and 3 the bends are fewer and less pronounced, and the pools become longer. The banks are generally earth and 10-15 feet high, broken at intervals by low rock formations along the shore. Higher, steeper hills rise occasionally at the bends. There are a couple of small bluffs, one large rock formation, and several pretty islands. The shores are heavily overgrown, and the overall sense is one of isolation and quiet beauty. The river is about 75 feet wide at the Section 7 put-in and gradually widens to about 90 feet at the end of Section 8 and 125 feet at the end of Section 9. The last two miles of Section 9 are pretty shallow.

See the take-out information for Section 6 for the put-in for Section 7. The take-out for Section 7 (or put-in for Section 8) has good off-the-road parking. There is a short embankment (about 20 feet) down to the river—steep but easily walked unless it's wet. This put-in (take-out) is in the clear-cut area, and the road to it is very good despite being dirt.

The take-out for Section 8 (put-in for Section 9) is a pretty drive through the woods, but only if the road is dry. The road is narrow and has some rutted places in it. Unless you have a four-wheel-drive vehicle, it would be best to stay off it when it's muddy. At the end of it is a turn-around place with parking for about six cars. You are still about 50 yards from the river. You can drive on down to within about 20 yards of the river, but it's a tight turn at the end and parking for only two vehicles. It would be best to check this last 30 yards of road, as there is one deeply rutted spot on it that a passenger car might not clear. The river landing itself is good—a nice shelving bar. The trail up to the parking place is easy and gradually sloping.

Take-out at Booths Ford (end of Section 9) is at a concrete slab across the river. There is limited parking (two cars) on the left but plenty of room for parking and turn-around on the right. In moderate water you can drive across the slab, but if you have any doubts, you might wait until someone local drives across it—or doesn't!

Shuttle Road.

SECTION 10

CAHABA RIVER 13.7 MILES

Booths Ford to County 65 (Piper) **Difficulty: 1**
Drop: 3 to Masena, 5 Masena to Piper **Hazards: Slab at**
Topos: Blocton, Montevallo (15 minute) **Marvel-Ardela Road**

This is a little longer run than most but can still be made easily in one day. This entire float is in an area that has been, and is, the scene of much strip mining activity. Several miles of the river bank have been ruined insofar as beauty is concerned, and when you run your shuttle, you'll see many acres of bare ground that have been stripped. Despite this, the run is a nice one and has some beautiful shoals, creeks, and scenery to enjoy.

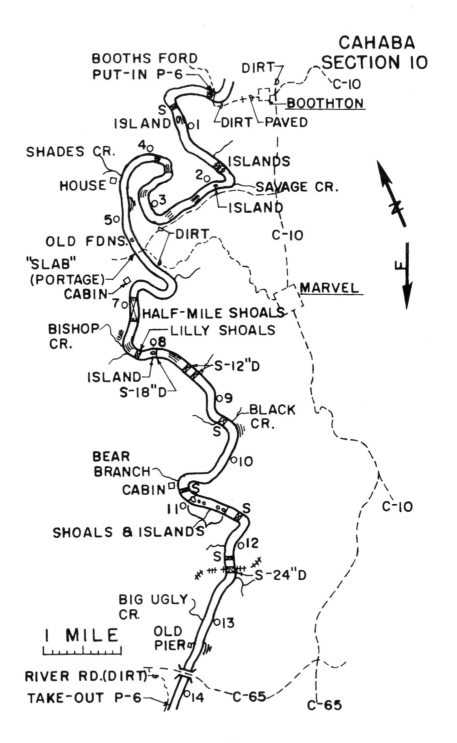

CAHABA
SECTION 10

BOOTHS FORD
PUT-IN P-6

DIRT
C-10
BOOTHTON

DIRT PAVED

ISLAND
S
ISLAND 1

SHADES CR.
4
ISLANDS

HOUSE
2
SAVAGE CR.

3
ISLAND

5
C-10

OLD FDNS.
DIRT

"SLAB"
(PORTAGE)
CABIN
7

MARVEL

HALF-MILE SHOALS
LILLY SHOALS

BISHOP
CR.
8

ISLAND
S-12"D

S-18"D
9

BLACK
CR.
S

BEAR
BRANCH
10

CABIN

11
S

SHOALS & ISLANDS

12
S
S-24"D

BIG UGLY
CR.
13

1 MILE
OLD
PIER

RIVER RD.(DIRT)
TAKE-OUT P-6
14
C-65

C-10

C-65

E

80

Access to the put-in at Boothton is down a narrow two-rut dirt road that ends at the ford. The ford is a concrete slab that crosses the river. There is plenty of parking room on the other side if the water is not too high to drive across the slab. Better judge by waiting until a local resident crosses—local residents are more familiar with when it's safe to drive across. There is room for about two cars on the Boothton side, but be sure to leave the road clear. If water is not completely over the slab, you will have problems with shallows all the way down.

Other than the small shoal at the slab, there are no obstacles between the Boothton slab and the Marvel-Ardela slab five miles down the river, except numerous shallows of various lengths in the first four miles. The river is generally placid and about 100-125 feet wide at the put-in, with low banks or small hills most of the way.

In this section you will see only a few not too noticeable strip mine dumps back away from the river until you approach the mouth of Savage Creek about three miles above the Marvel slab. From here on for the next 4½ miles you'll see a lot of strip mines right up to the bank of the river.

Your warning of the approach to the slab is two old stone railroad pilings in the river. Be extremely cautious if the water is flowing over the slab. Hug the shore (the right one is best), and take out in plenty of time to avoid being swept over. There is a dangerous hydraulic here at such times. If water is flowing only through the tubes, then you can paddle right up to the slab. Watch out for coal trucks! This is a private road, by the way, so don't use this slab as a take-out or as a put-in.

Another 1½ miles down the river will pretty well get you out of the strip mines and into the scenery. The river widens some, and you get back into the pretty, rocky hillsides so typical along this river.

Half-Mile Shoals is a walk-through in very low summer water—a swift ride with nothing to dodge at higher levels. Lilly Shoals has a long shallow, then a few eight to twelve inch drops just before and beside the island at mile 8. These drops are on both sides of the island but practically vanish on the right-hand side of the river.

At mile 11 you will find a string of small islands—breeding ground for many turtles in the spring and very picturesque at

81

A spot of nature rarely seen by the average traveler.

this time of year, also. A long shallow runs along beside them. Lest you look too closely at my map and note that I marked it "shoal," this is one of those places that I couldn't really decide which it was.

The only real drop you have is at the railroad trestle just past mile 12. Again—a series of small drops on the right, a chute with about a 24 inch drop immediately beside the left-hand foundation. In higher water this will have standing waves at its bottom and a powerful eddy behind the foundation.

The take-out is easy and low, on your right about 200 yards downstream from the County 65 bridge. There is turn-around room here. Be sure and park your shuttle cars so as not to block the river road. The numerous mud holes in the dirt road from the highway to the put-in are all hard-bottomed, so you shouldn't have any trouble with them.

SECTION 11

CAHABA RIVER 6.6 MILES

County 65 (Piper) to County 27 (River Bend)
Drop: 8   **Difficulty: 1**
Topos: Blocton (15 minute)   **Hazards: One 24 inch drop**

This section of the Cahaba contains the last large drops in elevation in this river. The drops are in the form of long shoals and are fairly even in their drop, the highest single abrupt change being the 24 inch drop shown on the map.

The first three miles of this trip are the shoal area, the first one being about ¾ mile from the put-in. Most of these shoals are covered with lilies in the late spring and early summer. In low water you'll have to thread a path down through these lily fields which is an interesting and pretty part of the trip, particularly if the lilies are blooming.

The river is about 125 feet wide at the put-in, widens out to about 200 feet at Hargrove Shoals, then narrows back to 125 feet at mile three, and holds this width to the take-out. See the take-out information for Section 10 for this put-in.

There is an orange painted water gauge on the downstream side of the left-hand bridge column at the take-out. The bottom mark is the lowest level at which this section may be floated with no difficulties at all. At four inches below this mark it can still be floated, but you'll have to do some picking. The map was made at this minus four level. Higher water will create standing waves in the shoals.

The terrain down to about mile 3 is steep, rocky, and wild-looking, but relatively low. There are numerous rock formations along the river's edge and low cliffs back from the banks. Several picturesque islands are in this part of the run, and there is one chute at about mile 1.3 that will call for a little caution at higher water levels. Hargrove Shoals between mile 2 and 3 is actually almost a mile long. In low water this is one of the places where you'll have to pick a path. At the end of this shoal is a 24 inch drop.

After mile 3 the river flattens out, the shoals become single, narrow lines of rocks across the river, and the wild-looking

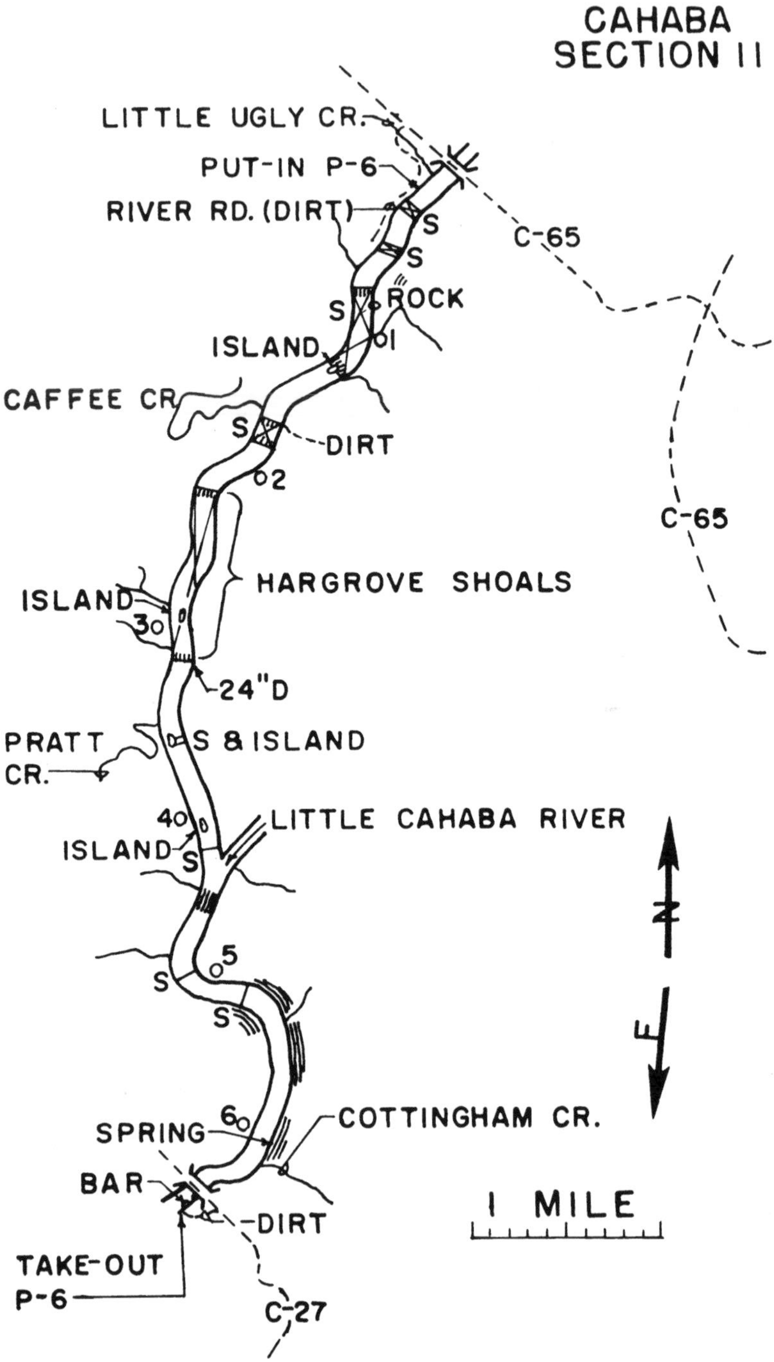

CAHABA
SECTION II

LITTLE UGLY CR.

PUT-IN P-6

RIVER RD. (DIRT)

C-65

ROCK

ISLAND

CAFFEE CR.

DIRT

C-65

HARGROVE SHOALS

ISLAND

24"D

PRATT CR.

S & ISLAND

LITTLE CAHABA RIVER

ISLAND

N

E

COTTINGHAM CR.

SPRING

BAR

1 MILE

DIRT

TAKE-OUT P-6

C-27

terrain settles into rolling hills with dirt banks broken occasionally by rugged cliffs. The most impressive of these cliffs are along the last 1½ miles before the take-out. If you paddle along the base of these formations, you'll find the spring shown on the map. Watch closely along here, and you may see some signs of other springs that bubble up in the main river. You will notice the Little Cahaba coming in on your left just past mile 4. This is a separate ride described elsewhere in this book.

The take-out is a low, gravel and sand bar on your left just below the bridge. There is a short carry (about six feet) up a bank to a level spot. In dry weather or with a four-wheel-drive vehicle you can drive down the dirt road from the highway to this level spot, but better check the ruts in the road first. There is plenty of room to turn around. You can also park by the highway in a cleared area at the upper end of this road.

SECTION 12

CAHABA RIVER 8.8 MILES

**County 27 (River Bend) to U. S. 82 (Centerville)   Difficulty: 0
Drop: Small   Hazards: One 24 inch drop
Topos: Blocton (15 minute). No others available**

This is a scenic, basically flat water stretch with just enough mild shoals and small drops to enliven the trip a bit. Many rock formations and low cliffs stud the shoreline. After Schultz Creek the shoreline becomes lower, and the rocks are generally replaced by dirt banks. The shore is heavily wooded, and you'll see no signs of civilization until you come to the house at mile 6½. The river is about 125 feet wide at the put-in and holds this to the take-out. See the take-out information for Section 11 for this put-in.

The cliffs at the beginning of the trip are very pretty and provide a nice backdrop to the view down the river from the put-in. The one shoal along this stretch has about an eight inch drop. On your left between mile 1 and 2 you'll see some of the shoreline rock formations that are typical along this stretch

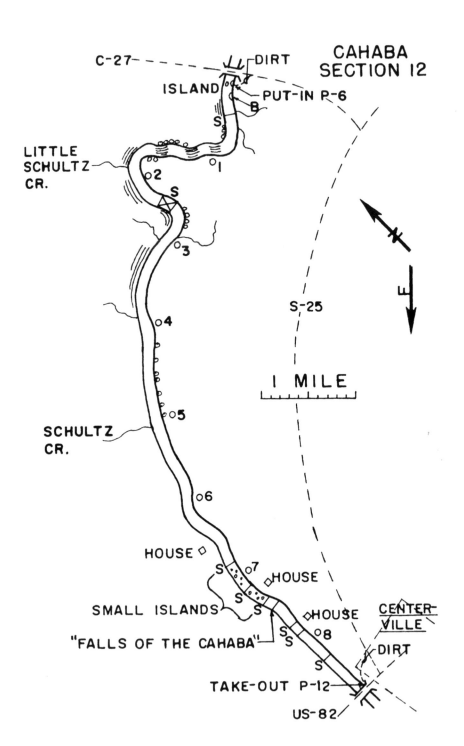

CAHABA
SECTION 12

C-27 — — — — — DIRT

ISLAND

PUT-IN P-6

B

S

LITTLE
SCHULTZ
CR.

2

1

S

3

E

4

S-25

1 MILE

5

SCHULTZ
CR.

6

HOUSE

7

HOUSE

S

S

SMALL ISLANDS

S

"FALLS OF THE CAHABA"

S

HOUSE

8

CENTER-
VILLE

S S

DIRT

S

TAKE-OUT P-12

US-82

down to about mile 6.

At about mile 2½ you'll come to a low grass island which will be covered at about one foot above the zero level. The cliffs and rock formations just below mile 8 are very pretty and a little unusual looking. From about mile 3 to mile 6½ you have a long pool through low rolling terrain. Schultz Creek enters on your right about halfway down this pool. This is a very scenic little creek about 30 feet wide. The water is clean and pretty, and you can paddle part way up it, if you want to fight the current. It's a fine place to wade on a hot summer day. At about mile 6¾ you come to almost a mile of low, grassy islands, shoals, and pools. These shoals are all very short with about six to ten inch drops. About mile 7½ you'll arrive at the "Falls of the Cahaba." This is a short shoal with a clear path on the right and a ragged drop of about two feet on the left. There is a clear path down this drop also, but you'll have to look to find it. The rest of the shoals are similar to those on the first part of the trip—very short and with low drops.

The take-out is on the left just under the bridge and is very steep. It also gets muddy rapidly after a few wet boats have gone up it. It's about a 25 yard haul up to a dirt road under the bridge but does have one plateau where you can rest. On your shuttle you will drive under this bridge from upstream and park just on the downstream side of it.

Water level for this run can be read on the downstream end of the second from the left bridge pier at the put-in. These red marks are graduated in tenths of a foot for three feet.

Linn Beck practices in a small drop.

SECTIONS 13-18

CAHABA RIVER 61 MILES

U. S. 82 (Centerville) to U. S. 80   Difficulty: 0
Drop: 1.3 (average for 61 miles)   Hazards: None
Topos: Summerfield, Selma. None available for Sections 13, 14,
     and part of 15.

This description covers the Cahaba River from Centerville to U. S. Highway 80. This is a distance of about 61 miles and is broken into six rides. Below Section 18 (U. S. 80) you begin to near the backwaters of the impoundment of Dannelly Lake, and the current flow gradually dies as you progress downstream.

The rides are all basically the same. Surprisingly, in normal water levels ("0" to about plus one foot), the current is generally not too much slower than the river above Centerville, and you don't have to paddle very much to make swift progress. In Sections 14, 15, and 16 particularly, many of the bends have gravel bars, and the islands are usually sand and gravel covered with willows and sycamores. The bars and many of the islands make good places to camp. Sections 13, 17, and 18 are not as blessed with these convenient camping sites. All of these sections have the advantage of always having plenty of water in them even in the dead of summer. There are no shoals or rapids, but there are numerous, easily negotiated shallows, most of which are associated with the bars. All of the bridges used as take-outs or put-ins are marked for water level indication down to the Radford Bridge (the end of Section 16). These are red marks graduated in tenths of a foot usually for three feet. You can float any of these rides with no trouble at all at the lowest mark. You can also float all of them at up to six inches below "0," but you'll have to be more selective of your path. Below the Radford Bridge there is never any water problem at all, so this bridge and those below it are not marked.

No topographic maps are presently available for the portions of the river covered by Sections 13, 14, and to mile 6.4 of Section 15, so these maps are not as accurate as most of those in this book. You'll have to be guided by the general curves of the river through these 29.4 miles!

Here is a synopsis of each of these six rides:

Section 13–U. S. 82 (Centerville) to Harrisburg Bridge. 11.7 Miles.

See the take-out information for Section 12 for this put-in. Water level indication is on the left-hand upstream bridge pier of the U. S. 82 bridge.

The banks are generally low and wooded with pastures beyond a fringe of shoreline trees in many areas. As you progress downstream, the bends begin to have higher, red dirt banks that come straight down into the water and are obviously well washed out when the water is up.

Many of the bends have gravel bars on their inside curves. Most of the islands would still be islands with plus two or three feet of water.

The river is about 125 feet wide at the put-in, narrows to 40 feet around the big island from mile 8.2 to mile 10, then spreads out to its original width from there to the take-out. Take the left fork around this island in the summer. There are a few small islands, bars, and logjams at this fork that may create a necessity for a lift-over at low water levels.

The take-out is on the right, 100 yards upstream from the Harrisburg Bridge. It has a short, easy slope up to a dirt road and has plenty of level turn-around space. The road from State 5 to the take-out bridge is a little hard to spot. You can identify it by a white, two-story, concrete block building located 1/10 mile north of the turn-off on State 5, on the west side of State 5. This building, as of this writing, is the "Young Merc. Co."

Section 14–Harrisburg Bridge to County 47 (Jericho) Bridge. 11.3 Miles.

See the take-out information for Section 13 for this put-in. Water level indication is on the right-hand, upstream bridge pier at the Harrisburg Bridge. Also see Section 13 for the location of the road to this bridge.

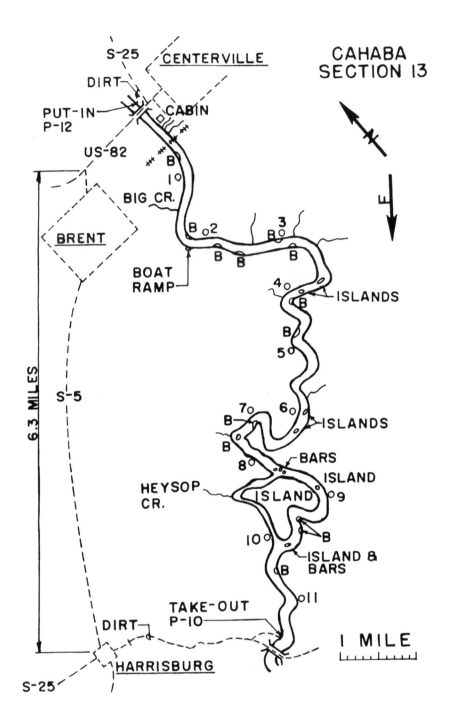

CAHABA
SECTION 13

S-25
CENTERVILLE
DIRT
PUT-IN P-12
CABIN
US-82
B 1
BIG CR.
BRENT
BOAT RAMP
B 2
3 B
B B B
4
ISLANDS
B
B
5
6.3 MILES
S-5
7
6
B
ISLANDS
B
8
BARS
ISLAND
HEYSOP CR.
ISLAND
9
10
B
ISLAND & BARS
B
11
TAKE-OUT P-10
DIRT
1 MILE
HARRISBURG
S-25

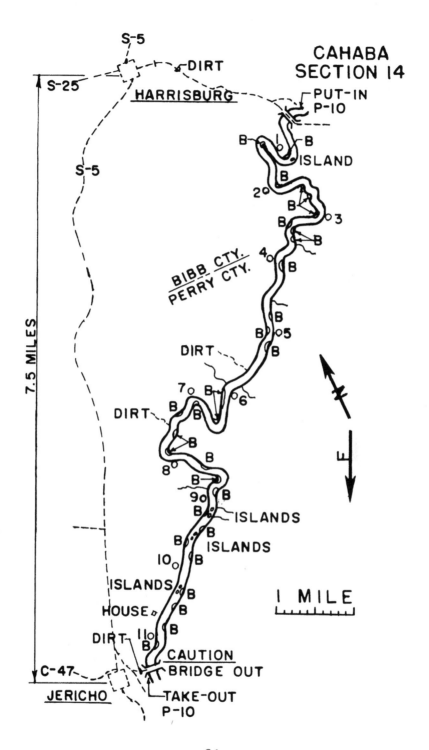

CAHABA
SECTION 14

S-5

DIRT

S-25

HARRISBURG

PUT-IN
P-10

B   B

ISLAND

B

2

B

3

B

B

BIBB CTY.
PERRY CTY.

4

B

B

B   5

DIRT

B

7   B

6

B

DIRT

B

B

8

B

9   B

B

ISLANDS

B

ISLANDS

B

10

B

ISLANDS

B

HOUSE

B

DIRT   11

B

CAUTION

C-47

BRIDGE OUT

JERICHO

TAKE-OUT
P-10

S-5

7.5 MILES

N

E

1 MILE

The banks in this area are almost all wooded and generally 10 to 15 feet high but sometimes as low as five feet. You will see short pasture areas at a few places. The land on top of the banks is flat and level, and the only hills in the area occur to the east at about mile 8, where a series of little round hills can be seen from the river. Almost every bend has a gravel bar on its inside curve—some of these are huge. About mile 9 and again near mile 10 the river widens out tremendously, and each location has several islands a few feet high. The only signs of civilization you'll see other than the pastures are two dirt roads (one with a pipeline crossing) and, down near mile 10, a small house on the right-hand bank.

The river is about 125 feet wide at the put-in and about 150 feet wide at the take-out. The take-out is on the right, downstream from the old, abandoned steel bridge, and at the construction location of a new bridge. The bank is low but steep for a few feet, and you then have about a 50 yard haul up a 40 degree slope to the parking place at the end of the old bridge. The road to this old bridge is closed, but you can drive around the sign. Just be sure you stop before the bridge—there's no bottom on it! Turn-around space is good.

Section 15—County 47 (Jericho) to State 14 (Sprott). 11.5 Miles.

See the take-out information for Section 14 for this put-in. Water level indication is on the *small* right-hand, downstream *old* bridge pier at Jericho. You should have no problem with this run up to about .6 feet below the bottom mark.

The section is about 150 feet wide at the put-in and holds this to the take-out, except near mile 8.3 where it widens out somewhat until the next sharp bend. This section is almost identical to Section 14 except the banks average more nearly 10 feet high with a few five foot sections on the left near the beginning and near mile 6.4 and 8.7. The usual terrain is the bank, then wooded flatland. The woods are fairly thick all along this section, but they get noticeably heavier just past mile 4 and remain so for about 2½ miles.

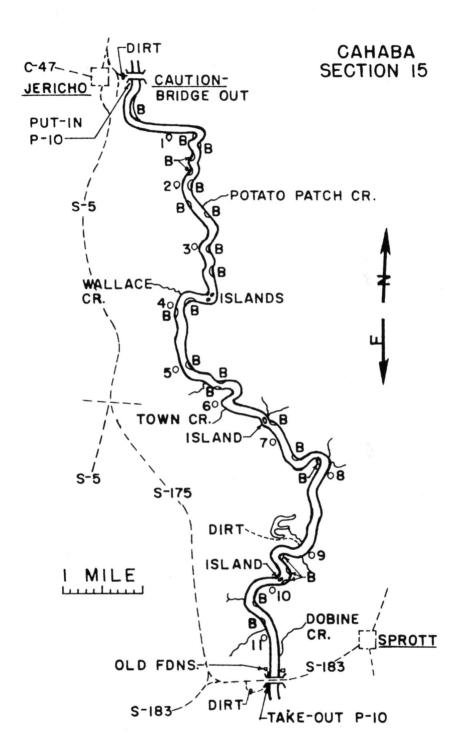

CAHABA
SECTION 15

DIRT

C-47

JERICHO

CAUTION—
BRIDGE OUT

PUT-IN
P-10

B

1 B
B
B

2 B

POTATO PATCH CR.

B

S-5

3 B

B

WALLACE
CR.

ISLANDS

4 B

5 B

B

6 B

TOWN CR.

B

ISLAND 7

B

S-5

8 B

S-175

DIRT

ISLAND 9

B

1 MILE

B 10

DOBINE
CR.

B

11 SPROTT

OLD FDNS

S-183

S-183

DIRT

TAKE-OUT P-10

93

You'll see a few obvious pasture areas. The first one is on your right just as you start the trip; another, about mile 1.8 on your right. One is on your left at mile 7.8, and the last one is at mile 9.4 on your right. Most of these have a thin fringe of trees along the bank.

There are a few ¾ mile-long stretches without bars, but, in general, almost every small bend has a gravel bar, some quite large. About mile 7 you will begin to notice more sand in the bars than you've seen in the preceding sections. Another sign of your southward path is an occasional cypress with its "knees" at the water's edge. The river and its banks are never actually swampy, but you will travel through an area near mile 8 much lower and wetter beyond the banks than the other parts of this run.

Islands are scarce on this run. There are a few on the left about mile 3.6 and a gravel island on the right just before mile 10. On the right at mile 7 there is a dirt road to the river; other than this and the pasture areas, the run is essentially wilderness. You'll see some old bridge foundations just before the take-out.

The take-out is on the right just upstream from the State 14 bridge. You drive under the bridge and nearly to the river on a fair dirt road. Access to the boats is good, and you'll only have about a 30 foot carry up a 35 degree slope to your car. The carry would be slippery if wet. Turn-around space is good.

Section 16–State 14 (Sprott) to County 30 (Radford). 7.3 Miles.

See the take-out information for Section 15 for this put-in. Water level indication is on the right-hand, upstream side of the middle bridge pier at the put-in. This is only marked for 2.6 feet; the lower .4 foot is omitted. You can easily float this run at up to 1.4 feet lower than the bottom mark.

This section has many more cypress trees and some Spanish moss. The bars are still basically gravel but with a lot more sand in and on them than the preceding sections and with some large, pure sand areas.

The earth banks start off about five feet high and have a

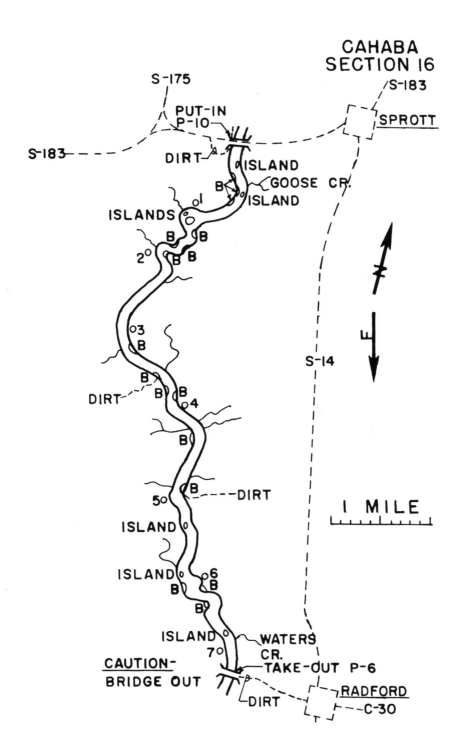

CAHABA
SECTION 16

S-175

S-183 /S-183

PUT-IN
P-10

SPROTT

DIRT

ISLAND

B GOOSE CR.

ISLAND

1

ISLANDS

B B

2 B B

3
B

S-14

DIRT B
B 4

B

B DIRT

5

ISLAND

ISLAND 6
B

B

ISLAND WATERS
7 CR.

CAUTION- TAKE-OUT P-6
BRIDGE OUT
DIRT RADFORD
C-30

1 MILE

95

few more five foot sections scattered along but are generally eight to ten feet high. All the shoreline is heavily wooded. A break in the general level terrain along the river occurs on the right from about mile 2.7 around the bend to mile 3.7. This is an area of low wooded hills. At the end of this section is a dirt bank that is unusual looking for this area. It almost has the appearance of rock.

There are several real islands in this section and also several gravel bar islands. About mile 6 the river widens out to about 300 feet with lots of bars and shallows. Just beyond this area the river narrows to about 100 feet and holds this to the take-out. Its average width from the put-in to this point is about 150 feet.

The take-out is on the left, upstream at the old abandoned bridge. It's steep (about 45 degrees) and slippery but only about a 25 foot climb to level ground. In low water (up to about plus two feet) you can climb out of your boat on conveniently located and shaped cypress roots. Parking is good and turn-around space adequate. The dirt road from the highway is narrow but level and firm.

Section 17–County 30 (Radford) to County 6 (Suttle). 9.1 Miles.

See the take-out information for Section 16 for this put-in.

This section's terrain is generally higher than Section 16. The eight to ten foot banks gradually build to 20-30 feet and average this for most of the run after mile 5.8, with some drops to five to ten feet and some dirt bluffs up to about 50 feet high. One of these bluffs near mile 4.6 has a small waterfall flowing over it.

Most of the right-hand shoreline is lightly wooded, often with a pasture behind a fringe of trees or, occasionally, clear and open. The left-hand shore is generally more heavily wooded but also has some pasture areas. In one area low wooded hills come directly into the river.

The banks on the outside bends are usually more in the nature of low bluffs. The lower five to ten feet of these dirt

CAHABA
SECTION 17

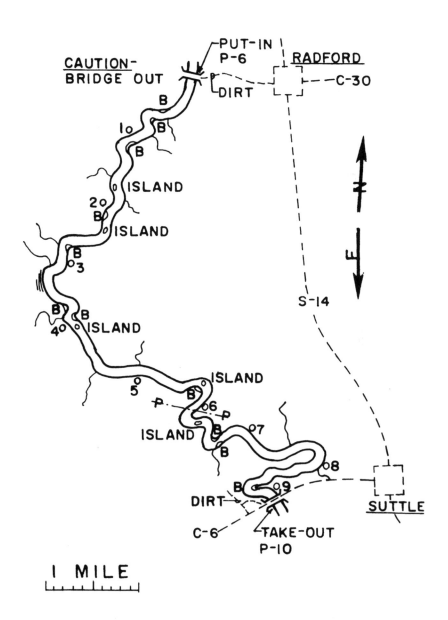

CAUTION- BRIDGE OUT

PUT-IN P-6

RADFORD

DIRT

C-30

B

I O

B

B

ISLAND

2 O

B

ISLAND

B

3

B B

4 O ISLAND

5

ISLAND

B

P P

6

ISLAND

B

7

B

8

B

DIRT

9

C-6

TAKE-OUT P-10

SUTTLE

S-14

N

E

I MILE

97

Waiting on the shuttle.

bluffs, especially below mile 5.8, are often made of compacted dirt that has all of the appearance of stone and probably is an early stage of a metamorphic process. At two places this "stone" protrudes from the bank in large slab-like shapes. One is about mile 2.5 on the left and the other near mile 6.6 on the right.

Camping spots are harder to find in this section. Most of the bars and islands are low and would be covered over at 12-24 inches more water than low summer levels. Others are often small in area. At mile 4 near Rice Creek are three good spots—two sand bars on opposite sides of the river and a small island between them. Another small island is at mile 6.3, and a sand bar is just downstream from it on the left at mile 6.6. Just across the river from this bar is a small pretty waterfall on an incoming stream. You'll see another small waterfall (about five feet high) about 20 feet up a stream coming in on the left just below mile 1.

The cypress trees and Spanish moss found in Section 16 are almost nonexistent in this stretch of the river. Most of the bars are pure sand with only an overlay of gravel on some of them.

The river is about 100 feet wide at the put-in and averages this to the take-out. The take-out is on the right under the bridge. Boat access is fair, and the 40 foot carry is up a sandy, moderate slope. You can drive under the bridge on a good dirt road almost to the top of this slope. Turn-around space is good.

Section 18-County 6 (Suttle) to U. S. 80. 9.7 Miles.

See the take-out information for Section 17 for this put-in.

This section is similar to Section 17 except the banks average 30-40 feet for almost the entire run and the bluffs are higher. As in the preceding section the metamorphic "stone" banks are present at many of the outside bends beginning at the put-in. The river is about 100 feet wide at the put-in and take-out, varying between 75 and 125 feet between the two points.

The banks (again more like low bluffs) are clear occasionally, but more often have a thin fringe of trees between the river and pasture areas or else are lightly wooded. The left bank is a little more forested.

Two bends have notable bluffs. At mile 1.3 the dirt wall soars upward about 100 feet as it rounds the bend. At mile 2.9 the bluffs are about 60 feet high with the lower 10 feet being the typical outside bend "stone." There is a big slab of this "stone" on the right at about mile 4.6.

The 50 foot high bluff in the big bend at mile 9 is an interesting sight. It slopes to a 10 foot wide flat at its base, then drops straight into the river. This flat runs at the same level for about a quarter mile around the bend, giving the appearance of a road paralleling the river. Both the "road" and part of the bluff behind it are the metamorphic dirt, and, at the start of this formation, there are layers of shale in it. Small waterfalls run off the "road" at two places, and one small stream runs in at river level through a peculiar cut in the formation.

Bars suitable for camping are both more frequent and bigger in this section. Most of the bars are pure sand, but some are overlaid with gravel. Near mile 1 there is a big gravel bar on the right. On the left just below it is a high, bank-hugging sand bar. Another big sand bar is just past the 100 foot bluff at about mile 1.4. On the right near mile 4.5 are two sand bars—one above and one below the "stone" slab you'll see there. There are other islands and bars which could be used, one an eight foot high gravel island at mile 2.3 on the right and another five-footer in the middle of the river at mile 4.6. These could vanish in the first flood, however.

Cypress trees and Spanish moss are scarce, although you'll see more between mile 5.2 and 5.8 than anywhere else on this

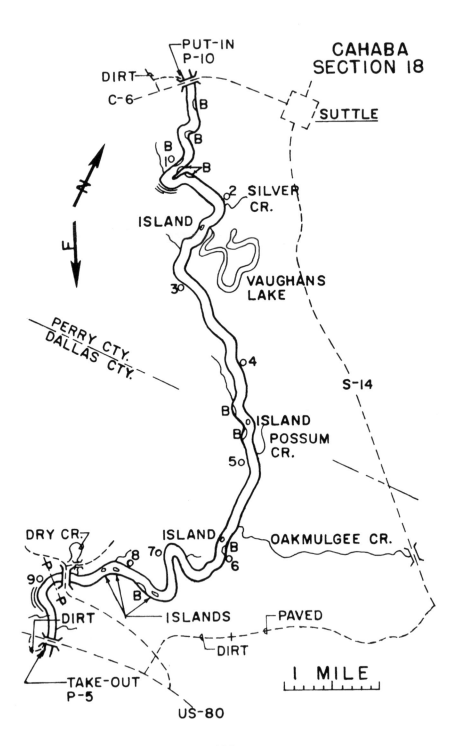

CAHABA
SECTION 18

SUTTLE

PUT-IN
P-10

DIRT

C-6

B

B

B

B
10

B

2 SILVER
CR.

ISLAND

N

E

30

VAUGHANS
LAKE

PERRY CTY.
DALLAS CTY.

4

S-14

B

ISLAND
POSSUM
CR.

B

50

DRY CR.

ISLAND

OAKMULGEE CR.

8

7

B

6

9

B

ISLANDS

PAVED

DIRT

DIRT

TAKE-OUT
P-5

US-80

1 MILE

100

run.

The clearing near mile 4 is a rather startling sight. As you round the bend, you'll see downstream on the right a low slope covered with neat rows of multicolored rectangles. These are old automobiles put there for erosion control and now half buried in the sand.

You can take out at the old steel bridge if you wish. It's still in use. Note just upstream from it what appears to be an old chimney on the right-hand shore. The U. S. 80 take-out is on the right under the bridge. It is not a great take-out, having a sharp slope right out of the water with the bottom several feet rather muddy. Luckily, it's only about 25 feet of gradually leveling path to flat ground. The road under the bridge is adequate, as is turn-around space, and you can drive right to the top of the take-out slope.

Solitude—one of the enjoyable aspects of canoeing.

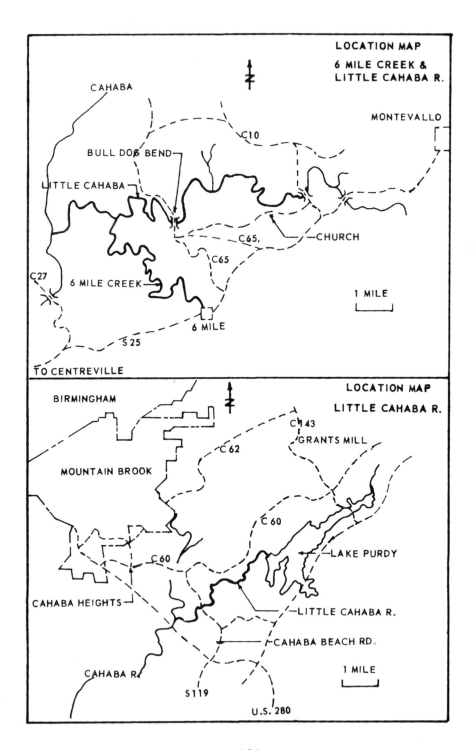

LITTLE CAHABA RIVER (LAKE PURDY) 4.7 MILES

Spillway Road to U. S. 280
Drop: 8.5 **Difficulty: 1**
Topos: Cahaba Heights **Hazards: Two low dams**

Several stretches of this run have privately owned gaze-boes, cabins, and cleared areas on the banks, but it's still a scenic, quiet little river where you can relax and be in relative solitude. Obviously you should respect the privacy of the developed property along the shores by not stopping there. This short run is a close-to-home trip for canoeists in the Birmingham area. The map and description cover all but the first half-mile below the Lake Purdy Dam.

In the summer this trip will usually require a lot of care in finding a floatable path. A good water level indicator is the slab in the river at the put-in. With six to twelve inches of water over the slab you'll have no trouble at all and can safely run the second dam. If water is just covering the slab, you'll still have a pretty easy ride as most of the shallow places will be underwater. With more than about four inches of slab showing above the water, you can make it but will have to hunt a path in many places.

The river averages about 25-30 feet wide and has several small drops and shoals. Two low, privately owned dams block it. The first dam is about five feet high and has a cottage and a waterwheel on the left. This is private property, so it's best to portage on the right unless you get permission to cross on the stonework on the left. As no one lives in the cottage, you'll have to get this permission ahead of time. The right-hand portage is steep and slippery but can be made in low water. In higher water (over the slab) you'll have to portage on the left, but do get permission first.

At present the second dam is leaking and you cannot run it. Normally it can be run if there is enough water flowing over the center of it. It's about a three foot drop that lessens to about two feet with a good water flow over it. Once you do paddle over it and are at the bottom, keep paddling until you clear the hydraulic which extends out about 12 feet. This will suck you back under the dam overflow and very quickly swamp you if you don't keep going. If you portage here, once more you will find a cabin at the dam. Get permission to portage first.

The trip can be shortened to 3.1 miles by getting out at the Cahaba Beach Road bridge. This is a rather poor take-out, however, with limited parking. Below this bridge the river levels out and begins to widen as it approaches the main Cahaba. Several scenic rocky hillsides are in this area.

The put-in is not a completely safe place to leave your vehicle, so be sure and lock it. It might also be a good idea to take your canoe racks off if they're easily removable. I've never heard of anyone having any theft or vandalism problems at the Highway 280 take-out. See the take-out information for Section 4 of the Cahaba for more on the take-out.

THE LITTLE CAHABA RIVER–GENERAL

The Little Cahaba River forms at the junction of Mahan and Shoal creeks about five miles southwest of Montevallo. The river flows almost due west. From the junction of these two creeks to its junction with the Cahaba River two miles above the County 27 (River Bend) bridge, the river is only about 17 miles long. The two trips described cover 13.3 miles of this length. One ride on Six Mile Creek, a tributary of the Little Cahaba, is also covered.

Averaging about 50 feet in width, the river is a picturesque blend of rocky shoals, small islands, drops, low falls, and quiet, slow moving pools. The banks are usually wooded and hilly with numerous boulder formations, low bluffs, and rocky hillsides along and just back from the river's edge to add scenic interest. In Section 2 the right bank is normally lower, with the wooded areas occasionally broken by the grassy slopes of pastures. Several small streams and creeks enter the river at various points, but only Six Mile Creek is canoeable for any length.

A few dirt roads touch the river between put-ins, and a few houses or cabins can be spotted from boat level. Other than

104

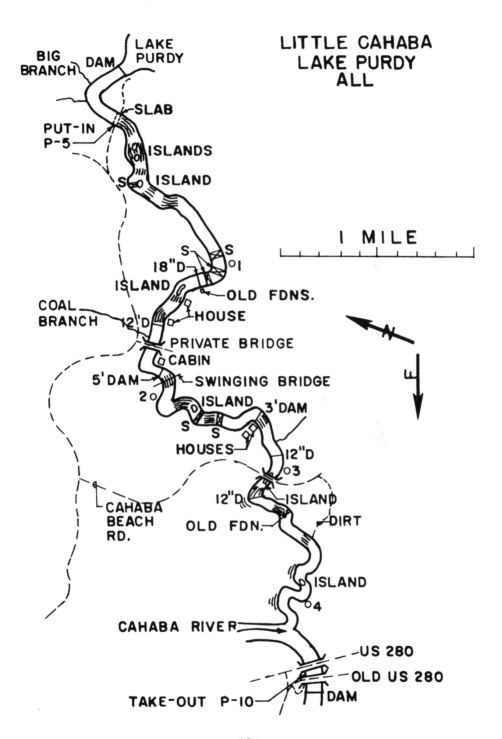

LITTLE CAHABA
LAKE PURDY
ALL

1 MILE

these intrusions the stretches are fairly empty of signs of civilization. This river is popular for short inner tube and raft trips and is also waded and float-fished by local fishermen. Despite this, however, it is definitely not crowded.

Watch out for hornet nests in low hanging tree limbs. Several stretches also have large, flat shelf-like rocks just under the surface. These present no danger. They are just something to avoid hitting. In very low water the shallows and many of the shoals are not floatable except by canoe or kayak. A good combination trip for a weekend is to float Section 1 on one day, camp at Bulldog Bend, then run Section 2 on the next day. This way you can leave your camping gear at the camp and have two enjoyable floats with an empty boat.

Parking for take-out of Section 1 and put-in of Section 2 is at Bulldog Bend Park—a privately owned campground on the river. There is a small fee for parking but plenty of room for at least 20 or 30 vehicles. No camping is allowed along the river but you can camp at Bulldog Bend. Much of the river is in a game management area so no firearms are allowed either.

SECTION 1

LITTLE CAHABA RIVER 6.7 MILES

Cahaba Valley Church to County 65 (Bulldog Bend)
Drop: 6.8 (approximately)   Difficulty: 1
Topos: Montevallo, Blocton (15 minute)
                            Hazards: Two low waterfalls

The put-in is between the church and the river just north of a picnic pull-off on your left as you come from County 65. You'll see the first shoals as the road approaches the river; put-in above them. Don't park in the picnic area. There's room for only about three cars to pull off the road at the put-in, so unload, run your shuttle, and, if possible, only leave one car there.

This section is both very scenic and a little exciting. There are enough shoals, drops, and falls to keep you on your toes and

106

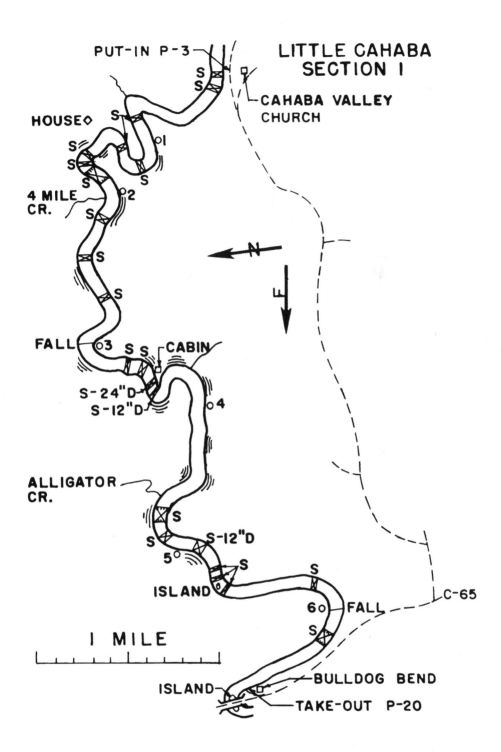

LITTLE CAHABA
SECTION I

PUT-IN P-3

CAHABA VALLEY
CHURCH

HOUSE◇

4 MILE
CR.

FALL

CABIN

S-24"D
S-12"D

ALLIGATOR
CR.

S-12"D

ISLAND

C-65

FALL

1 MILE

BULLDOG BEND

ISLAND

TAKE-OUT P-20

N

E

107

yet enough quiet places to let you sit back and relax and enjoy the scenery.

Water level indication is a gauge at Bulldog Bend. You can easily run Section 1 solo at a reading of 1.5. You can also run it tandem at this level, but not as easily. About the minimum level for *any* float on Section 1 is 1.0; below this you just won't enjoy it unless you like to wade some. (Section 2 is runnable at 1.0 with only minimum difficulty.) One advantage on this river—as of this writing you can telephone Bulldog Bend Camp for the gauge reading and possibly save yourself a trip.

The shoals from the put-in to the first fall will present no problems. The one just above Four Mile Creek is long and will require some care in selecting a path in low water. The first fall may be run about anywhere except on the extreme left if there is enough water to cover the tip of the fall. In very low water there is a path on the far left that will at least give you wet rocks to slide on, or you can go through a chute on the extreme right that has about a two to three foot drop.

The mile 3.4, 24 inch drop is really a two-step, sloping drop with a total descent of about three feet. This can be run anywhere except about 15 feet from the left bank where a curl of water invites you to run through it. Don't—there is a rock under all that pretty froth. The next two drops are low.

Through the ride so far you have passed cliffs and boulders and rock formations. You now enter a long quiet pool with some lovely low cliffs on one or both sides of the river. At the end of it, just past Alligator Creek, is a long shoal with a few sharp drops. You may enjoy a few hundred yards of scenic trip up Alligator Creek if there's enough water in it. The shoals from here to the last fall will vary in difficulty depending on the water level, but none are real problems.

The last fall is about a three foot sloping drop over a ragged line of boulders and sharp-edged rocks. In low water just give up and carry over it. In higher water it can be run without turning over but only in a few places. One is in the center on a diagonal from left to right. It would be well to get out and scout this one. The current for the last 10-15 yards above the fall is very swift, so if you can't back up or stop, make sure you've lined up on the slot. The danger here is the lack of smooth lip on the fall and the piles of rocks below what would normally be the lip. From here to the take-out are only a few easy shoals and a pool.

The take-out is a gently sloping beach at Bulldog Bend Park. You can park close to the river.

An early evening stop and dinner on the ground.

SECTION 2

LITTLE CAHABA RIVER 8.6 MILES

County 65 (Bulldog Bend) to County 27 (River Bend)
Drop: 6.9 (approximately)   **Difficulty: 1**
Topos: Blocton (15 minute)   **Hazards: None**

This scenic section is studded with more shoals than Section 1, but they are all mild and easy. The few drops are about 12 inches high. The drop at about mile 2½ is a peculiar-looking rock formation. It is so perfect a line that it looks as if it were man-made. As the river descends and travels toward the main Cahaba, the banks become less and less rocky and the hills more rounded. After Six Mile Creek the shoals almost disappear into long shallows that are **very** shallow in summer's low water levels. The only places (in normal water) that will take even a modicum of maneuvering are at the two islands (mile 1¼ and 4). You might also find it interesting to paddle the ¼ mile up Six Mile Creek to the first shoal. Almost nine miles of this creek are also covered on a separate ride in this book. After you enter the main Cahaba, you will soon see some cliffs on your left. See Section 11 of the Cahaba for comments on this area and on the take-out.

The put-in is at Bulldog Bend campground. See the general comments on the river. When you leave Bulldog Bend, it is best to go to the right of the island under the County Road 65 bridge if the water is low.

Bob Howe and Folboat on the Little Cahaba.

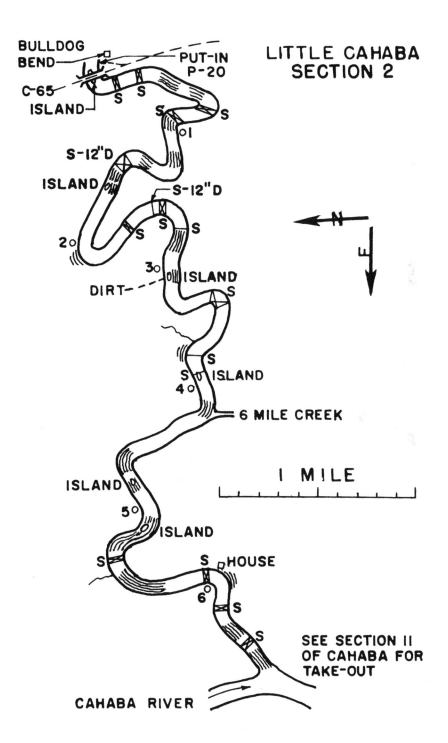

LITTLE CAHABA
SECTION 2

BULLDOG BEND
PUT-IN P-20
C-65
ISLAND
S S
S S
○1
S-12"D
ISLAND
S-12"D
S S
2○
3○ ISLAND
DIRT
S
S ISLAND
S
4○
6 MILE CREEK
1 MILE
ISLAND
5○
ISLAND
S S HOUSE
S
6○
S
S
SEE SECTION II
OF CAHABA FOR
TAKE-OUT
CAHABA RIVER

N
E

111

SIX MILE CREEK 9.8 MILES

Six Mile (State 25) to Coosa Road   Difficulty: 1–2
Drop: 10.7   Hazards: Sharp bends,
Topos: Blocton (15 minute)   narrowness, the "Sinks"

Six Mile Creek is narrow and winding with numerous cliffs and rock formations along its shores. It is unique (at least in this book) in the fact that most of it vanishes underground for a short distance. The run is interesting and pretty but has some built-in hazards that require caution at water levels of .6 and that would make the trip unsafe for a novice at 1.0 or higher.

The "Sinks" and the bends are the only problems on this creek. All of the shoals are easy, most of them with one to three foot drops spread out gradually, many with low 12 to 18 inch vertical drops with clear chutes. The hardest one is at mile 4.1 where an island in the middle combined with short drops and rock slabs makes a long series of turbulence, but this one is also simple. As this is such a narrow creek, however, you should keep your eyes open for possible logjams.

The put-in is down the concrete embankment by the State 25 bridge. This is about 12 feet high and on a 45 degree angle. It's slippery when wet and overgrown with kudzu in the summer. Watch out for broken glass on the slope. There's no room to park, and the shoulder is just barely wide enough to pull off the road. You can park in the store parking lot across the bridge if you ask permission and if you park out of the way.

Water level can be read on the downstream side of the left-hand bridge pier at the put-in. These yellow marks are graduated in tenths of a foot for a distance of two feet. The bottom mark is the minimum water level at which you can *float* the entire stretch; however, you can also run the trip at four inches below this mark if you're willing to get out and wade some.

The banks on this run are generally rocky and hilly with some lower areas on the inside of the bends. Some of the cliffs are solid rock; others are composed of large boulders. There are also a lot of large boulders and slabs along the shoreline. The bluffs vary from about 30-50 feet high; two of these are seen in the first mile. The highest and most impressive bluffs are at about mile 2.6 and are about 75 feet high. Some 50 foot bluffs in the bend at and just below mile 5 plunge straight into the water. This would be a dangerous place in higher water because the combination of a very narrow passage and very sharp bend could easily sweep you into the cliff face. Enter this bend cautiously when the water level is 1.0 or higher and learn to "ferry" before you start the trip at all.

There is a cave in the cliff on your left at mile 1.3. Just upstream from it is a spring running out of the rocks. This spring is actually an underground stream in the cave. There is also a vertical shaft running from the cave roof up to the top of the cliff, and someone uses this as a shaftway to pump water from the stream. The main cave goes off a short distance to your right.

Just after the tight bend at mile 4.7 is an alternate take-out on your right. This area is used as a Boy Scout weekend camp and can be recognized by the steps leading down the bank.

The "Sinks" is an interesting place. It's in a bend, but only a small amount of water flows around the bend. Most of it flows straight into a 10 foot wide by 30 foot high hole in the face of the cliff. A boulder has dropped down and wedged in this hole about 12 feet off the river *leaving plenty of space for a boat to be swept in under it.* This is a real danger at a level of 1.6 or higher and even at lower levels if you are not expecting it. Stay on the inside of this bend as you approach it.

There are two markers you can use to forewarn yourself of the arrival of the "Sinks." One is "Monster" Rock on your right at about mile 5.7. This is called "Monster" Rock because it juts out about 10 feet over the river and looks like an upper jaw with a few teeth in it. Don't get swept under it. You'll only have about four feet clearance at a level of 1.0. Just downstream on your left there is a 10 foot high boulder in the creek. The "Sinks" are now in the bend right in front of you and on your right. Depending on the water level, you may have to wade around the bend after the "Sinks." After you go all the way around the bend, you'll see the main flow of the river come out from under a rock overhang on your right.

Below the "Sinks" the terrain changes to rocky hillsides and a lower shoreline with fewer boulders and only a few low

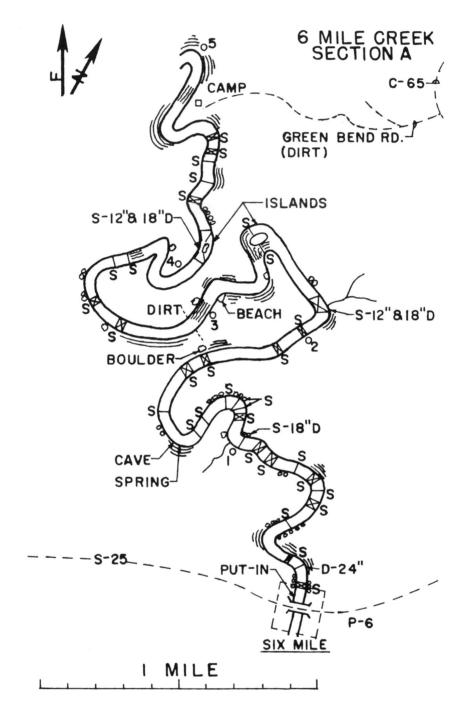

6 MILE CREEK
SECTION A

114

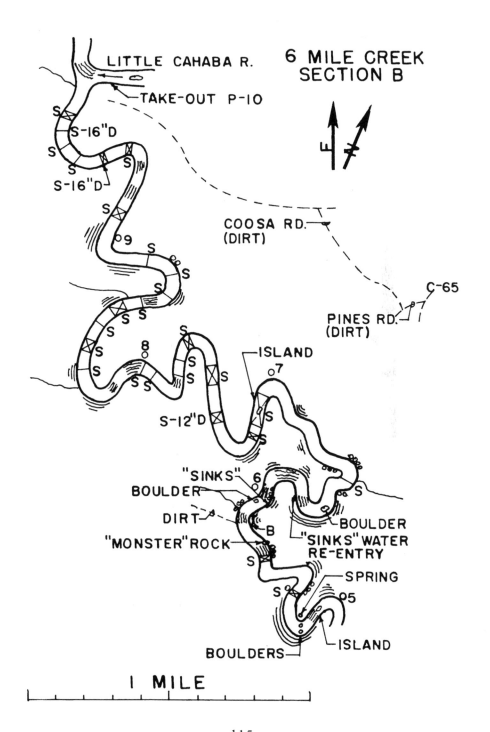

6 MILE CREEK
SECTION B

LITTLE CAHABA R.

TAKE-OUT P-10

S-16"D

S-16"D

COOSA RD.
(DIRT)

C-65

PINES RD.
(DIRT)

ISLAND

S-12"D

"SINKS"

BOULDER

DIRT

"MONSTER" ROCK

BOULDER

"SINKS" WATER
RE-ENTRY

SPRING

ISLAND

BOULDERS

1 MILE

bluffs. The high rocky hill on your right at about mile 9.4 is not only the highest one you'll see on the trip but also the last one before you reach the take-out.

The take-out is about 50 yards up the Little Cahaba River. You'll see a path. It's steep for about 30 feet, then levels off. There's a total carry of about 50 yards up to the road, which is dirt but in excellent shape.

READ THIS: During non-hunting season this take-out road is closed, and you will have to take-out either at the junction of the Little Cahaba and the main Cahaba rivers or at River Bend Bridge (County 27) on the main Cahaba. See Section 2 of the Little Cahaba and Section 11 of the Cahaba for information on this part of the trip.

THE LOCUST FORK OF THE WARRIOR—GENERAL

The Locust Fork of the Warrior begins near the town of Snead and flows generally southwestward until it runs into Bankhead Lake near Port Birmingham. Forty-eight miles of the main river and 17 miles of one of the tributaries are covered in this book. There are several bridges above Section 1, and the river is perfectly floatable, but the put-ins are either very rough—all of them steep and overgrown—or else they're on private property.

The Locust is basically a rocky river and, as such, has many shoals, rapids, cliffs, and rock formations. The part covered in this book also has two waterfalls. The river is essentially uninhabited, and public access is limited to the highways and county roads. The shores are forested, wild life is frequently seen, and the runs usually uncrowded except for a few of the "whitewater" sections which are heavily used by canoeists and kayakers when the water level is up. Overall the river is wild, scenic, unlittered, and well deserving of respect for its beauty and power.

The Locust has an accessible water level gauge at the State 79 bridge and the reading on this gauge is used for most of the rides on the river. Parking space at all the put-ins and take-outs is generally adequate and carries to the river are pretty easy.

The Locust offers a variety of types of water and scenery. Section 1 has small shoals and pools; Section 2 offers harder shoals, a few rapids, cliffs, and a waterfall. Section 3 is the whitewater section with rapids up to heavy class 4 ratings and some spectacular cliffs, while Section 4 has cliffs and another, higher waterfall. The rapids in this section gradually taper into shoals and shallows leading into Section 5 which is mostly a long pool with high banks. Section 6 gives you shoals and lower cliffs once more, and Section 7 is basically a wooded flat-water stretch.

The Locust is usually low in the summer and fall, occasionally falling to the non-floatable point. Use of the gauge or one of the bridge markings will keep you from hiking when you want to be floating, so I'd advise you to use it. Also use it when the water is up as parts of the Locust can be very dangerous. I suggest that you read and believe the warnings under Sections 3

117

and 4 particularly.

The rides on the Locust may seem to be peculiar lengths, but there is a good reason for it! I try for an average length ride of about seven to ten miles, but this has to be broken into available, fairly decent put-ins and take-outs. I consider 15 miles on a river with a low water level too much of a one day trip for enjoyment. Thus Section 1 is short, Section 2 the right length, Sections 3 and 4 are very swift trips in high water, if you're experienced. To the not so experienced, or in low water, these sections may be all day trips. Section 6 is a good length, but this means Section 7 comes up short—and so on. If you don't like the short trips, I'd suggest that you combine them. I've run the combined Sections 2, 3, and 4 in one day but wouldn't really want to do it again!

SECTION 1

LOCUST FORK OF THE WARRIOR 5.5 MILES

Wards-Bridge to Dirt Road
Drop: 7.4   Difficulty: 1
Topos: Susan Moore, Blountsville   Hazards: None

This is a pleasant, easy run with frequent small shoals and a few harder ones thrown in for interest. Water level is best read on the gauge on the left-hand upstream side of the State 79 bridge. The minimum to float this trip with no problems is 1.4, but you will have to be a little selective of your path in places at this level. A level of 1.6 should give you an easy float.

The river is about 50 feet wide at the put-in and holds this width to the take-out. This stretch is typified by eight to ten foot high dirt banks, usually steep and usually going back in a flat to very low hills off the river. There are also a few low cliffs off the river. The shores are heavily forested, mostly hardwood, and the ride is pretty and interesting. There is a great variety of trees on this run and quite a few relatively rare cardinal flowers.

The put-in has very limited parking, only about three vehicles on the put-in side and two more across the bridge. It is pos-

118

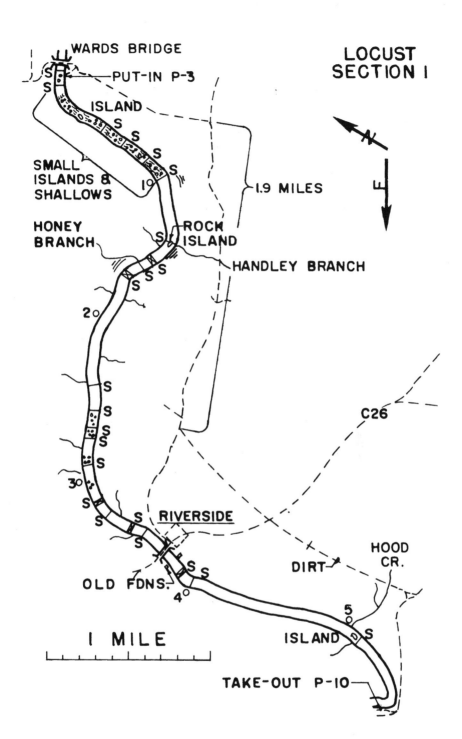

WARDS BRIDGE

PUT-IN P-3

LOCUST
SECTION I

ISLAND

SMALL
ISLANDS &
SHALLOWS

HONEY
BRANCH

1.9 MILES

ROCK
ISLAND

HANDLEY BRANCH

N

E

C26

RIVERSIDE

HOOD
CR.

OLD FDNS.

DIRT

1 MILE

ISLAND

TAKE-OUT P-10

sible to park on the side of the road, but if you do this, squeeze over as far as possible as the road is narrow. The put-in is easy— a good trail gradually sloping to the river and about 50 feet long.

The 3¾ miles from the put-in to the County 26 bridge have numerous small shoals, rocky peninsulas, and islands. These peninsulas and islands would require some care at higher, swifter water levels.

The first mile of the trip is a series of very small shoals with the area in between filled with small grass islands, small rocks, and rocky peninsulas out from the shore. I've made no attempt to show these on the map. Many would become shallows or vanish at a level of about 1.8. These shoals are all very easy with gradual drops not exceeding about 12 inches.

At the end of the long pool there is a rock island in the middle of the river with upturned 36 inch high slabs on it. Watch this in higher water. On the left by the next pool you'll see the only large rock formation on this stretch, and past the next shoals you can spot a low line of cliffs off the river on your right.

The next couple of shoals are a little harder and would probably have standing waves at higher water, but they're still very easy.

After the next long quiet pool you will find several more of these island, shallow, small shoal areas. These are a little longer but simple, as are the shoals following them. As you come in sight of the County 26 bridge, there is a shoal with about a 24 inch gradual drop. Another similar shoal is just below the bridge. Both would probably have standing waves at higher water.

Just below the bridge, note the old concrete-filled 24 inch steel pipe bridge foundations. The ones on the left shore are still standing, but the ones on the right have fallen into the river and could be a definite hazard at about 2.4 and up.

You'll notice that the County 26 bridge is neither a good put-in or take-out. The banks are high, very steep, and densely overgrown. From the shoal below this bridge on down to the take-out is a long pool with only two minor shoals. You'll notice some clearings and fields on your left slightly back from the river.

The take-out is easy. A gradual dirt bank and only about a 25 foot carry. Parking is down a little dirt road off the main dirt road with room for about six vehicles and no turn-around space. Again you can park on the side of the main road but get off of it as far as you can.

SECTION 2

LOCUST FORK OF THE WARRIOR 10.2 MILES

Dirt Road to U. S. 231 (S79)
Drop: 9.8   Difficulty: 2
Topos: Susan Moore, Blountsville
Hazards: One 5 foot waterfall, two Class 2 rapids

This is a pretty stretch of the Locust and forms a prelude to the "whitewater" of Section 3 by gradually leading you from shallows to shoals to harder shoals to rapids. The put-in is easy—dirt shelving into the river and only about a 25 foot carry to the water. See the take-out information for Section 1 for this put-in.

Water level can best be read off the gauge upstream on the left above the State 79 bridge. This map was made at a level of 1.3, and the trip required a great deal of dragging and picking. The minimum level to float this section is 1.5.

The river is about 50 feet wide at the put-in, holds this average width for a few miles, then gradually widens out to about 100 feet at the take-out. For the first three miles of the run, the banks are mainly dirt, rather low, and wooded. A few rock formations and one group of bluffs can be seen off the river. At the end of the first mile, the shallows begin to turn into shoals. Many of these shoals and all of the shallows would vanish at a level of 1.8 or better.

After mile 3 the terrain begins to change to some very pretty bluffs and more rock formations. Some of the shoals are a little more difficult but still no real problem.

Your signal of the waterfall's approach is the two islands just above it, one large and the next small. The waterfall is in a

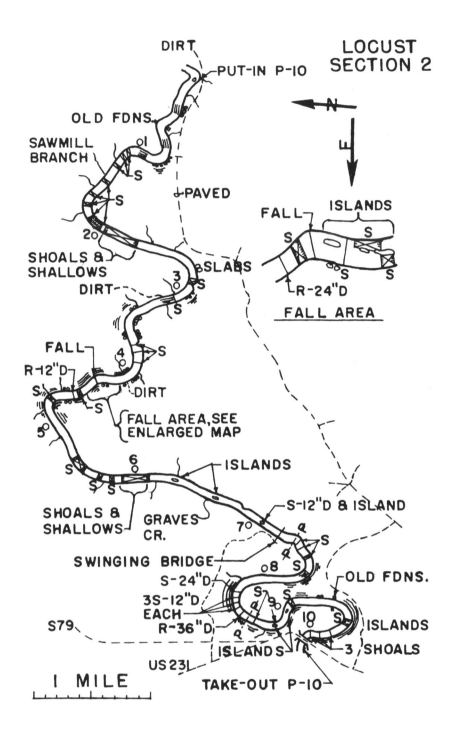

LOCUST
SECTION 2

DIRT
PUT-IN P-10

N

E

OLD FDNS.

SAWMILL
BRANCH

S

S

2

SHOALS &
SHALLOWS
DIRT

3
SLABS
S

S

PAVED

FALL
ISLANDS
S

S

R-24"D

FALL AREA

FALL
R-12"D
S
S

4
S

DIRT

FALL AREA, SEE
ENLARGED MAP

5

6
S

S
S

ISLANDS

SHOALS &
SHALLOWS

GRAVES
CR.

7

S-12"D & ISLAND

S

SWINGING BRIDGE
S-24"D

3S-12"D
EACH
R-36"D

S79

US 23

ISLANDS

8
S

S
S

9

OLD FDNS.

10
S

ISLANDS

3 SHOALS

TAKE-OUT P-10

1 MILE

122

very pretty set of bluffs with some large, flat rock slabs on the right just above it. The fall itself extends all the way across the river, and it's quite possible to be swept over it at higher water levels. The left-hand side is a straight down drop, but the extreme right is more of a stairstep affair that is runnable after scouting and if there's enough water over it. On the other hand, at higher water levels beware of a possible hydraulic at the bottom of the fall. There is a good portage on the right if you want to walk around it.

The fall is in sort of a rocky canyon, and below it are a couple of rapids, both with small drops. Both are short and runnable, but you need to go through the slots and should scout them first or at least be cautious in your approach. The "canyon" ends about mile 5 and the shoals and shallows from here to the bend (about mile 7 2/3) will be hidden at higher water levels. From mile 7 2/3 to the end you have more bluffs and cliffs, slightly rougher shoals, and more frequent low drops, but none that are of any real consequence.

The take-out is just downstream of the State 79 bridge and on your left. It is a good landing place but a steep climb up to the road on a path under the bridge. If you wish to drift down through the first shoal below the bridge, there is an equally easy take-out and a longer but gradual path to the highway. Parking is on the side of the highway, but there is plenty of room.

SECTION 3

LOCUST FORK OF THE WARRIOR 3.6 MILES

State 79 (U. S. 231) to Swann Covered Bridge
Drop: 23   Difficulty: 2–3
Topos: Blountsville, Cleveland   Hazards: Up to Class 4 rapids

This section of the Locust Fork is the "whitewater" part and can range from a bottom-dragging, rock-picking trip up to Class 4 rapids depending on the water level. The rapids occur from the State 79 (Section 3) put-in to Skirum Bluff (Section 4); after that there are shoals only to just below the County 160 bridge.

The miles for the map of Section 3 and Section 4 are numbered consecutively because these two trips are often run as one. Usually whether this is done or not depends on water level and the skill of the floater. This map was made at a water gauge reading of 2.1. At this level you can float through everything, and the rapids (Class 1 and 2) are no particular hazard although they are still perfectly capable of destroying your boat. The water gauge is on the left-hand bank just upstream from the put-in bridge. It would be well to look at it before you start down the river.

THIS IS NO STRETCH TO BOAT ALONE! Only skilled river canoeists should venture on it at a level of 2.6 or better. Above 4.0 it's best to stay off of it.

The put-in is under the 231 bridge or just downstream on the left. Directly under the bridge is steep but short. The other put-in is a trail through the woods on the left bank at highway level that is gradual but longer. Take your choice. Parking is on a very wide shoulder, so you won't have any problems being well off the road. **WARNING!** Some vandalism (cars broken into, windows broken) has been experienced at this put-in! The river is about 100 feet wide at the put-in but averages 50-75 feet with much "necking down" to less than this by rocks out from the shore. This is an extremely scenic stretch. Numerous rock formations occur in the river and on the shore, and there are some quite pretty sand beaches scattered along. Several high cliffs plunge straight into the water, and a lot of lower ones pretty up the hillsides back off the bank. There are no signs of civilization except the bridges themselves, and the whole valley is lovely.

Most of the shoals and rapids have a very noticeable drop in elevation; a few have an abrupt drop. At higher water levels many of them will have big standing waves that are quite likely to swamp an open boat.

The first rapid likely to cause you any trouble is House Rock, so named because of the enormous boulder on the left of the river and just below the rapid. Rock formations on the right squeeze the river to the left toward House Rock. When running this, stay to the right side of the rapid (about a five foot, 45 degree drop). If you go to the left side, you may be swept **under**

124

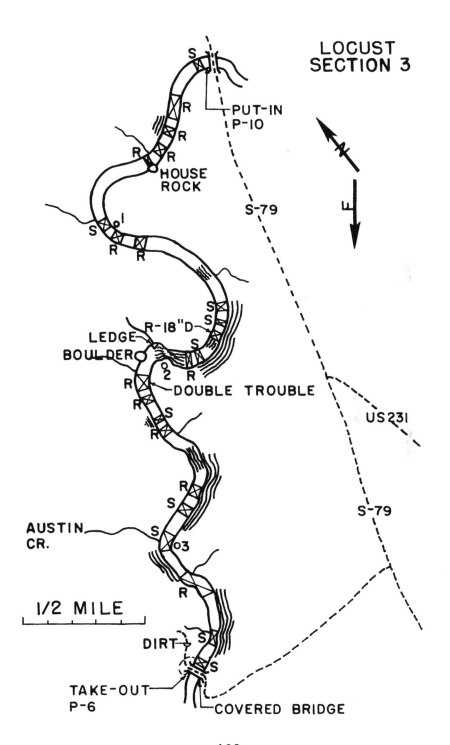

LOCUST
SECTION 3

S
R
R PUT-IN
R P-IO
R
HOUSE
ROCK
S-79
S
R
R
S
S
R-18"D
LEDGE
BOULDER
R DOUBLE TROUBLE
R
S
R
R
S
R US231
S
AUSTIN
CR.
S S-79
DIRT
S
TAKE-OUT S
P-6
COVERED BRIDGE

N
E

1/2 MILE

House Rock. Watch for the powerful eddy on the right side below the rapid. It, too, can flip you.

At mile 2 the river takes a long downhill curve. The rock ledge on the map has to be avoided by ferrying to the left. This is complicated a bit by having to enter the stretch on the right because of the shallowness of the water. If you just follow the outside of the curve, you'll be swept over the ledge. Immediately below this curve is "Double Trouble"—so called because it is two trouble spots separated by a short pool. The upper part is in a blind curve to the left. Pull out on the left and scout it if you've never run it before. To run it, approach it as close to the rocks on the left as you can. You may run to either side of the pyramidal rock halfway down the drop, but don't rely on the current to take you by it—it won't. At the end of the pool you may run through the rocks and far to the left and have a 12 inch drop or less, depending on the water level, or run just to the left of the big boulder on the right-hand shore. By just to the left, I mean practically scraping. This is about a 30 inch straight down drop, but the slot is clear. Most of the rest of the rough spots from here to Swann Bridge should give you no great trouble. The rapid just past mile 3 is best run on a long diagonal from right to left. All of them will have big standing waves at 3.0 or better.

Some of the prettier places along here are the high cliffs on your left just above mile 2 and mile 3 and the sand beaches on your left at mile 3. The most spectacular cliffs are about .3 mile above Swann Bridge on your left.

The take-out is on the right just at the covered bridge. Parking under the bridge is easy, and you can drive right around in a circle and back onto the road. This is one of the few remaining covered bridges in Alabama.

SECTION 4

LOCUST FORK OF THE WARRIOR 4.2 MILES

Swann Covered Bridge to Nectar Covered Bridge
Drop: 25 (first 2.4 miles) 1 (last 1.8 miles)   **Difficulty: 1−2**
Topos: Cleveland, Nectar   **Hazards: 8 foot waterfall**

This section ranges from wild to peaceful as you can probably guess from the drastic change in drop between the first and last parts of it. The drop is actually about 25 feet from Swann Bridge to mile 4.4, 16 from there to the County 160 bridge, and something like 22 on to the island at about mile 6.3. At least eight feet of the 16 foot drop section is concentrated in a waterfall. The rest is pretty evenly distributed. After mile 6.3 the river is practically flat to the take-out. See the take-out information for Section 3 for this put-in. Water level is a matter of experience unless you want to drive to the U. S. 231 bridge and read the gauge. If the gauge reads less than about 1.6, you'll have floating problems. See the warning in Section 3 for higher water levels. The river is about 50 feet wide at the put-in, spreads to about 75 feet near the 160 bridge, then narrows back down to about 50 feet, and holds this to the take-out.

All the rapids are milder than in Section 3. High cliffs and a placid pool at mile 4.6 are both scenic and the announcement for an eight foot, 60 degree waterfall. This waterfall can be run on the **RIGHT SIDE ONLY**. There is a big rock island splitting the fall. You can portage down the island if you wish or run the fall on the right a little left of its center. Be careful when you land on the rock island—its sloping and the current will try to sweep you to the right and over the falls. Just before you get to Skirum Bluff pool there is an 18 inch drop and a rough little rapid. Skirum Bluff and its pool are very scenic places. There's a nice beach on the left, and the bluffs are high and plunge straight into the water. This is a good place to stop and swim in the summer. The river necks down at the end of this pool and has a right-hand bend. In higher water levels this could be a tricky place if you can't ferry. At the lower end of the bluff is a pretty little waterfall running out of the cliff, and just below this on your left are some attractive rock formations.

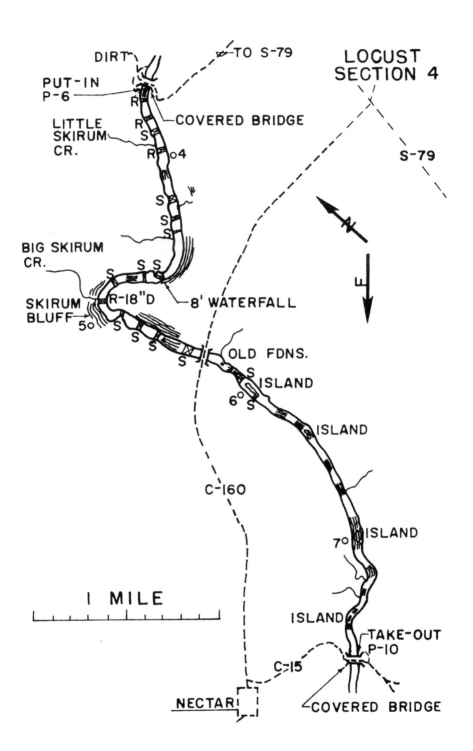

DIRT

TO S-79

LOCUST
SECTION 4

PUT-IN
P-6

R

COVERED BRIDGE

LITTLE
SKIRUM
CR.

R

S

R o4

S-79

S

S

S

BIG SKIRUM
CR.

S S

SKIRUM
BLUFF

R-18"D

8' WATERFALL

5o

S

S

S

OLD FDNS.

S

ISLAND

6o

S

ISLAND

C-160

7o ISLAND

1 MILE

ISLAND

TAKE-OUT
P-10

C-15

NECTAR

COVERED BRIDGE

The shoals are very mild from here on and turn into shallows at the end of the island at mile 6. As you pass under the County 160 bridge you'll see why this is not used as a take-out—it's **very** steep and overgrown. The islands shown are pretty, and the ride from here to the take-out is cool and shady between shore lines that are lower and made of dirt instead of rock and sand as in Section 3.

The take-out is a sand beach, a low bank (short but slippery), and a well-beaten, gradually sloping, easy path for about 75 feet. Parking is limited, but it's easy to get completely off the road. Don't block the dirt road going into the woods. The bridge at the take-out is another of the few remaining covered bridges left in Alabama and is the longest of its type construction in the United States.

SECTION 5

LOCUST FORK OF THE WARRIOR 5 MILES

Nectar Covered Bridge to County 15 (Shoal Creek)
Drop: 2   **Difficulty: 0**
Topos: Nectar   **Hazards: None**

This is a slow-moving, peaceful stretch of river with a few minor shoals usually consisting of a single line of rocks across the river. The river is about 50 feet wide at the put-in and gradually spreads to about 125 feet at the take-out. See the take-out information for Section 4 for this put-in.

Water level can be read on the gauge at the U. S. 231 bridge if you want to drive that far. This map was made at a reading of 2.2. You should be able to easily float this section as low as 1.5. If you don't wish to drive to the gauge, there is a yellow mark on the upstream end of the right-hand bridge pier at the take-out. The bottom of this mark is 2.2, and you can judge from there.

The banks in this section are earth, heavily overgrown, about six to eight feet high, and go back to flat areas on the right. The left-hand shore has some small ridges set back from

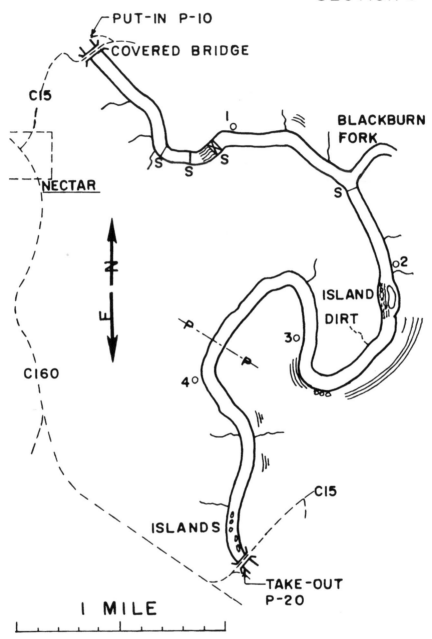

LOCUST
SECTION 5

PUT-IN P-10
COVERED BRIDGE

C15

NECTAR

BLACKBURN
FORK

N

E

C160

ISLAND
DIRT

C15

ISLANDS

TAKE-OUT
P-20

1 MILE

the shoreline. At two places there are rock formations and bluffs along these ridges, the major ones being between mile 2 and 3.

At mile 1½ you'll see Blackburn Fork come in on your left. This is a pretty stream, and you may want to spend a while paddling up it. Two rides on it are covered in this book. The two islands shown on the map just before the take-out are so close to the left hand shore that they are hard to distinguish as islands. The grass islands upstream are only a few inches high and are actually weed grown shallows. The group about ¼ mile before the take-out may have lilies blooming on it in the late spring and early summer.

The take-out is a slab of rock next to the bridge pier. There is a well-beaten, not very steep path up to the parking area. The parking area itself is a local picnic spot and is clear and open. You may prefer to drift on down about 25 yards and take-out just as easily at a clearing on the bank. Either way, when you park, don't block the picnic area road.

SECTION 6

LOCUST FORK OF THE WARRIOR 10 MILES

County 15 (Shoal Creek) to Vaughns Bridge
Drop: 6.0   **Difficulty: 1**
Topos: Nectar   **Hazards: Low bridge at mile 5.7**

This is a scenic, relatively peaceful stretch of river despite the appearance of the shoal just below the put-in. The river is about 125 feet wide at the put-in but gradually narrows to about 60 feet at the first low water bridge and holds this width to the take-out. See the information for Section 5 for this put-in.

Water level can be read on the upstream end of the right-hand bridge pier at the put-in bridge. The bottom mark is 2.2. You can *just* barely float this entire section at 1.2 if you very carefully select a path.

The banks in this section are generally low with alternating

131

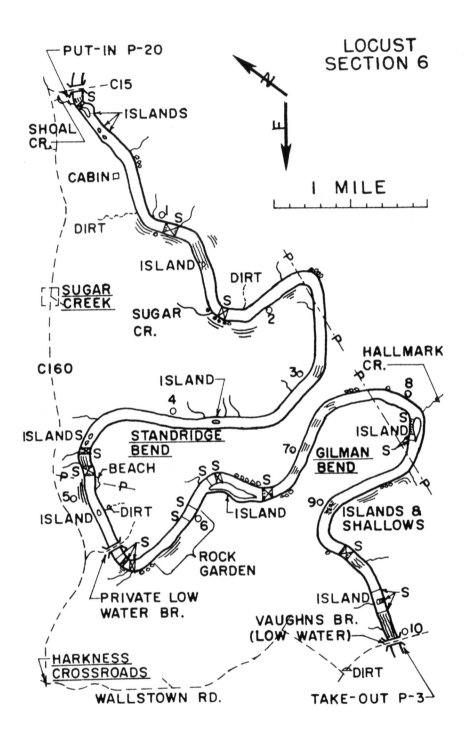

LOCUST
SECTION 6

PUT-IN P-20

C15

ISLANDS

SHOAL CR.

CABIN

DIRT

1 MILE

SUGAR CREEK

SUGAR CR.

ISLAND

DIRT

C160

ISLAND

HALLMARK CR.

ISLANDS

STANDRIDGE BEND

BEACH

GILMAN BEND

ISLAND

ISLAND

ISLANDS & SHALLOWS

DIRT

ROCK GARDEN

PRIVATE LOW WATER BR.

ISLAND

VAUGHNS BR. (LOW WATER)

HARKNESS CROSSROADS

DIRT

WALLSTOWN RD.

TAKE-OUT P-3

132

15 foot high banks and low hills. It is pretty well forested, with some signs of fields and pastures along the way. Below the private low water bridge the forest is thicker, the hills steeper, and there are very few signs of civilization.

One word about this private bridge: It *is* private as is the road to it and the land by it. On the Nectar map it is identified as a covered bridge. If you decide to use this as an alternate put-in or take-out, then get permission *first*. The owner has been very nice about this so far, and canoeists and floaters can keep it that way by being courteous, asking permission, and leaving *nothing* on this property but tire tracks by his bridge.

One other word: Both this bridge and the take-out bridge have only about six feet of clearance between them and the *bottom* of the river. Hence the name "low water" bridge. They are covered up at high water. Being low, they present two hazards to the boater—for one they create logjams, and for the other, there may not be enough clearance below the bridge to float under it. Both cases could result in broadsiding, capsizing, and drowning. So at a water level of about 3.0 or higher be very cautious. Make sure that you can *stop* the boat if you need to and that you can control it well enough to go to shore and portage if necessary. And don't get overconfident—it's not easy to halt a boat in a fast flowing current.

The shoals in this section are generally easy. The first one below the put-in is the hardest you'll have, although at some water levels the ones at about mile 1.8 and 4.0 could be a little turbulent and tricky. The rest of the shoals will be no problem at all; in fact most of them will vanish at a level of about 2.0.

There's a long "rock garden" for about 1/3 mile above mile 6. Again, a level of 2.0 will wipe this out for the most part. Run by to the left of the big island below the private bridge, to the right of the second one, and on the left again around the last little island. There are a lot of small grass islands and shallows by the big island, and you'll have to find your own path here unless the water is high enough to cover them.

Scenery on the river is mostly forest, but there are a few low cliffs and rock formations of interest. One of these cliffs is at about mile 1. There is usually a small waterfall off the low ledge on your left about mile 1.8. At mile 4.8 there is a tremendous rock formation on your right—a solid sloping boulder with

133

a waterfall right down the middle of it. Don't look for this fall in the dead of summer though. The most impressive cliffs are those about mile 5.7, slightly back off the river. Watch for them just after the huge boulder on your right about 1/8 mile below the private bridge.

The take-out is on the left downstream side of the bridge. It's a short (about 20 foot) carry to the vehicles. This carry will be extremely slippery if it's wet. Parking is very limited, but there is room to get completely off the road. If you prefer you can unload, then drive about 50 yards further and park on a paved road, but if you do, then park well to the side.

The last ½ mile of road to the put-in is on a sharp slope and will present problems if it's muddy. If it is, I suggest you buy a topo map and come in to the river on the other side.

SECTION 7

LOCUST FORK OF THE WARRIOR 9 MILES

Vaughns Bridge to County 121 (Trafford)
Drop: 2.2   **Difficulty: 0**
Topos: Nectar, Trafford, Warrior   **Hazards: Low water bridge**
and boulders in river

This section is a little faster moving than Section 6 because of the width of the river. Its 75 foot put-in width necks down to about 50 feet and holds this to the take-out. See the take-out information for Section 6 for this put-in.

Water level can be read on the marks at the Shoal Creek put-in (See Section 5 or 6). This map was made at a reading of about 1.2, and you can easily float the section at this level.

The banks in this section are earth, fairly overgrown, and about 15 feet high. From Vaughns Bridge to Deans Ferry Bridge they are usually low, with a few small hills scattered along and one set of 20-30 foot bluffs at mile 3. Below Deans Ferry Bridge the first 3/4 mile on your right is pasture, but after that the shoreline is more rugged and frequently has a bank, a flat area, and then a line of hills that are sharper and steeper than

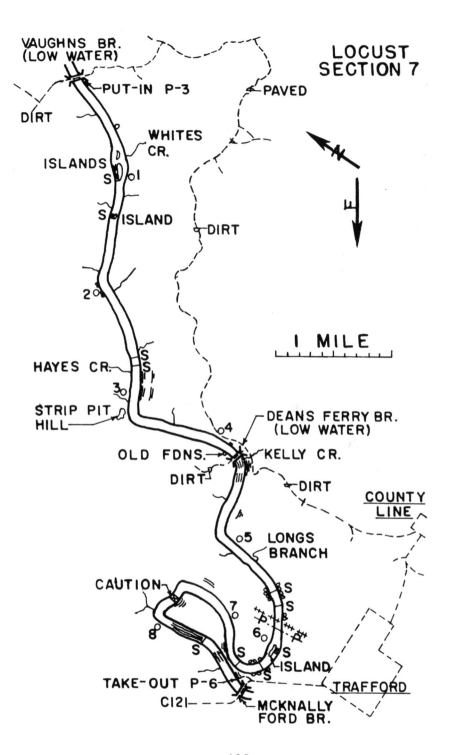

LOCUST
SECTION 7

VAUGHNS BR.
(LOW WATER)
PUT-IN P-3
PAVED
DIRT
WHITES CR.
ISLANDS
S 1
S ISLAND
DIRT

1 MILE

2

HAYES CR.
S S
3
STRIP PIT HILL
4
DEANS FERRY BR. (LOW WATER)
OLD FDNS.
KELLY CR.
DIRT
DIRT
COUNTY LINE
5
LONGS BRANCH

CAUTION
7
S
S
8
6
S S
S ISLAND
S
TAKE-OUT P-6
TRAFFORD
C121
MCKNALLY FORD BR.

135

the upstream four miles.

You will begin to see strip mines at mile 4 and will see them on and off from here to the take-out. Much of the bend between miles 5 and 7½ has been stripped. This is either obvious through the thin fringe of trees along the bank or else because the land has been stripped right to the river. The first instance of this stripping to the bank is just above the railroad. You'll see it again at miles 7¾ and 8½.

The stripped area at mile 7¾ is the only danger spot on this run (if you've read the low water bridge warning under Section 6). Five foot high boulders have rolled into the water here, and you will have to snake your way through them. At water levels of 2.5 and up they could create a maneuvering problem as well as serve as a foundation for a logjam.

Despite the strip mines, the ride is very pretty and peaceful. The few shoals are small, with about a 12 inch elevation drop, and the shallows are not so shallow as to offer problems. The two islands just before mile 1 should be run on the left for the first one, on the right for the second one. The island shown at mile 6 is not an island except at a water level of 3.0 or better. Run to the left of it in any event.

There are a few rock formations and cliffs along the river, all of them relatively low and most of them back off the bank except those at mile 3 and just below Deans Ferry Bridge. The highest bluffs are about 50 feet tall, on your left at about mile 4¾, and off the river.

The take-out is disconcerting-looking from County 121 but isn't as bad as it looks. Take out on your left about 100 yards upstream from the County 121 bridge. You'll have about a 100 yard carry up a trail with a 20 degree slope to the dirt road running under the bridge. The trail is good and so is the dirt road, but the road will be slippery if it's wet, so you'd better check before driving down it.

BLACKBURN FORK–GENERAL

Blackburn Fork runs out of the Inland Lake dam near Inland Junction, Alabama, and about two miles downstream passes under the State 75 bridge. From here it flows approximately 9.9 miles to a confluence with Calvert Prong. From this point on, it is known as either Blackburn Fork or the Little Warrior River depending on which map you study. I prefer to call it Blackburn Fork to avoid confusion with several other rivers that are all known locally as "The Little Warrior." The stream then flows another 6.8 miles to a junction with Section 5 of the Locust Fork of the Warrior River. All but the first two miles (from the dam to State 75) are covered in these rides.

All of Section 2 and most of the last half of Section 1 are in a remote-appearing forest area. There are areas of high bluffs and rock formations, but these are pretty well localized. Section 2 (an actual eight mile run on Blackburn Fork) is a nice, easy, peaceful, and scenic wilderness ride with small shoals gradually giving way to low islands and shallows. After Blackburn Fork enters the Locust Fork, you will have to paddle 3.2 miles on down to the Shoal Creek Bridge for a take-out and a total ride length of 11.2 miles.

The first and last halves of Section 1 are so different that I've made two maps of them, and, although I count them as one ride, they can be conveniently split into two. **Part A** is through pasture land with numerous farms and dwellings, very small shoals, and slight elevation drop. **Part B** can be very dangerous at water levels of plus two feet or more, and the area shown as the "Narrows" should be approached with extreme caution at this level or higher. There is no way to run the first blockage in

Blockage on Section 1B of Blackburn Fork.

the narrows at any water level, and **IT MUST BE PORTAGED!** You should *scout* the half-mile stretch below the blockage before attempting to run any of it. You will find (depending upon water level) rapids up to Class 4 in this short ¾ mile stretch.

SECTION 1 (Parts A and B)

BLACKBURN FORK 8.7 MILES

State 75 to Little Warrior Bridge
Drop Part A: 8.7   Difficulty: Part A: 1
Part B: 42 in 2 miles, 24 average   Part B: 1-3, 4
Topos: Remlap, Cleveland   Hazards: Part A: 0
                                    Part B: Class 2-3-4 rapids

This section of the Blackburn Fork is described in two parts. Please read the *cautions* in the general comments on this river.

Water level for all of Section 1 can be read on the downstream side of the left-hand bridge pier at the take-out. These red marks are graduated in tenths of a foot for three feet. The bottom mark is the lowest level for the trip if you're *solo.* You'll need about .4 foot more for tandem floating. The put-in for the section is good—a level and firm dirt road with good turn-around room. You'll have about a 60 foot carry to the water on a gently sloping path.

PART A

This part is about 35 feet wide at the put-in, narrows to 25 feet at some of the bends, spreads to 60 feet much of the time, and is about 50 feet wide at the low water bridge which marks the start of **Part B**. All of the shoals are very easy, but you should be cautious at the tight bends in higher water as this is where the river necks down to 20-30 feet.

Almost the entire right-hand shoreline to mile 4 is pasture with generally five to ten foot high dirt banks and then level

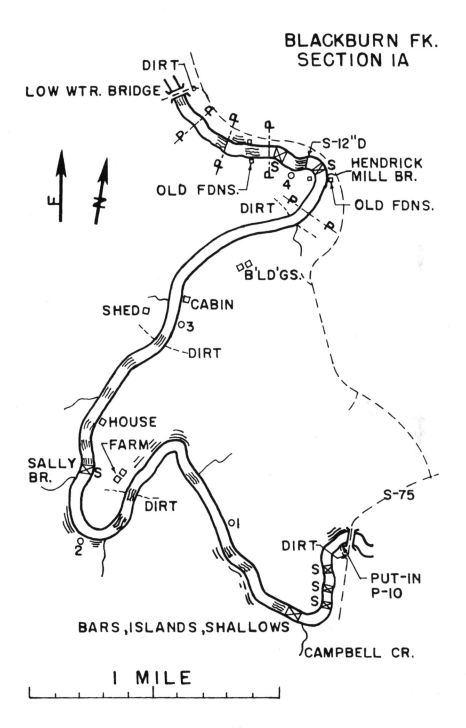

BLACKBURN FK.
SECTION IA

DIRT

LOW WTR. BRIDGE

S-12"D

HENDRICK
MILL BR.

OLD FDNS.

OLD FDNS.

DIRT

B'LD'GS.

CABIN

SHED

3

DIRT

HOUSE

FARM

SALLY
BR.

S

DIRT

S-75

1

DIRT

2

PUT-IN
P-10

S
S
S

BARS, ISLANDS, SHALLOWS

CAMPBELL CR.

1 MILE

land beyond. Some of the banks are overgrown slightly or have a fringe of trees, but much of it is obviously pasture land. The left shoreline also has a lot of pasture land and the same type of bank but is rougher and broken up by wooded areas and low hills, some with some rugged looking rock formations on them.

You'll see a few low bluffs and rock slabs here and there, but basically this first four miles is an uncluttered ride with only a small elevation drop and with numerous indications of civilization. One of these indications is very interesting. About mile 2 you'll begin hearing a peculiar rhythmic clanking sound. Then on your left at about mile 2.2 you'll see a small concrete structure part way up a low bluff on your left with a pipe running out of it, under the river, and out again on the right-hand shore at a pasture. If you'll watch the pipe, you'll notice it quivers each time you hear a "clank." This is a water ram that some ingenious person has rigged up to pump water. The concrete structure is a reservoir, and the source of power is the water itself.

From mile 4 to the low water bridge you'll find a little more elevation drop and a few small shoals. Notice the old foundations at Hendrick Mill Branch. This used to be a covered bridge, and a road ran along the shore and crossed the river at another bridge around the bend at about mile 4.2. I mention this because at the second crossing there is an old stone roadbed out from the left-hand shore, and there are two 18 inch spikes sticking up out of it. At plus 12 inches of water you could float right into them.

The river narrows to 25 feet at the bend at mile 4 and the rock formations are quite pretty. Just below them, the bluffs are about 75 feet high and plunge straight into the water. The low water bridge has about six feet clear under it at the "0" level. Be cautious at higher levels. If you decide to take out (or put-in) here, there's a good dirt road, adequate turn-around space, and easy access to the water.

PART B

Immediately after passing the low water bridge, you'll notice that the elevation drop is obviously greater. Go to the left of the big island at mile 5. The channel is about 30 feet wide here. Just below the island you'll start to approach the very rocky, narrow, and turbulent part of the ride. The next two bends have 75-100 foot bluffs into the river with big, tumbled boulders on the right shoreline. The second set of bluffs (about mile 5.4) overhangs the water. After passing these you'll enter an area of large boulders that neck the river down. The first three foot drop is through a 12 foot gap in these boulders. The "pool" below is littered with them also—once more leaving about a 12 foot wide path. Once clear of this you'll find the river *blocked* to floating by boulders about four to seven feet high (at "0" level). This is the real start of the "Narrows." Portage on the left just before the blockage. The bank is steep and slippery, but the portage path is not too bad and is about 30 feet above the water.

From here on for approximately ¾ of a mile the shoreline and riverbed are studded with boulders, twisting water courses, drops, and small hydraulics even at "0" level. A lot of this *can* be run, but you *must* portage this first blockage. The total drop at this blockage is about 25 feet in a very short horizontal distance, and all of it is down through a mass of solidly packed boulders. The *final* drop at this blockage is about 10 feet high and 80°. Below the blockage there is a twisting path through boulders, then a rapid with an 18 inch drop, four more with a drop on the last one of three feet, and another 18 inch drop. You'll see an absolutely enormous boulder on your left, thread through a "rock garden" by it, and come to a stairstep rapid with a four foot drop at the top, then a two foot one—all in a horizontal distance of about 15 feet. The next rapid has about a two foot drop. All of this is in an area littered with boulders on the shore and in the water that makes a *selection* of path quite necessary, but as you progress downstream, the rocks in the water become smaller and fewer. There are picturesque 100 foot bluffs on your right and left in the curves, just before and after the particularly big boulder.

After the rapid with the two foot drop, the rapids begin to space out and drop down to about Class 2, but all require some maneuvering. They begin to change over to shoals about mile 6.5, and these continue on to about mile 6.7, getting easier as you go downstream. The river broadens back out to an average of about 50 feet but still narrows down to 25 feet in the bends

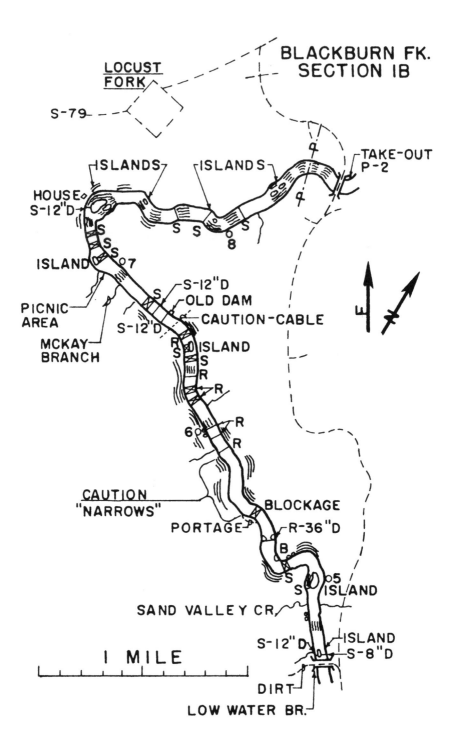

BLACKBURN FK.
SECTION 1B

LOCUST FORK

S-79

ISLANDS   ISLANDS

TAKE-OUT
P-2

HOUSE
S-12"D

S
S
S
ISLAND   7

S

PICNIC
AREA

S-12"D
OLD DAM
CAUTION-CABLE

S-12"D

MCKAY
BRANCH

R
S   ISLAND
S
S
R

R

R
6

R

CAUTION
"NARROWS"

BLOCKAGE

PORTAGE   R-36"D

B

S   5
S   ISLAND

SAND VALLEY CR.

1 MILE

S-12"D   ISLAND
S-8"D

DIRT

LOW WATER BR.

142

and around the islands. You also get out of the high bluffs after the 75 foot high ones overhanging the water at mile 6.4.

The only caution below this point is a cable across the river just above the old dam. This is about six feet off the river at "0" level. Watch it at higher water. You could use the picnic area as an alternate take-out if you wished.

The real take-out is poor. It's just upstream of the bridge pier. You have a few feet of sloping bank that's slippery when wet. The path is not well beaten out and has a lot of brambles and vines. You can walk around the concrete riprap under the bridge to the steps leading up to the highway, but it's easier to just drag your boat up the face of it. Parking is very limited—a stub of a dirt road about 40 yards north of the bridge. There's not room to park on the shoulder.

SECTION 2

BLACKBURN FORK 11.2 MILES

Little Warrior Bridge to Section 5 of Locust Fork
Drop: 6.1   **Difficulty: 1**
Topos: Cleveland, Nectar   **Hazards: None**

See the take-out information for Section 1 for this put-in. Water level can be read on the downstream side of the left-hand bridge pier at the put-in. These red marks are in tenths of a foot for three feet, and this ride can be run at the "0" level. The river is about 50 feet wide at the put-in, gradually spreading to about 70 feet at its junction with the Locust Fork.

After passing through the low wooded hills and pastures between the put-in and the State 79 bridge, the river flows in a virtual wilderness area for the rest of its length. The banks are usually five to ten feet high with occasional low, rolling hills generally with a flat area between the bank and the hills.

There are numerous bluffs but none as high as those in Section 1 and most of them off the river, although some do approach to within a few feet of the water. The most picturesque ones are on the right near mile 3.3. They are about 50

143

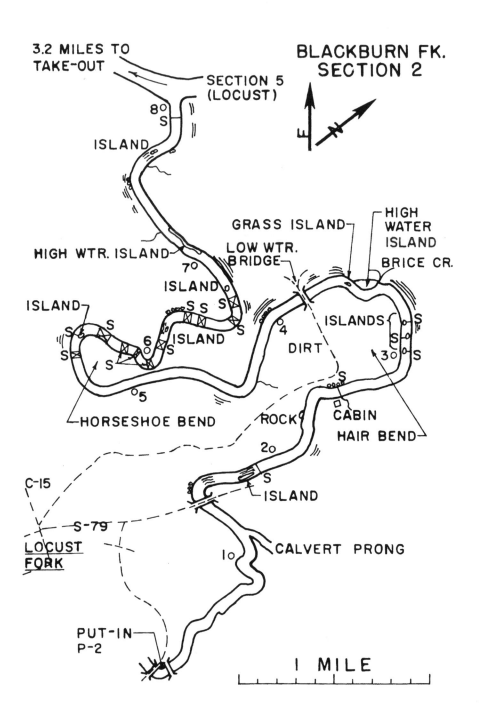

3.2 MILES TO TAKE-OUT

SECTION 5 (LOCUST)

BLACKBURN FK. SECTION 2

E

8 S

ISLAND

GRASS ISLAND

HIGH WATER ISLAND

LOW WTR. BRIDGE

BRICE CR.

HIGH WTR. ISLAND

7 ISLAND

ISLANDS

S S S

ISLAND

4 DIRT

S S

3

ISLAND

S S S

6 ISLAND

S

S

5

HORSESHOE BEND

ROCK

CABIN

HAIR BEND

C-15

2

S-79

S

ISLAND

LOCUST FORK

CALVERT PRONG

1

PUT-IN P-2

1 MILE

feet high and end in a series of overhangs just before the entry of a small stream at this point. Some rock formations and boulders also occur. Most of these and the bluffs are in the big bend between mile 2.5 and 4.5.

The islands in the first 1½ miles below State 79 and some of the rest of them are real islands, particularly those below mile 5.5. Others are low grass islands that would be covered at higher water, and still others are islands only *at* higher water.

All of the shoals are easy; the biggest one has only about a two foot elevation drop. The hardest ones are near a cabin at mile 2.5, by the first two islands about mile 3.0, and just below the big boulder near mile 6.3.

The only two signs of civilization you'll see are the cabin and the concrete, low water bridge. There is one particularly pretty place along this stretch. At the end of the bluffs above mile 3.5 there is a stream coming in on the right through a deep, wide channel. There is a nice, level beach with a natural tree seat and all backed up by the ends of the bluff. It's clean now so if you stop there, please keep it so.

After the Blackburn Fork enters the Locust Fork, you'll have a 3.2 mile paddle down to the next take-out. For information on this part of the trip and on the take-out, see Section 5 of the Locust in this book.

The Mulberry Fork of the Warrior begins near the town of Arab and flows in a southwesterly direction to a junction with the Sipsey Fork below Smith Lake. The combined rivers then run into the backwaters of Bankhead Lake near Gorgas. The general bed of the Mulberry parallels that of the Locust Fork.

From Arab to Center Hill, the Mulberry is very small, narrow, and shallow. Near Center Hill the addition of the equally small and narrow Duck River almost doubles its flow. The Broglen, which comes in some four miles further downstream, adds even more.

Below I-65 the river's average drop is small, the current slower, and the bed almost totally unobstructed. This part is floatable, pleasant, and relatively remote appearing. It is fished rather heavily. I have included in this book only the 22.1 miles from Center Hill to an old bridge just above I-65.

The portion of the Mulberry covered here is rocky with many shoals, rapids, and bluffs. In general, the rides are through scenic, relatively undeveloped forested areas, but you will see numerous signs of civilization scattered along.

These two rides are not dangerous at low water levels ("0" up to about plus 12 inches). Above this, however, Section 1 can become very tough due mostly to standing waves, velocity of water, and narrowness of rocky passages, all or any of which could swamp you, drown you, or destroy your boat. I recommend that your first few trips on this section of the Mulberry be in the company of experienced people. Section 2 is much easier.

The Mulberry, like the Locust, sometimes falls to the nonfloatable point in the summer, so I advise that you pay attention to the bridge markings that indicate water level.

SECTION 1

MULBERRY FORK OF THE WARRIOR 11.3 MILES

Center Hill-Blountsville Road to U. S. 31
Drop: 8.8   Difficulty: 1–2
Topos: Garden City, Nectar   Hazards: Class 1 and 2 rapids

This is a very scenic run from the standpoint of bluffs, cliffs, and rock formations. The river is about 30 feet wide at the put-in, broadening to about 75 feet after the Broglen River enters it, and about 150 feet at the take-out. Water level can be read on the center span of the old U. S. 31 bridge. These red marks are for four feet. The lower two feet are in one foot increments and the upper two feet are in tenths of a foot. This section can be run at six inches above the "0" level.

Neither the put-in nor the take-out is good. Both involve a climb up a steep bank. Parking at the put-in is in a large clearing by the highway. You can slide your canoe down the bank here—it's easier than carrying it down.

The river has an irregular rock bottom, and most of the "shallows" shown are really areas where you will be hitting the bottom with the tip of the blade as you paddle. I haven't shown all of them as you'll find many short areas like this. The river banks are generally low for the first 3¾ miles. After that, and to the end of the trip, they range from low to rolling hills except where the cliffs and bluffs occur. The entire river shoreline is practically deserted of signs of civilization and is heavily overgrown.

The first 3¾ miles are relatively flat water paddling except for a few mild shoals. Some of the islands are grass hummocks that would be covered at higher water levels. Just before mile 3 there is a group of islands, not all shown on the map. You will have to thread your way through the numerous small shoals around them. This area could be tricky at higher water as it requires some sharp bends and the ability to ferry. You'll pass some pretty bluffs just past mile 3.

Just before you get to the Broglen River entrance, you'll see some bluffs about 100 feet high on your left. At the end of them is a rapid followed by a pool. After this point the shoals

147

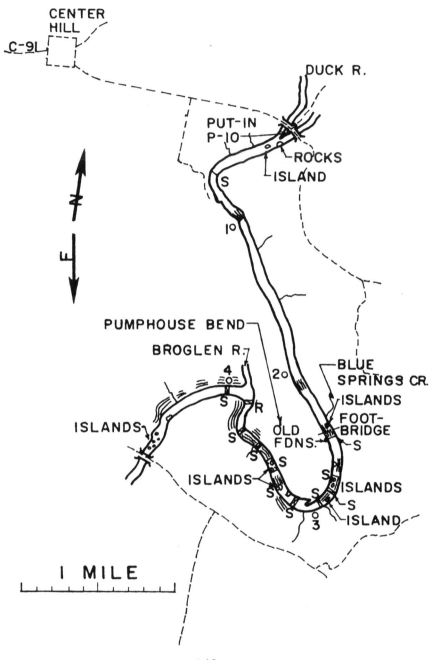

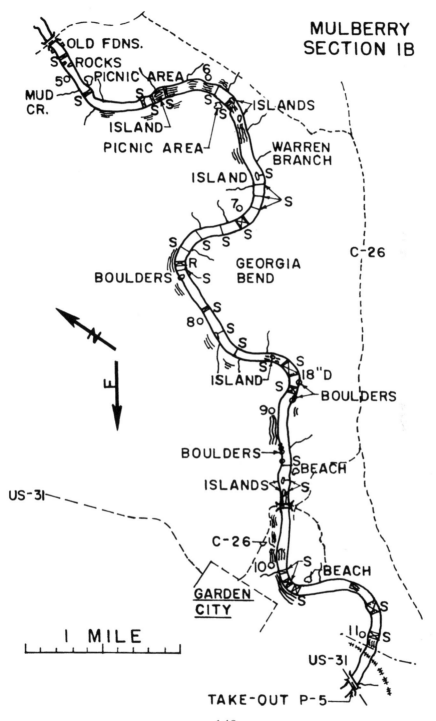

MULBERRY
SECTION 1B

GOLD FDNS.

S ROCKS

5 PICNIC AREA

MUD
CR.

6

ISLAND

ISLANDS

PICNIC AREA

WARREN
BRANCH

ISLAND

S

7

S

S S

GEORGIA
BEND

C-26

BOULDERS

R
S

S
8 S S

ISLAND

S

18"D

S

BOULDERS

9

BOULDERS

BEACH

ISLANDS

S

US-31

C-26

10

S

BEACH

GARDEN
CITY

S

S

11

S

US-31

1 MILE

TAKE-OUT P-5

get harder, many of them being Class 1 rapids at this water level and Class 2 at higher water levels, and you'll also have to watch out for the rock formations that jut into the river and will be all or partially covered when the water is up.

Most of the shoals after this point have a noticeable drop in elevation, but there is only one actual drop. This is the 18 inch one at mile 8¾. Just before the bridge at mile 4¾ there is another maze of islands surrounded by shallows, through which you will have to find your own path.

As you paddle along, you will catch glimpses of bluffs back off the river, and there are numerous rock formations in the river and on the shore. Rock "peninsulas" neck the river down frequently, particularly at the shoals. Many of these are only a few feet high and are mentioned before as requiring caution at higher water levels. I have shown a few of them. Just before mile 5 there is one of these formations of rocks extending halfway across the river from the right and just below this a similar formation from the left. You will have to take an "s" course through them.

After mile 7 2/3 there are some big boulders on the right, apparently broken off the cliff line behind them long ago, as full grown trees are now growing in and on them. Another noteworthy formation is at the end of the bluffs at mile 9. Here are a group of three gigantic boulders, then a space, then another huge boulder. Still another is the group just before mile 10.

The sand beaches shown are pretty and make good stopping points. The picnic areas are sand and are undeveloped clearings except for the one at mile 5. All are reachable by local dirt roads, but finding these local roads is a matter of stopping and asking someone.

The take-out is another steep place, about a 50 yard carry up a narrow trail to the highway. Parking is on a narrow shoulder of the highway, so park as far off the edge of the road as you can.

SECTION 2

MULBERRY FORK OF THE WARRIOR 10.8 MILES

Old U. S. 31 to bridge above I-65
Drop: 9.2   Difficulty: 1–2
Topos: Nectar, Blount Springs   Hazards: Class 1 and 2 rapids

See the take-out information for Section 1 for this put-in and for water level indication. The river is about 150 feet wide at the put-in, narrows to 50 feet, spreads back to 100 feet about mile 3.5, then progressively narrows to about 50 feet at the take-out. This section can easily be run at the "0" level.

The river is continuously rock-bottomed to mile 9 when it abruptly becomes sandy. You'll find some shallow areas where the bottom is level, but you don't have a paddle-blade length of water under you at "0" level. Much of the first 1¼ miles is like this. Those shallows shown on the map usually have an uneven bottom and will require a little selective path finding at low water levels.

Low hills backing up two to five foot sloping banks and interspersed with stone bluffs, generally 20-40 feet high but ranging up to 100 feet, make up the usual terrain. Steeper and higher hills occur in the bends, and large slabs and boulders and low-lying rock peninsulas are scattered along the run in the river and along the shoreline. In the last four miles, the terrain begins to shift over to 10-15 foot high dirt banks with low hills or flat areas beyond the shoreline. The cabins and trailers and the plant (sewage disposal, I think) are your biggest intrusions on solitude.

Some of the shoals are single lines of rock; others would wash out at higher water levels. All are easy to run. There are three Class 1 and two Class 2 rapids. The Class 1 rapids have good water volume and lots of rocks to dodge. The one at mile 1.9 has several four to five foot boulders on the right and an "s" curve around the boulders into a chute. The chute will carry you right through even though it looks as if it will sweep you right into the lower boulder.

The hardest Class 2 rapid is at mile 5.9. It has a strong current even at "0" level and requires a lot of maneuvering. The

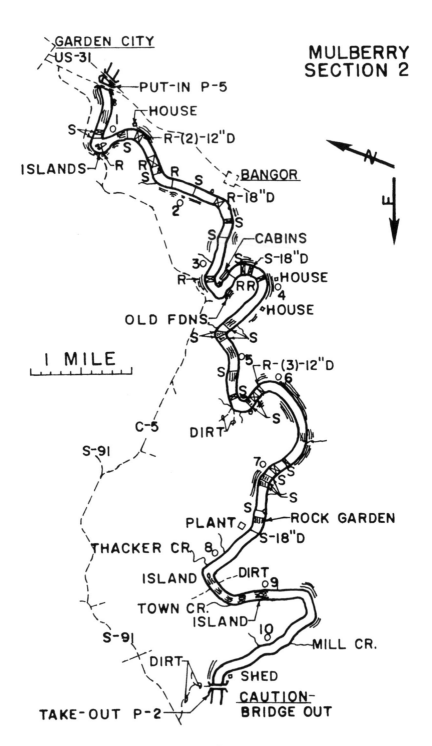

MULBERRY
SECTION 2

GARDEN CITY
US-31
PUT-IN P-5
HOUSE
S
R-(2)-12"D
ISLANDS
R R R R
S
S
BANGOR
R-18"D
2
S
CABINS
S
S-18"D
3
R
R R
HOUSE
4
HOUSE
OLD FDNS
S
S
S
5
R-(3)-12"D
S
6
S
S

1 MILE

C-5
DIRT
S-91
7
S
S
S
PLANT
ROCK GARDEN
S-18"D
THACKER CR. 8
ISLAND
DIRT
9
TOWN CR.
ISLAND
10
MILL CR.
S-91
DIRT
SHED
TAKE-OUT P-2
CAUTION-
BRIDGE OUT

N

E

other one at mile 2.4 has a total drop of about 36 inches.

Section 2 has some very interesting bluffs and rock formations. Some of the prettiest (although not the highest) are the
40 foot rock shelves on the right at mile 3.2, the 70 foot bluffs
at mile 5.9 on the left, and the long line of 10-15 foot formations bordering the river on the right near mile 7.3. The
"shelves" have the remains of an old stone wall on them.

Another picturesque spot is the waterfall on the right
about mile 1.8. The little stream runs off a pair of four foot
stone steps into the river.

A not so picturesque spot are the bluffs on the right in the
first sharp bend on the ride. These are a shining example of con-
cern for the outdoors with their big pile of garbage dumped
over the edge from the road above!

The take-out is on your right just downstream from the
old bridge. The bank is low but you have about a 100 foot
carry up to the road through a gradually sloping but heavily
overgrown field with one five foot vertical rise in it. There is no
turn-around space—you'll have to back up about 50 yards to get
out. Park in the road. The bridge is out, and you can't drive
over it. Neither can you put-in or take-out on the other side—
the road and property right to the water is all posted.

SECTION 1

WEST FORK OF SIPSEY 8.8 MILES

**County 60 (Sipsey Recreational Area) to low water bridge near
State 33   Difficulty: 2
Drop: 4.5   Hazards: One Class 1 rapid
Topos: Bee Branch, Grayson, Double Springs, Houston**

A very scenic ride. The river is about 35-50 feet wide and
holds this width throughout the section. In higher water the
narrowness and swiftness of the river will require a little skill in
the handling of a canoe and the one rapid will be a strong class
2 with high standing waves. Water level can be judged by the
flow at the low water bridge at the take-out. If there is just

153

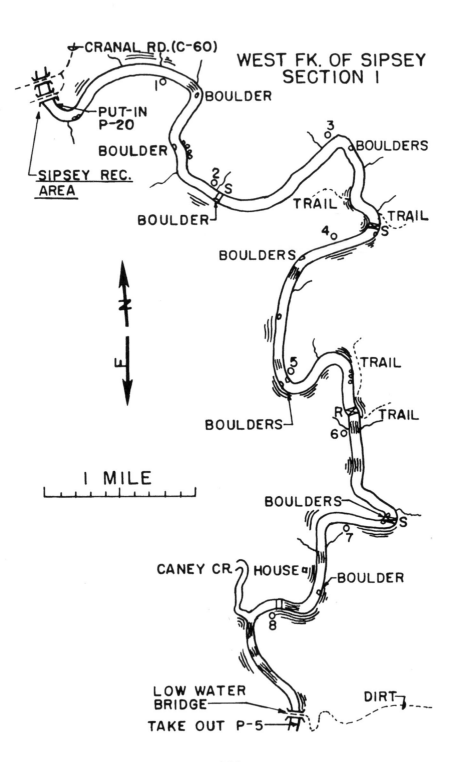

WEST FK. OF SIPSEY
SECTION I

CRANAL RD.(C-60)

BOULDER

PUT-IN
P-20

BOULDER

SIPSEY REC.
AREA

BOULDER

BOULDER

BOULDERS

BOULDERS

TRAIL

TRAIL

BOULDERS

TRAIL

TRAIL

BOULDERS

BOULDERS

CANEY CR. HOUSE

BOULDER

LOW WATER
BRIDGE

TAKE OUT P-5

DIRT

1 MILE

N

154

enough water flowing under this bridge on the left for you to float through, then you can **just** float the entire section. This is low water. If the water level is such that there is about three feet clearance under the bridge, then the rapid will become Class 2. As this clearance between water and bridge decreases, the standing waves and the length of the rapid increase.

The put-in has plenty of paved parking, but the last 50 feet of the path down to the river is rather steep and over big rocks. Once at the river level, there is a nice put-in.

In the first two miles you'll see many bluffs back from the river and large boulders in the water and on the riverbank. Some of these boulders are tremendous. Just past mile 3 you'll pass some high bluffs right on the water's edge and then some low ones on your right. If you'll watch closely as you pass the next banks of bluffs on your left, you'll spot a cave-like opening with a waterfall over the edge of the cliff. This is only about 30 feet back from the river and is a cool, nice place in the summer. In the winter it is a glittering mass of ice crystals created by the freezing spray of the waterfall coating trees, rocks, and cliffs—a really pretty place.

You can spot some inviting-looking overhangs under some of these bluffs as you go on down the river. One such place is just before mile 5 on your right. You can identify the location by a big rock in the river. Notice the enormous boulder on the river bank on your right at mile 5; it's a split rock now with trees growing in the split. Here also, the river is nearly blocked with boulders. Another overhang right at the river is just around the next bend and on your right.

You now come to the rapid. There's an old road on the bank on the right if you want to portage. In low water your only difficulty will be finding a floatable path. Usually you can make the run by staying on the right, but watch out for the nearly submerged rock at the very end of it. At higher water levels you'll have a few more rocks to watch for and will need to bear to the left to avoid the low trees growing on the island just below the rapid. This, of course, is only if the water is high enough to submerge the island. You'll have some shallow spots on and off for the next few miles. The bottom is rock, and in the summer you may have to get out and wade and tow your boat.

Just before mile 8 you'll see a very high bluff on your left that plunges straight into the water. There's a lovely pool at its foot. This is probably the most photographed bluff on the section and is well deserving of a few shots. Below Caney Creek the shallow stretches are more frequent but the water deepens before the take-out. Be cautious at the low water bridge in high water. It constitutes a real danger. You could easily be broadsided on it and rolled under. As it also serves as a stop for floating logs and trees, you could also be **caught** under it and drowned. In low water you can go under it on the left. The take-out is gently sloping. The road to the bridge is often washed out in the spring floods, so you may have to carry about 100 feet to your vehicle.

When you get out, walk over the little dirt bank on your left just above the bridge. There's a shady cove, a sand-bottomed pool, and a low waterfall off a rock bluff. A private place—cool and nice on a summer day.

SECTION 2

WEST FORK OF SIPSEY 5.4 MILES

Low water bridge near State 33 to Grindstone Creek Road
Drop: 0.5   **Difficulty: 0**
Topos: Double Springs, Houston   **Hazards: None**

If I were rating trips as to the beauty of their scenery, then the first 1½ miles of this section and, to a lesser extent, the next 2½ miles would be rated tops. High bluffs plunging into the river, undercuts, large boulders, and small waterfalls combine to make this an extremely scenic ride. The river starts off about 50 feet wide but gradually widens as it goes toward Smith Lake, reaching about 200 feet in width at the take-out. Use the low water bridge at the put-in as a water gauge. If you can float under it on the left, then this stretch will be no problem. See the take-out information for Section 1 for this put-in.

The bluffs just above, under, and downstream from the State 33 bridge are possibly the most magnificent. The ice cold

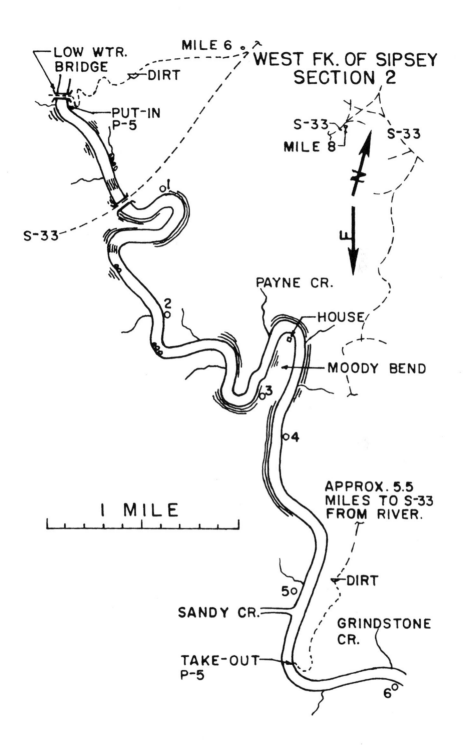

LOW WTR. BRIDGE

DIRT

MILE 6

WEST FK. OF SIPSEY
SECTION 2

PUT-IN P-5

S-33

S-33
MILE 8

S-33

E

S-33

PAYNE CR.

HOUSE

MOODY BEND

APPROX. 5.5 MILES TO S-33 FROM RIVER.

1 MILE

DIRT

SANDY CR.

GRINDSTONE CR.

TAKE-OUT P-5

157

spray of a waterfall falling off the top is a delight to paddle through on a summer day. Farther down you pass large boulder formations on the bank and in the river. Unfortunately, the current nearly dies about mile 2, so in normal water the rest of the trip is strictly a "paddle" and not a "float." There is a big shelter undercut in the low bluffs on your left at about mile 2½, and immediately around the bend are high undercut bluffs on your right, often with several small waterfalls off them. On your left just past Payne Creek is an absolutely delightful place. Watch in the low bluffs on your left, and you'll see a small stream about six feet wide. Paddle up it, and there's a beautiful little rock-ringed cove with a low waterfall off the bluffs. The waterfall hits a sloping rock then goes into a sand-bottomed pool. The rock makes a good "sliding" rock into the pool. This is one of the river's real treasures—please leave it spotlessly clean—it's a jewel. Just downstream at the next little stream on your left is a similar cove and waterfall.

By now you're in the slack waters of Smith Lake. Bluffs on your right are very scenic and stretch down the river almost a mile. Watch out for Sandy Creek—the take-out is just past it on your left. The take-out is low and sloping, and you can drive almost to the water, but you'll have to back up to turn around. The take-out road is long and may be impassable if wet unless you have four-wheel drive. Grindstone Creek road is not the real name of this road, but it runs near Grindstone Creek. Locally it is known by another name, so be prepared for a few blank stares if you ask directions.

BLACKWATER CREEK—GENERAL

Blackwater Creek is a relatively narrow stream, although it's as large as some other bodies of water called "rivers." It flows through a section characterized, for the most part, by rocky hills, bluffs, and wild and rough terrain, although there are a lot of pasture areas along the first few miles of Section 1. The creek is rocky-bottomed from beginning to end and is generally picturesque from a scenery standpoint and interesting for its shoals and rapids. These rides cover 23.8 miles of the creek, the final take-out being about 1/8 mile before the creek runs into the Mulberry Fork of the Warrior River.

Section 1 has the most shoals and rapids, particularly below the County 41 bridge where you will find seven of the hardest ones on this creek concentrated in one ½ mile stretch. Section 2 is a more remote appearing part of the creek, and is very similar in appearance to Section 1 of the West Fork of the Sipsey, flowing as it does through a rock-walled valley. This section of Blackwater Creek, however, has far more shoals than the West Fork. In Section 3 the creek begins to level out, and the rock formations and bluffs become fewer. The last two miles are a peaceful, scenic, flat water run.

The only fault with any of these runs is the put-ins and take-outs. There isn't any run that has a good situation at both ends. The Section 1 put-in is bad from a parking and unloading standpoint, but the take-out (Section 2 put-in) is good. An alternate run with a better put-in could be from the County 41 bridge down. However, this cuts the run in half. The Section 2 take-out (Section 3 put-in) is badly overgrown in the summer, very steep all the time, and has virtually no parking space. But Section 3 has an excellent take-out.

Start of a ride. Note the piroque in the foreground.

159

SECTION 1

BLACKWATER CREEK 8.9 MILES

State 195 (Manchester) to Walston Bridge
Drop: 9.9 to County 41, then 15   Difficulty: 1—2
Topos: Manchester, Sunlight   Hazards: Class 2 rapids

The put-in road is narrow with *just* enough room to get your vehicle out of the traffic. Unloading will require your walking in the road, so be cautious and unload as rapidly as possible. I suggest that you get permission from the owner of the store about 1/10 mile north of the bridge to park there after you unload. It's gently sloping under the bridge, and boat entry is easy.

Water level can be read on the left-hand bridge pier at the put-in. It's marked in tenths of a foot for 2.6 feet. The lower .4 foot down to "0" is not marked. You can easily run the section at "0" level or at down about .4 below "0" if you take care in selecting your path.

The creek is about 40 feet wide at the put-in but gradually widens as you approach the dam at mile 1.3. The first part is a combination of woods and pastures with one pretty bluff. The eight foot dam is just below the second footbridge. You can portage it on the far left-hand end at the dam unless the water is high, in which case approach cautiously and portage sooner. This is private property, so don't stop and don't delay your portage. Try to be as unobtrusive as possible.

The creek narrows back to about 50 feet below the dam and varies between 50 and 80 feet to the County 41 bridge. The shoreline down to mile 2 is fairly wooded with low hills or eight to ten foot high banks, numerous rock formations, and 10-40 foot and some 75 foot bluffs both on and off the creek. The shoals and longer shallows have a definite drop in elevation. All are easy, but most of the shallows do have enough small protruding rocks in them to keep you on your toes.

From mile 2 to the County 41 bridge the terrain is lower and more open with pasture on your right, wooded shores on your left, and some sheds and farm buildings on both sides.

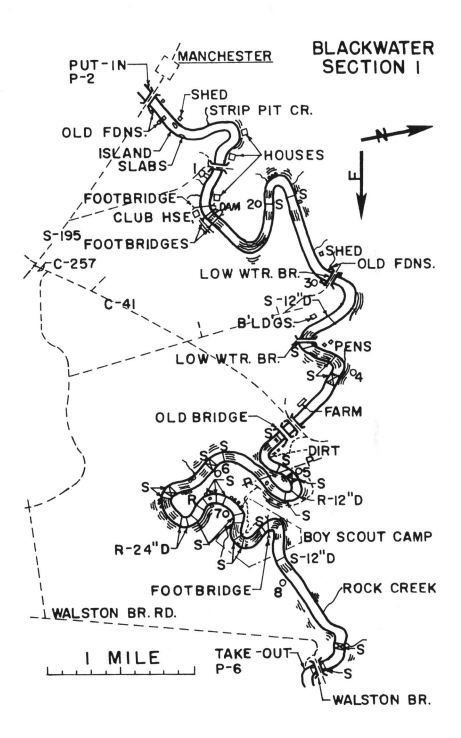

BLACKWATER
SECTION I

PUT-IN
P-2

MANCHESTER

SHED
STRIP PIT CR.

OLD FDNS.

ISLAND

SLABS

HOUSES

N

E

FOOTBRIDGE

CLUB HSE.

DAM 20 S

S-195 FOOTBRIDGES

C-257

C-41

LOW WTR. BR.

SHED

OLD FDNS.

30

S-12"D

B'LDGS.

LOW WTR. BR.

PENS

S

S 04

OLD BRIDGE

FARM

DIRT

S S

S 05

S 6 S R

S R R-12"D

R

S

R-24"D 70 S

BOY SCOUT CAMP

S S-12"D

FOOTBRIDGE 8

ROCK CREEK

WALSTON BR. RD.

1 MILE

TAKE-OUT
P-6

S

S

WALSTON BR.

161

There is a small rapid just below the low water bridge at mile 3. The rapid is simple with several well-defined paths. At mile 4 you'll see a fine sample of preserving nature—some beautiful bluffs that someone uses for a garbage dump!

Below County 41 is more of a wilderness. The creek runs in a sort of wide gorge with much higher, steeper, and more heavily wooded hills, most of which are topped with low bluffs. Other bluffs, some up to 75 feet high, parallel or touch the creek, and the shoreline and creek bed have many more rocks and boulders in and on them.

From County 41 to mile 6.6 the creek has more shoals and one small rapid. All are easy and some are only single lines of rocks across the creek. Others will require more care than those upstream. You should be cautious of boulders and slabs in the water at higher water levels. The long shoal about mile 6.7 will require the most care as the creek narrows to about 40 feet here, and the shoal has about three feet total drop and lots of rocks.

Between mile 6.6 and 7.0 the creek narrows to 30 feet, and there are seven rapids or hard shoals in succession. The first one (Class 2) has a slot running diagonally right to left in the middle. Run the next one on the left. After the shoal is a rapid with a 12 foot slot between boulders. It's clear but has standing waves even at "0" level. After the next shoal the creek opens back up to about 50 feet. You'll have two more shoals, the second one being a little harder than the first one.

The camp and swinging bridge you see is a Boy Scout camp. Notice the bluffs on the left in the curve at mile 7.7. The scouts have made rooms under the natural overhang and use the bluff face for mountain climbing practice.

From here to the take-out is a flat, scenic paddle. The take-out is just below the Walston Bridge on the right. A dirt road leads from the highway. The road is rutted and steep at the highway, but if you can make it down and up this first incline, you'll have no problem. The take-out is good. You'll have about a 50 foot carry up a gentle slope with only one short, steep part. Parking is good, and turn-around space is adequate.

SECTION 2

BLACKWATER CREEK 7.6 MILES

Walston Bridge to State 69
Drop: 7.6   Difficulty: 0–1
Topos: Sunlight, Cordova   Hazards: None

See the take-out information for Section 1 for this put-in.
Water level can be read on the downstream side of the left-hand
bridge pier. These red marks are in tenths of a foot for 2.6 feet.
The lower .4 foot is not marked, but the section can be run
down to what would be the "0" level. The creek is about 50
feet wide at the put-in, varies from 30 to 75 feet, and is 50 feet
wide at the take-out.

This section runs through a wide, heavily wooded, and
rocky valley for most of its length. Except for an old mine on
the right just below the put-in, a cabin at mile 1.2, and a power
line crossing, the run is basically in a scenic wilderness area.
Where the bluffs occur they are usually almost continuous on
both sides of the creek. The shoreline averages about eight to
ten feet high at places, sloping gradually back to the bluff-
topped hills that form the valley and, at other locations, having
low hills that run directly into the creek. At many spots there is
a second line of low bluffs closer to the water, and there are a
few huge, picturesque, solitary rock formations. Both the shoreline and the creek bed have an abundance of rocks, boulders,
and slabs on and in them.

The first three miles of the paddle are in this bluff-lined
valley. All of the shoals and shallows are easy but are frequent
and close to each other Most of the shoals are single lines of
rock across the creek, and only two (mile 1.6 and mile 2.6) have
any abrupt vertical drops. On the left at the mile 1.6 shoal the
lower line of bluffs has a break that makes a picturesque point.
You'll see several of those along the creek.

The shoal in the bend at mile 2.6 has two small islands
with a drop at the top of the shoal and one at the islands, followed by a shallow. On the right at this shoal is a nice overhang
suitable for camping.

From mile 3 to 4 the valley opens out, with the bank going

163

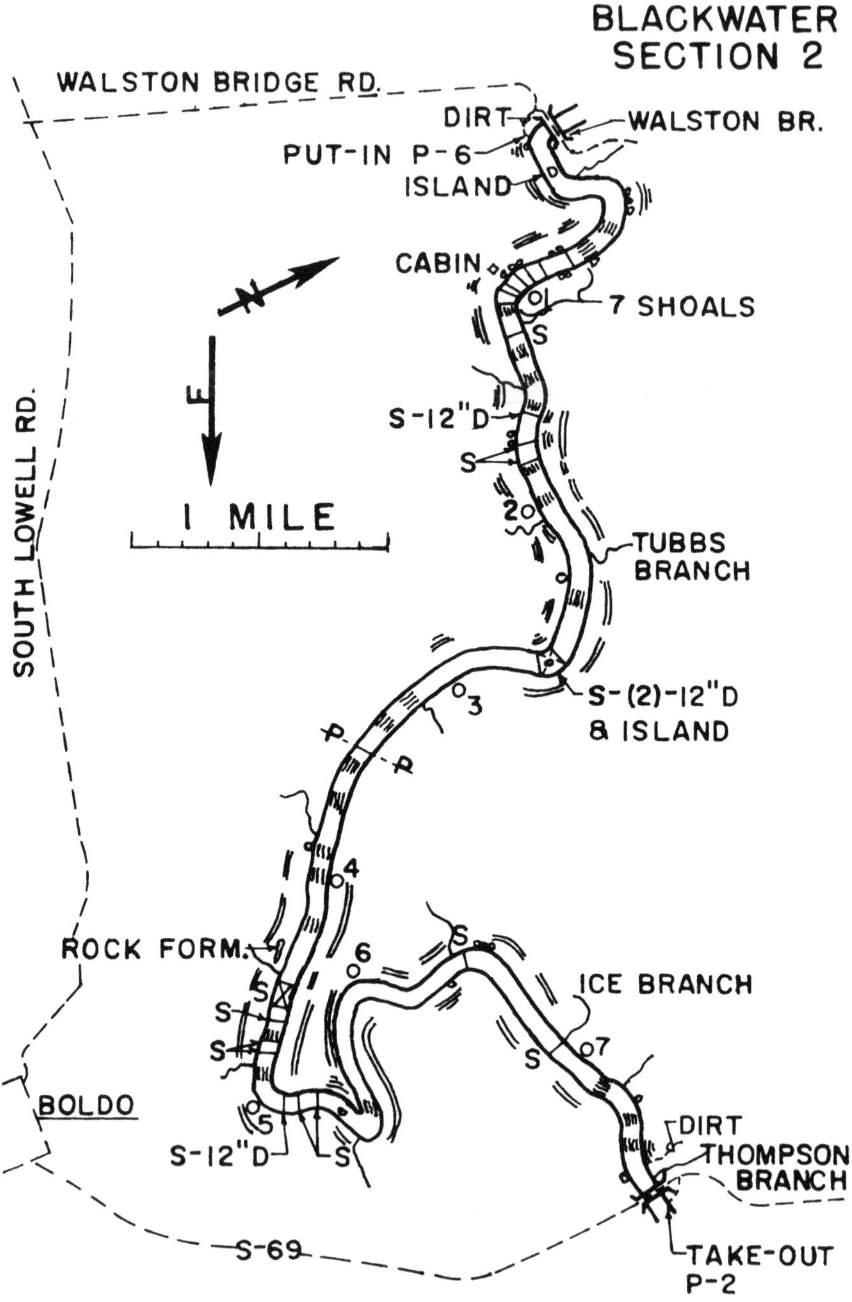

BLACKWATER
SECTION 2

WALSTON BRIDGE RD.

DIRT

WALSTON BR.

PUT-IN P-6
ISLAND

CABIN

7 SHOALS

S-12"D

SOUTH LOWELL RD.

N

E

1 MILE

2

TUBBS
BRANCH

3

S-(2)-12"D
& ISLAND

P
P

4

ROCK FORM.

6

ICE BRANCH

S

7

S

BOLDO

S

DIRT
THOMPSON
BRANCH

S-12"D

S

S-69

TAKE-OUT
P-2

back in a flat, wooded area. At mile 4 you enter the valley again. Watch on the right about mile 4.5, just above a stream coming in; you'll see a trail going up to a very pretty 100-yard-long rock formation that has a good camping spot along its base. At its upper end there is a tunnel completely through the formation. Another overhang is visible from the creek at mile 4.8 on the right, just above another stream entry.

The creek narrows to about 50 feet at this point, and you'll have to do a little picking at the next three easy shoals. There's another pretty point about mile 7.1 on the right. The bluffs end here, and the shoreline changes to low hills at the take-out bridge.

The take-out is bad. It's on the left just below the bridge and is a rough, steep path about 50 yards long up beside the bridge to the highway. There is room (barely) for two cars to park off the road and no turn-around except in the highway itself.

SECTION 3

BLACKWATER CREEK 7.8 MILES

State 69 to County 22
Drop: 7.9   Difficulty: 0-1
Topos: Sunlight, Cordova   Hazards: None

See the take-out information for Section 2 for this put-in. Water level can be read on the left-hand downstream bridge pier (the pier closest to the bank). These red marks are in tenths of a foot for 2.6 feet. The lower .4 foot is not marked, but the section can be run at up to six inches below what would be the "0" level. The creek is about 50 feet wide at the put-in and gradually widens to about 90 feet at the take-out.

This run has numerous small, easy shoals alternating with flat water sections. As you progress downstream, the flat water sections get longer. All of the shoals are easy, but, as is usual in this creek, most of the shallows have small rocks that will usually require some maneuvering.

165

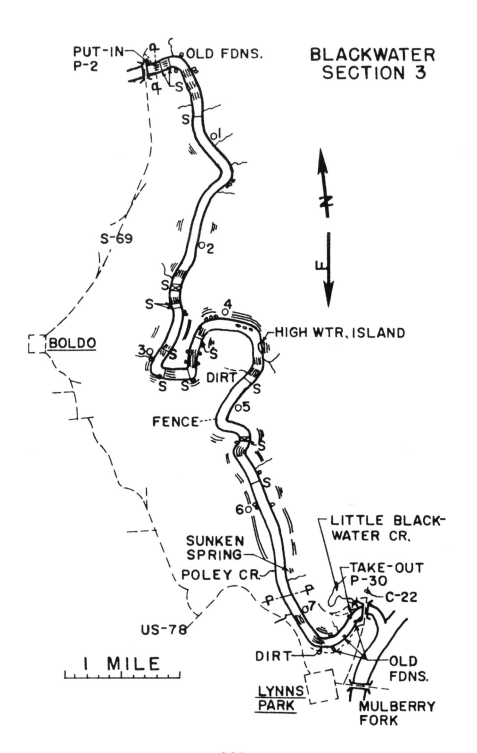

BLACKWATER
SECTION 3

PUT-IN
P-2

OLD FDNS.

S-69

BOLDO

HIGH WTR, ISLAND

DIRT

FENCE

LITTLE BLACK-
WATER CR.

TAKE-OUT
P-30

C-22

SUNKEN
SPRING

POLEY CR.

US-78

1 MILE

DIRT

LYNNS
PARK

OLD
FDNS.

MULBERRY
FORK

166

This section flows in a wide valley with low hills that frequently merge into the water. The hills are topped with low bluffs in some areas. In places there are eight to ten foot high banks with a small flat area between the shoreline and the hills. There are fewer boulders and rocks in and on the river than in Section 2, but they are still numerous in some locations.

The shoreline in the first 2.5 miles of the ride is mostly hilly or low banks with only a few bluffs here and there. The old highway (if you could call it that) crossed the creek just around the bend below the put-in. You'll see the foundations for it. About mile 2 the creek widens to 70 feet, and on the right about mile 2.2 you'll see a huge, solitary rock formation that would offer a good camping area.

From this point on for the next few bends you'll have more bluffs, scattered boulders, and a much rockier shoreline. At mile 3 on your right is a stream that has a beautiful cascade when water is running in it, and just around the bend below it is an overhang close to the creek—another camping spot.

The rocks in the creek near mile 4.2 are about three feet high and could be trouble at higher water levels. You'll find still another overhang on the left at mile 4.4, and on around the bend is an old bridge foundation on the left and a dirt road on the right. This is a pasture area, and you'll see a farm building up on the hill on the right.

About mile 5.4 you'll begin to see 15 foot high bluffs paralleling the river on both sides. Some of these have very pretty points on them. From here on, the ride is essentially a flat water paddle. Watch on the left about mile 6.5 just below the last of these low bluffs—there's a peculiar sunken opening in the rock just off the shore and just visible above the 10 foot high bank.

The left-hand shoreline gets lower here, and low hills line the right side of the creek. The old foundation you see at mile 7.4 used to be a dam and mill; the mill was on the right. There's another old stone foundation and some old bridge foundations just above the take-out.

The take-out is excellent. It's a dirt boat ramp into the water just around the bend past the old bridge foundations. There is plenty of parking and turn-around room, as this area is used for a boat launch and picnic area.

167

TALLAPOOSA RIVER–GENERAL

The Tallapoosa River is, at the time of the writing of this book, free-flowing from its headwaters in Georgia to its entrance into Martin Lake below State 49 east of Alexander City. However, the construction of a dam above Malone, Alabama, will flood the river almost back to the Georgia line and leave only 42 miles still open. These 42 miles are covered in the rides in this book. As this dam is not due to begin backing up water until late 1976, I have also included an additional 9.5 miles above the dam site. Hopefully, you can see this beautiful section of the river before it vanishes forever.

My descriptions and maps were made from floats on the river *before* the dam was built. Although the dam will not change the basic features of the river below it, the water flow will definitely be affected, so bear this in mind as you float down the river and read my comments.

The Tallapoosa is generally a slow moving, shallow river, averaging about 225 feet wide but ranging down to 100 feet and up to over 300 feet at some of the island locations. The bottom is basically rocky, and the river contains numerous small shoals and shallows, all of which are floatable even at very low water.

The shoreline is wooded, the banks being 10-15 feet high and usually having either a bank and then a flat area going back to low hills or, in some sections, a larger flat area used as pasture. The hills are rocky; wild life is fairly abundant; and it's an excellent camping river.

If you're looking for the thrills of whitewater, then the Tallapoosa is not an exciting river. If you're looking for an easy, relaxing, peaceful, solitary float, then it may just suit you exactly.

Where a strong back stroke comes in handy.

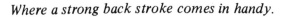

SECTION 1

TALLAPOOSA RIVER 7.5 MILES

State 48 to Dirt Road
Drop: 2.6   **Difficulty: 0**
Topos: Ofelia   **Hazards: None**

NOTE: This entire section will be flooded by Lake Wedowee.

This is a peaceful, slow-moving stretch of river with minor shoals, usually consisting of a single line of rocks across the river. The river is about 225 feet wide at the put-in, widens out to 300 feet at the island near mile 6, then narrows back to 200 feet, and holds this width to the take-out.

The put-in is the old ferry road reached from the west end of the State 48 bridge. The road is paved to the river, and the put-in is about 1/8 mile above the bridge. There is plenty of turn-around and parking room. Access to the water is easy and gently sloping. Water level can be read on the right-hand bridge pier of the State 48 bridge. These are red markings graduated in tenths of a foot for three feet. At the lower mark you can float this entire section.

The banks are earth and about 10 feet high. Low, rocky hills reach the river in places, but the general shoreline has a flat wooded area between the bank and the hills. There are some big, rough rock formations off the river on your left starting about mile 3 and continuing around the bend to mile 3.7. There is also one low bluff. Fox Creek at mile 4.4 is an attractive place for lunch and also has a good flat camping spot on top of the river bank. The islands at mile 6.5 are four to five feet high and flat on top.

All of the shoals are easy, usually with only a six to ten inch drop and all with a choice of clear paths. At mile 5 there is a "rock garden," consisting of 12-24 inch high boulders widely scattered in the water. Again there are many wide, clear paths, but this area would be a little turbulent with a few feet more of water.

169

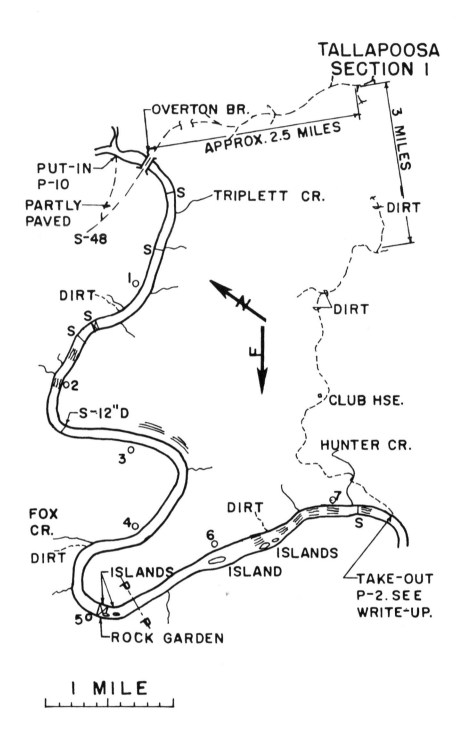

TALLAPOOSA
SECTION I

OVERTON BR.

APPROX. 2.5 MILES

3 MILES

DIRT

PUT-IN
P-10

S

TRIPLETT CR.

PARTLY
PAVED

S-48

S

DIRT

1

DIRT

DIRT

S

S

E

2

CLUB HSE.

S-12"D

HUNTER CR.

3

7

FOX
CR.

4

DIRT

S

DIRT

6

ISLANDS

TAKE-OUT
P-2. SEE
WRITE-UP.

ISLANDS

ISLAND

5

ROCK GARDEN

1 MILE

The take-out is a dirt road on your left and is a rather poor excuse for a put-in or a take out. The road is not visible from the river, so you'll have to keep a sharp eye out for the correct place on the map. It's also *off* the river somewhat, so you'll have to go to shore and start looking. And finally, when it's wet, it's doubtful that a two-wheel drive vehicle will make it all the way.

SECTION 2

TALLAPOOSA RIVER 9 MILES

Dirt Road to County 15 (Malone)
Drop: 4.4   Difficulty: 0
Topos: Ofelia, Wadley North   Hazards: None

NOTE: The first two miles of this section will be flooded by Lake Wedowee.

This stretch of the river is through wilder and more rugged terrain than Section 1. The hills are generally steeper and more rocky, and there are more large rock formations and low bluffs. There are only three small shoals on this run, the last one being just before the take-out and having a 12 inch drop to it.

The river is about 200 feet wide from the put-in to the take-out. (See the take-out information for Section 1 for this put-in.) Water level can be read on the State 48 bridge markings (see Section 1) or on the bridge at County 15. The marks on the County 15 bridge are on the right-hand, downstream bridge pier, graduated in tenths of a foot for three feet and are red. This section can easily be floated at the lowest mark.

The banks, flats, and hills are similar to Section 1 except the hills in the upper few miles are somewhat sharper, and all the banks are 10-12 feet high. There are some rough, picturesque hills just below the put-in on your left and some occurrences of low bluffs and large rock formations, usually slightly off the river. The topo map of this area shows an island in the river about mile 1.7. Don't look for it—it's not there.

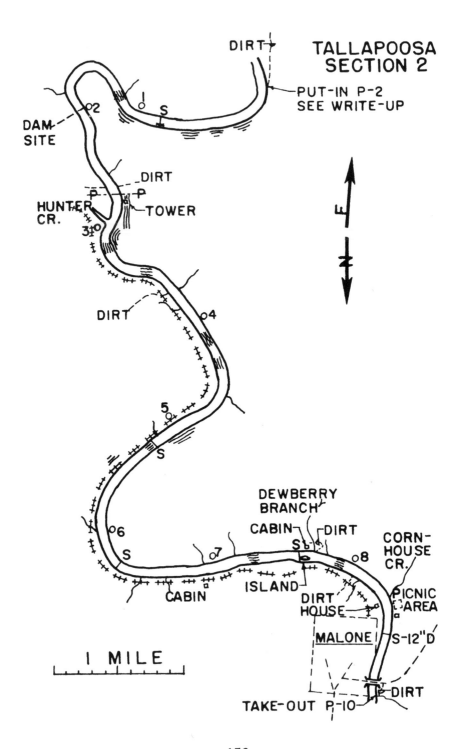

TALLAPOOSA
SECTION 2

DIRT

PUT-IN P-2
SEE WRITE-UP

DAM SITE

2

DIRT
P   P
HUNTER CR.   TOWER
3½

DIRT   4

5
S

DIRT

6
S

E

7

DEWBERRY BRANCH
CABIN   DIRT
S   8
CORN-HOUSE CR.

CABIN   ISLAND   DIRT HOUSE   PICNIC AREA

MALONE   S-12"D

TAKE-OUT P-10   DIRT

1 MILE

172

You'll pass the dam site at mile 2. It's unmistakable with its cleared bank and bare graded hillsides. Just below it, near Crooked Creek but on the left bank, is an old 20 foot concrete tower. I have no idea of its real purpose, but it's now serving as a giant hornets' nest, so be careful if you stop to investigate. The tower is backed up by one of the prettiest rock formations on the section. This 100 foot rocky hill continues on around the bend past the tower.

Below mile 3 the land begins to flatten out a bit and looks more like Section 1. You will see a railroad and its cuts following the river bank on the right from Crooked Creek to the end of the trip. From about mile 7 on to Malone there are scattered cabins along the shore, most of them on your left. At Cornhouse Creek there is a town park area and also the shoal with the 12 inch drop. You'll also pass the old bridge foundations just above the take-out point.

The take-out is on the left, downstream of the new bridge. It's a public park type area with a short and good dirt road leading to it. There is plenty of parking and turn-around space, and although the bank is a few feet high, access to the water is easy.

SECTION 3

TALLAPOOSA RIVER 6.5 MILES

County 15 (Malone) to State 22 (Wadley)
Drop: 3.0   Difficulty: 0
Topos: Wadley North, Wadley South   Hazards: None

This is a flatter stretch of country than the upstream trips, but the river has more shoals in it. The section starts and ends about 200 feet wide but spreads to about 350 feet at mile 1.5 and to 250 feet at mile 4.5. See the take-out information for Section 2 for this put-in. Also see County 15 bridge marking comments in Section 2 for water level indication. This section can be easily floated at the lowest mark.

The shoreline has eight to ten foot wooded banks and is almost consistently flat for a considerable distance back from

173

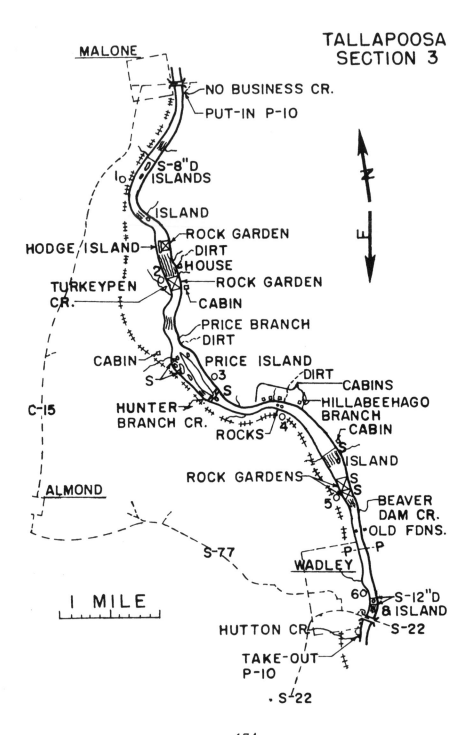

TALLAPOOSA
SECTION 3

MALONE

NO BUSINESS CR.
PUT-IN P-10

S-8"D
ISLANDS

N

E

ISLAND

ROCK GARDEN
DIRT
HOUSE
ROCK GARDEN
CABIN

HODGE ISLAND

TURKEYPEN
CR.

PRICE BRANCH
DIRT

CABIN

PRICE ISLAND

3

S

DIRT
CABINS

HILLABEEHAGO
BRANCH

CABIN

C-15

HUNTER
BRANCH CR.

ROCKS

S

4

ISLAND

ALMOND

ROCK GARDENS

S
S

5

BEAVER
DAM CR.
OLD FDNS.

S-77

P P

WADLEY

1 MILE

6

S-12"D
& ISLAND
S-22

HUTTON CR.

TAKE-OUT
P-10

S-22

174

the banks, particularly on the right-hand shore. A few low hills, some more or less rocky, occur here and there. A railroad generally follows the right-hand shoreline along this entire section.

There are several large islands and a number of smaller ones in this run. Some of the shoals and "rock gardens" occur at these islands. Go left of the small island at mile 1.3. Hodge Island at mile 1.5 has a "rock garden," but the widely spaced 12-24 inch high rocks have lots of clear paths on the left of the island. The river is about 250 feet wide here. The "rock garden" is followed by a long shallows and a series of smaller islands.

Price Island is a large picturesque island with about seven smaller ones scattered around it. Price is wooded and about 10 feet high and has a nice flat, solid rock slab on its upstream end that makes a good lunch or camping spot at low water levels. There are very small shoals to the right and left of this group of islands and one harder one at the end of the main island between it and the upstream end of the little island below it.

On your left around mile 4 you'll see some big six foot high slabs in the river. These slabs point upstream. You'll also see some cabins on the shoreline. Just downstream the river widens out to about 300 feet with a small shoal, a shallow, and another "rock garden" with two small shoals in it. The boulders here are 12-60 inches high, but the river is pretty clear on the left, and there is a choice of wide paths.

Notice the old bridge foundations just before the take-out. The one in the middle is rock and is a very old-style construction. The upstream end has partially collapsed. A six inch steel pipe now runs across the top of these foundations.

The take-out is easy. It has a short (about 10 feet) bank that flattens out and ends in a good dirt road. There is a turnaround area about 50 yards up this road. You should have no particular problems with the mud holes just before the turnaround areas.

175

SECTION 4

TALLAPOOSA RIVER 11.5 MILES

State 22 (Wadley) to Bibbys Ferry
Drop: 3.6   Difficulty: 0
Topos: Wadley South   Hazards: None

This section of the river winds through pasture land for much of its length. The shoals are much more abrupt than in the upstream floats. The river is about 200 feet wide at the put-in but narrows to about 100 feet at the take-out. See the take-out information for Section 3 for this put-in.

Water level can be read on the right-hand, upstream pier of the State 22 bridge. These red marks are graduated in tenths of a foot for three feet. You can just float this entire section at the lowest mark.

The banks in this section are 10-12 feet high, going back to wooded flat land with a very few low, wooded hills. Much of the shoreline after the first two miles (beyond the railroad bridge crossing and continuing to Muleshoe Bend) is pasture, but most of it has a thin fringe of trees on the bank. Camping spots are limited in this section because of these fenced pastures. Muleshoe Bend is the point on this run at which the river begins to narrow down and get deeper and slower. Rock formations and bluffs are rare on this stretch, but there are some low, pretty, and rugged ones on your left about mile 3 and on your right about mile 5.6.

Despite the flatness of the area some of the shoals are sharp, and at certain water levels they would become strong Class 1 rapids. Two of these are on the left by the large island at mile 1. The upper shoal is more of a "rock garden," with 12-36 inch high widely scattered boulders. The shoal at the end of this island has a 36 inch horizontal drop and is sharper than the upper one. There's another "rock garden" at mile 8 with most of the rocks toward the left bank. Watch out for some big, upturned four foot high rocks at mile 8.5 in higher water. Most of the other shoals have about a 12 inch drop and are very mild except for the one just past the big island near mile 10.5. This one has about a four foot horizontal drop and would, with

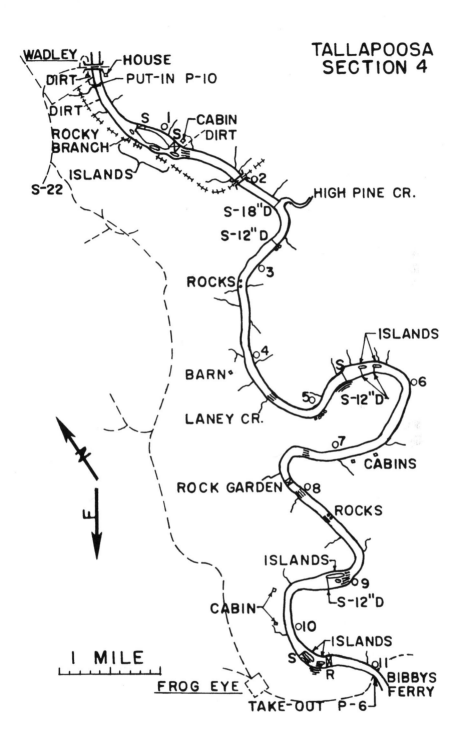

TALLAPOOSA
SECTION 4

WADLEY — HOUSE
DIRT — PUT-IN P-10
DIRT
ROCKY BRANCH
ISLANDS
S-22

S I
S
CABIN
DIRT
○2
HIGH PINE CR.
S-18"D
S-12"D
ROCKS
○3

BARN
LANEY CR.
○4
○5
S
S-12"D
ISLANDS
○6

ROCK GARDEN
○7
CABINS
○8
ROCKS

ISLANDS
CABIN
○9
S-12"D
○10
ISLANDS
S
R
○11
BIBBYS FERRY

1 MILE

FROG EYE
TAKE-OUT P-6

about a plus-one foot water reading, be a low Class 2 rapid.

The take-out is the ferry ramp and is good and easy. It's a very gradual slope into the water, and there's enough room to turn around at the parking area. Parking is on a little hill overlooking the ferry or on the wide, grass shoulder of the road. Don't block access to the ferry.

SECTION 5

TALLAPOOSA RIVER 8.1 MILES

Bibbys Ferry to Everglade–Buttston Road
Drop: 2.4   Difficulty: 0
Topos: Wadley South, Dudleyville, Buttston   Hazards: None

This is a generally deep and flat stretch of the river about 100 feet wide at the put-in and gradually widening to about 175 feet at the take-out. No water level indication is necessary for this run as it would take exceptionally low water to prevent its being floated. A small motor could be used in much of it most of the year.

The shoreline on both sides of the river averages eight to ten feet high, with some rises to 15 feet in the first five miles and up to 20 feet in the last three miles. These 20 foot banks are usually in two steps—a 10 foot bank, a short flat area, then another 10 foot rise. The general aspect of the shore is a bank, then flat land beyond, although there are a few scattered locations where low hills rise beyond the flat area or occasionally go directly into the water. The banks are earth with a few low rock formations usually occurring at the bends. The biggest and prettiest of these are about 50 feet high and on your left ½ mile below the put-in.

Down to mile 5 the left-hand shore is almost totally wooded and the right-hand shore, almost all pasture. Below mile 5 both sides of the river are mostly pasture. A fringe of trees along the shore usually screens the pastures, but they are sometimes clear to the bank. The lines of pastures are broken up by a few wooded sections.

178

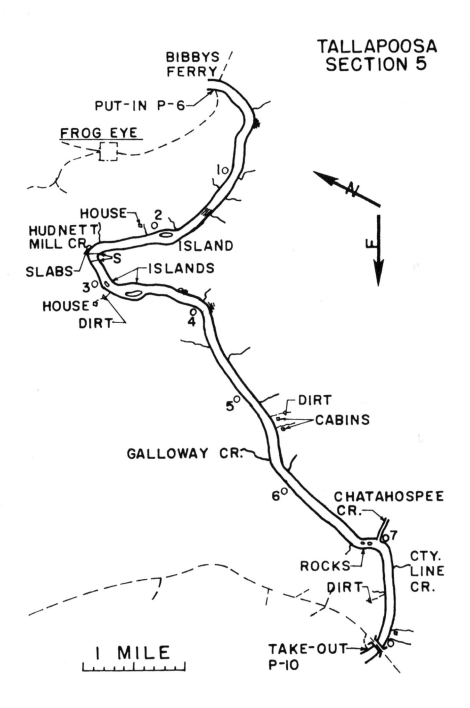

TALLAPOOSA
SECTION 5

BIBBYS FERRY

PUT-IN P-6

FROG EYE

1

HOUSE
HUDNETT MILL CR.
2
ISLAND

SLABS
S
ISLANDS
3
HOUSE
DIRT
4

5
DIRT
CABINS

GALLOWAY CR.

6
CHATAHOSPEE CR.
7
ROCKS
CTY. LINE CR.
DIRT

1 MILE

TAKE-OUT P-10

179

The few shoals are single lines of rocks across the river. There are some low rocks in the river which, like the shallows, would become more obvious at lower water levels. The two foot ones in the middle of the river about mile 6.9 are the highest.

Except for the pastures, the section is fairly deserted. All of the islands are high, wooded, and suitable for camping. The one at mile 3.4 has several low sand islands at its upper end. You might want to take a short side trip up Chatahospee Creek; it's a big and pretty stream.

The take-out is excellent. It's a concrete boat ramp on the right, just downstream from the bridge. There is plenty of turn-around and parking space.

SECTION 6

TALLAPOOSA RIVER 9.2 MILES

Everglade—Buttston Road to State 49 (Horseshoe Bend)
Drop: 2.2   Difficulty: 1
Topos: Buttston   Hazards: Griffin Shoals

Except for Griffin Shoals, Section 6 is very similar to Section 5, differing only in being wider. See the take-out information for Section 5 for this put-in.

The river is about 175 feet wide at the put-in, spreads to 300 feet at the small shoal at mile 1.4, spreads to over 500 feet at Griffin Shoals, then narrows back to an average of 250-300 feet, and holds this to the take-out. No water level indication is necessary as only the shoal area would offer any problems at low levels. A small motor could be used for most of the run.

The banks are dirt, about 5 feet high on the left, and five to ten feet on the right down to Griffin Shoals. Below the shoals both banks are eight to ten feet high to the take-out. A few low hills are scattered along, but, in general, the terrain is flat except for slightly steeper hills on the left at Griffin Shoals and just before the take-out. Both shores are wooded except for a pasture just before the put-in on the right, a farm and pasture on the left at mile 3 (where the pasture is cleared to the water),

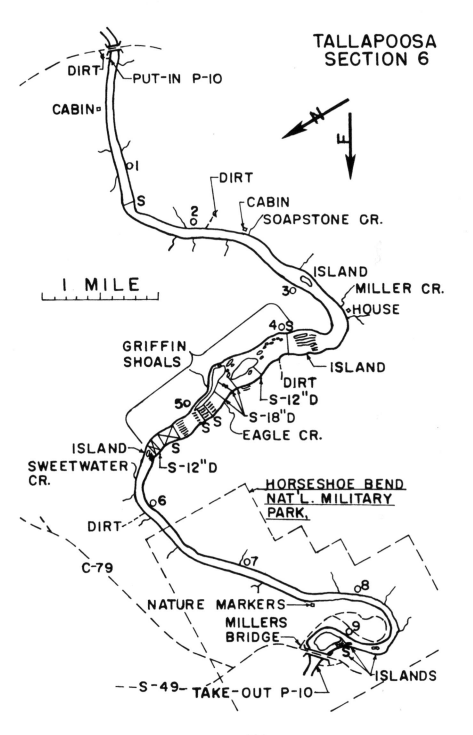

DIRT

PUT-IN P-10

CABIN

1 MILE

DIRT

CABIN

SOAPSTONE CR.

ISLAND

MILLER CR.

HOUSE

GRIFFIN
SHOALS

ISLAND

DIRT

S-12"D

S-18"D

EAGLE CR.

ISLAND

SWEETWATER
CR.

S-12"D

HORSESHOE BEND
NAT'L. MILITARY
PARK.

DIRT

C-79

NATURE MARKERS

MILLERS
BRIDGE

ISLANDS

S-49 TAKE-OUT P-10

181

Flying high—Ed and Pearl Hawkins in some standing waves.

and another small pasture on the left just below the shoals.

At Griffin Shoals the left shore is lined with fairly steep but low hills that are wooded and rocky and have some pretty, but not spectacular, scattered rock formations. The shoals themselves are 1.8 miles long. All of the islands are wooded and on the right-hand side of the river. There are eight shoals with 12 to 18 inch drops, depending on where you run them, and all with easy, clear chutes. Most of the shoals have shallows between them that would be *very* shallow in the summer. The last two shoals are long. There are several protruding rock formations in the shoals up to about three feet high.

Eagle Creek at mile 4.7 is pretty. The island at mile 3 is wooded and could be camped on. You enter the "Horseshoe" about mile 7.5, although you've long been on the National Military Park property. About mile 7.6 you'll see on your right, on the shore, what looks like a tombstone behind a fence. It's not—it's a nature walk sign cautioning you against slippery river banks!

You can go to either side of the big island just before the take-out. There are a lot of one to three foot high boulders protruding from the water between the two islands. At higher water levels this could be a *very* turbulent area.

The take-out is good. It's a concrete boat ramp on the left just below the bridge. There is plenty of parking and turnaround space. After the trip you might want to visit the park on the other end of the bridge.

Hatchet and Weogufka Creeks run parallel to each other south of Sylacauga. Both terminate in the backwaters of Lake Mitchell, and both flow through mostly forested areas that are rather remote in appearance. No large towns are close to either, so the creeks are relatively clean. Public access is good on both for the rides included. In general, Hatchet is the more peaceful; Weogufka, the more interesting.

HATCHET:

Hatchet Creek is a rocky stream with headwaters in the Talladega National Forest. The whole creek is about 41 miles long. Hatchet is basically wide and shallow with numerous shoals and a very few rapids. Section 2 is probably the most popular and most floated section. It's in this section that you see most of the picturesque shoal areas with protruding rocks that seem to be typical of published photos of this creek. Most of the land surrounding the creek is relatively low or with low hills.

About 35 miles of the creek are floatable, but access is a problem above the U. S. 231 bridge because of privately owned property, so only the lower 15.6 miles, broken into two rides, are covered in this book.

Wildlife is abundant on the creek, particularly in Section 1, and a quiet float down it will probably reward you with some good close-up looks.

WEOGUFKA:

Weogufka Creek is narrower, generally rockier, and has more shoals and rapids than Hatchet Creek. It has a lively current and generally flows through more remote-looking terrain. In Section 2 the scenery gets more rugged and wild looking the farther downstream you go, gradually building into areas with high, very steep, and rocky hills resembling a narrow valley. This is accompanied by a gradual increase in average drop.

Weogufka starts near U. S. 280. Only the 19.8 miles below County 29 are covered in this book as much of the upper reaches are generally very flat and shallow and through or along populated areas. Like Hatchet, the nearness of Lake Mitchell to the end of Section 2 doesn't seem to affect the flow at all. You'll have a good current right to the take-out.

SECTION 1

HATCHET CREEK 6.8 MILES

U. S. 231 to Rockford—County 29 road
Drop: 8.8   Difficulty: 1
Topos: Rockford, Flag Mountain   Hazards: Old Dam

This is an easy, basically wooded section. The put-in access is good. You can park on the wide shoulder of the highway or drive down an easy slope and park under the bridge. The bank is about 10 feet high, but once down it, boat entry is easy.

Water level can be read on the left-hand, upstream bridge pier. These red marks are in tenths of a foot for three feet. The trip can be easily floated *solo* at "0" level. You'll need about .4 foot more for an easy tandem float. The creek is about 75 feet wide at the put-in, spreads to about 100 feet in a couple of places and 175 feet at the mile 3.6 shoals, then narrows to about 75 feet at the take-out.

Down to about mile 2.5 the shoreline is usually six to ten feet high with flat, wooded areas beyond the bank, some low hills, and a few open pastures. Below this point the hills become more frequent both at the water and backing up the flat areas beyond the banks. This whole lower stretch is much more heavily wooded than the upper few miles and is almost deserted.

There are very few rock formations on this run after the first mile. You might glance up the side stream near mile 5.7. It has a very pretty series of low drops forming picturesque little falls.

Most of the shoals are easy with clear paths, but some will require a little maneuvering. The old dam site offers the only rapid—a Class 2 by virture of drop and velocity. About 20 feet are missing from the center of this once 10 foot high dam. Large

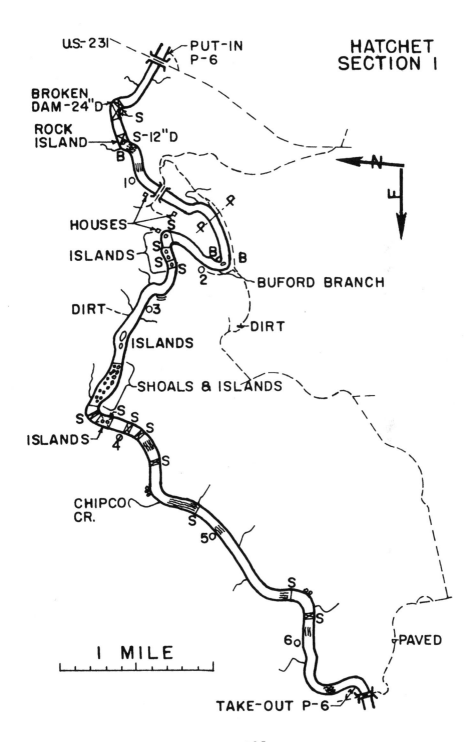

rocks in the water above the dam force you to go to the right of the break, then curve back to the left down the chute. There's a quick two foot elevation drop followed by 18 inch standing waves (at "0" level). Just as you come out of the chute, you'll have to do some rock dodging in the shoal just below the dam and in the next one just downstream from it. About mile 3.4, the creek widens out and for about ½ mile you'll have a complexity of small, low wooded islands, shallows, and small shoals, through which you can pick your own way. Just around the bend from this section are four shoals in a row—all easy, all with obvious elevation changes. The third one is the hardest. All the other shoals are small.

The take-out is on the right just around the bend above the bridge. At "0" level there's a sandbar on the right with a steep eight foot bank behind it which has several low places in it. At above "0" level you'll *have* to get out at one of these lower places. There's about a 20 yard carry through level woods to a dirt road off the main road. Don't block the main road at the bridge—park on this stub road in the woods. You can turn around at the end of this stub road, but it's easily blocked by a parked vehicle, so don't get yourself boxed in.

SECTION 2

HATCHET CREEK 8.8 MILES

Rockford--County 29 road to County 29
Drop: 6.8   Difficulty: 1
Topos: Flag Mountain, Richville   Hazards: One Class 2 rapid

See the take-out information for Section 1 for this put-in. Don't let the appearance of the old steel bridge over the creek scare you—it has stood up so far. Water level can be read on the right-hand upstream pier. These red marks are in tenths of a foot for three feet. Below the "0" level you will almost surely hang up in places. You'll have to climb down the bank near the bridge to read this gauge; it can be seen from the sandbar.

The creek is about 75 feet wide at the put-in and only wid-

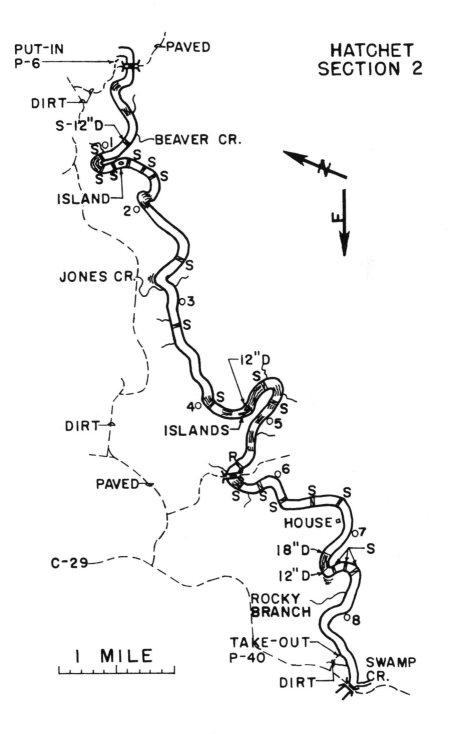

PUT-IN
P-6

PAVED

HATCHET
SECTION 2

DIRT

S-12"D

BEAVER CR.

S

S S

S S S

ISLAND

2

JONES CR.

S

3

S

12"D

S

4 S

S

5

ISLANDS

R

6

PAVED

S S S

HOUSE

7

C-29

18"D S

12"D

ROCKY
BRANCH

8

TAKE-OUT
P-40

SWAMP
CR.

DIRT

1 MILE

ens a little more at the take-out despite its proximity to Mitchell Lake. You will have current all the way. The shoreline is generally low with rolling hills, and only occasionally do you see a high, steep slope coming into the river.

Most of what you'll have from the put-in to the rapid just above the bridge at mile 5.6 are shallows, small shoals, and low eight to twelve inch drops. All of these will require a lot of picking in low water, but none of them are any hazard whatsoever. Many of the shoals are preceded or followed by shallows, so you may well disagree with some of my designations on the map. Some of these shoals are studded with boulders out in the creek.

In a bend just before mile 3 there is a low hillside on your right with some large scenic rock formations on and in the river. Just below this, a small stream comes in on your left and a large one on your right. There is a pretty little five foot waterfall up the small stream that is visible from the main creek.

At mile 4 is one of the shoal-shallow combinations with large rocks in the river. The islands just beyond them are surrounded by shallows all the way across the river, but there is a little more water on the right side of the biggest island. There is a small 12 inch drop at the end of the islands and then more shallows.

Just as you come in sight of the bridge at mile 5.6, you will find the only real rapid on this creek. Despite its roar, froth, and foam, it's an easy rapid, but you should pull over on the right shore and scout it because the speed of the water as it goes through here is very fast. In normal water you can sneak around the whole rapid on the far right if you're careful not to be swept from your boat by overhanging bushes and limbs. If you want to run it, there are two good places a little to the right of the middle. One of these just takes you on down the first drop, scoots you across a long ledge (about 40 feet) and then across the final 12 inch drop. The other—just a foot or so to the left—is more fun but a bit trickier. As you go off and your bow drops down, another current of water coming in from the right slams your boat in the side and jerks it around to the left. If you're ready for it, it's fun; if you're not, you get wet.

After you pass under the bridge, and from there on to the take-out, the shoals are a little harder than in the upper part and the drops, a little larger. The shoal at about mile 6½ has a 2½ foot total drop, but this is spread out over the length of the shoal.

On your left just before mile 6 you'll see one of the few big hills in this stretch. The only other ones are down at about mile 7½. Here, too, you'll find some very pretty low cliffs on the right—about the only ones on this trip.

From mile 7½ to the take-out is a long pool. The take-out is on your right about 1/3 mile above the County 29 bridge and will surprise you. It's a paved parking area with a nice low, sloping shoreline that more than makes up for the put-in.

SECTION 1

WEOGUFKA CREEK 10.2 MILES

County 29 to Low Water Bridge
Drop: 9.8   **Difficulty: 1**
Topos: Flag Mountain   **Hazards: Class 1 rapids**

This is a pretty run with a lot of small shoals, a few rapids, and some rugged, wooded scenery. The put-in is good—a gently sloping bank and a 40 foot carry to under the bridge. The shoulder is too narrow to get your vehicle completely off the road, so you'll have to park on a stub of a road about 50 yards north of the bridge.

Water level can be read on the right-hand bridge pier. These red marks are in tenths of a foot for two feet. The lower 12 inches down to "0" is not marked. This run can easily be made at "0" level. The creek is about 50 feet wide at the put-in and averages this for the run except for spots that neck down to 25 feet and one that spreads to 100 feet.

Except for the "valley" area between miles 3.5 and 5.5, the section usually has five to ten foot wooded banks with a flat area beyond them. Low hills occur in the bends, and there are a few pasture areas along the shore, particularly after the bridge at mile 7.4. In the two mile long "valley" area, the hills close in on the creek, get higher and steeper, and are rocky and heavily

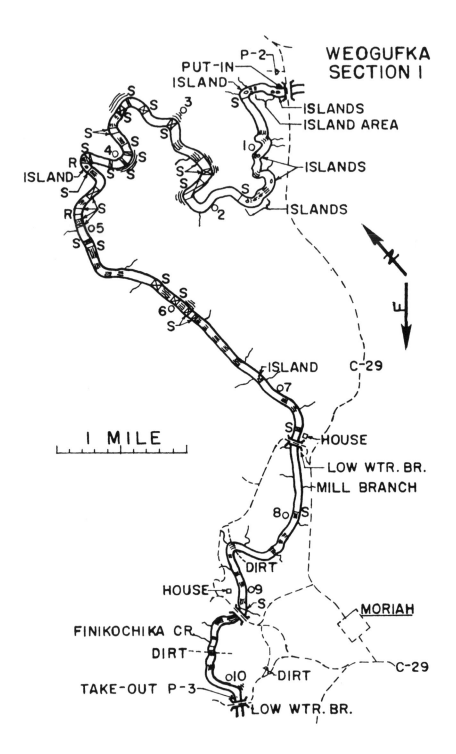

WEOGUFKA
SECTION 1

PUT-IN ISLAND
P-2
ISLANDS
ISLAND AREA
ISLANDS
ISLANDS
ISLAND
1 MILE
C-29
ISLAND
HOUSE
LOW WTR. BR.
MILL BRANCH
DIRT
HOUSE
MORIAH
FINIKOCHIKA CR.
DIRT
C-29
TAKE-OUT P-3
DIRT
LOW WTR. BR.

190

wooded. You'll find a lot of rocks in the creek and along the shoreline, and the only prominent rock formations on the run occur in this section. Here, too, are most of the places where the creek narrows to 25 feet.

The very beginning of Section 1 may look discouraging. Just below the put-in is a maze of small islands and shallows to pick through, and the whole first 1½ miles are subject to logjams that may take some dragging over at low water and could be quite hazardous at higher levels. After mile 1.5, however, the creek is clear.

The shoals are all easy, and most of them are small, but many will require minor maneuvering. The shoal at mile 3.6 is a little harder as it's in a narrow area and has a higher water velocity. The Class 1 rapid at mile 4.4 is a rapid only on one side of the island. It's a shallow on the other side. The one at mile 4.8 is the same way, less the island. Shallows almost replace the shoals after mile 6.4. Most of the shallows on the whole run will require a little path selection at "0" level.

Bill McGowan in a small shoal on Weogufka Creek.

The two low water bridges could be hazardous at higher water. The one at mile 7.4 only has 2½ feet clear below it, and the take-out bridge has five feet clear—both at "0" level. Obviously, you can't float under the first one at any level. A powerful current and standing waves build up at both of these locations at higher water levels, and neither bridge has a good stopping place above it, so approach both with caution when the water is up.

The take-out has about a four foot bank up to the road. Parking is limited to the edge of the narrow road, but you can get completely off it if you drive about 50 feet north of the bridge.

SECTION 2

WEOGUFKA CREEK 9.6 MILES

Low water bridge to Ford
Drop: 14.6   Difficulty: 1−2
Topos: Flag Mountain, Mitchell Dam N.W.   Hazards:
                                              Class 1 rapids

See the take-out information for Section 1 for this put-in. Water level can be read on the left-hand side of the left bridge pier. These red marks are in tenths of a foot for three feet. This run can be easily floated at "0" level.

The creek is about 40 feet wide at the put-in, necks down to 20 feet in a few spots, and spreads to 75 feet, but averages 50 feet and is this width at the take-out.

If a single word were used to describe this section, it would be "rocky." Except for a small pasture area near the put-in, the run is almost completely wooded with five to ten foot banks or low rocky hills in the straight parts and on the inside of the bends, and high, steep hills covered with, based by, and often topped with massive rock formations on the outside of the bends. Some of these plunge straight into the water and are very pretty. You might particularly note the pine-covered reddish-brown sloping cliff near mile 6.9. There are only a few vertical

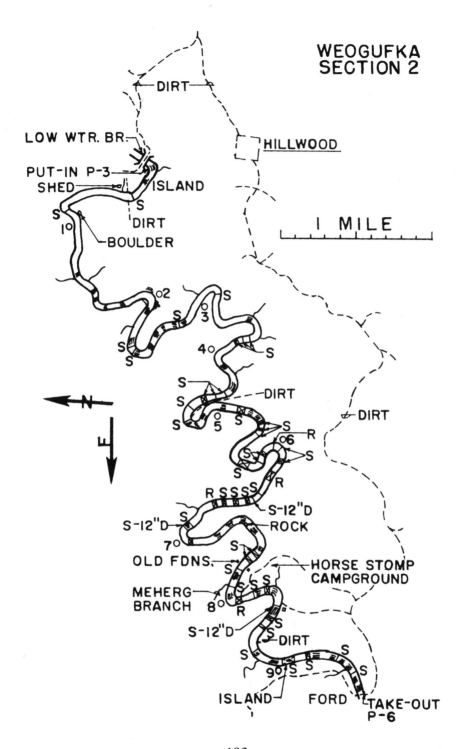

DIRT

HILLWOOD

LOW WTR. BR.

PUT-IN P-3

SHED

ISLAND

1 MILE

S

1°

DIRT

BOULDER

°2

S

°3

S

4°

S

S

S

S

DIRT

DIRT

S

S

°5

S

S

R

°6

S

S

S

R S S S

R

S-12"D

S-12"D

S

ROCK

7°

S

OLD FDNS.

S

HORSE STOMP
CAMPGROUND

MEHERG
BRANCH

8°

S

R

S-12"D

S

DIRT

S

S

9°

S

S

S

ISLAND

FORD

TAKE-OUT
P-6

193

bluffs, and these rarely exceed 50 feet high, but the large boulders and stone outcrops combined with the steepness of the higher hills and the tight bends in the creek all give the impression of a rock-walled valley. Some of the hillsides are clear except for pines; others are covered with tangles of laurel. The creek bed is rocky and has numerous boulders along its banks. The entire run is very scenic, rugged, and remote-appearing.

All of the shoals are simple and easy to mile 6 except for a few near mile 4. The area between mile 6 and mile 8 has harder shoals and some Class 1 rapids. These rapids are at about miles 6.0, 6.2, 6.6, and 8.1. The one at mile 6.0 is the hardest one on the run. It's in one of the most scenic bends, has protruding rocks in the water, and takes a good amount of maneuvering. The mile 8.1 rapid is a rapid by virtue of drop and water velocity. It's in a curve, the creek is necked down, and the elevation changes swiftly, but there's nothing to dodge. The shoal at mile 6.5 has 24-36 inch high rocks in it and would be a rapid at slightly higher water levels. Below mile 8.1 all of the shoals are very small.

In this same area (about mile 5.5 to 8.1) is some of the most rugged and picturesque-looking scenery in this run. On the left at mile 6.0 (by the rapid) a narrow 20 foot high waterfall runs off the low bluffs. You'll see another waterfall on your right near mile 4.7.

Three places look like caves. One is on the left just below mile 6 near the top of the high hill. From the water it has every appearance of a cave, but it's only an overhang. Another opening is lower and on your left near mile 4.3. This one is bush-covered and may be either an overhang or a cave. Still another is near mile 7.6 on the left.

You can either take out at Horse Stomp campground or float on down to a better take-out at the ford. The ford is concrete, and you can take-out on the left. There is off-the-road parking and good turn-around space. The bank slopes very gently into the water, and you, obviously, can drive right to the ford for loading your boat. Horse Stomp itself is a nice, clean, quiet, very woodsy, and primitive campground.

LITTLE RIVER–GENERAL

Little River is unique in being one of the few rivers that forms and flows for almost all of its length on *top* of a mountain. It is also well known because it flows through Little River Canyon, a 700 foot deep gorge some 12 miles long.

Little River is formed from its east and west forks. The east fork flows out of Lake Lahusage near Mentone, Alabama, and the west fork forms in Georgia, flows down into Alabama, drops over DeSoto Falls, and junctions with the east fork to form Little River about 8.5 miles below Lake Lahusage. The river then flows about seven miles to Little River Falls just below the State 35 bridge. These 60 foot falls mark the beginning of the canyon. The runs described here are on the east fork, on Little River to just above the State 35 bridge, and from Eberharts Point, six miles down the Canyon, to the Canyon Mouth Campground at the end of the canyon.

Sections 1 and 3 can be dangerous, and even Section 2, while basically mild, has a few places that offer hazards. All three runs are in scenic wilderness, Sections 1 and 3 in a rugged rock-walled gorge or valley with a rocky, much obstructed river bed and Section 2 in a broader, more open, but heavily forested, valley.

You may notice that I have omitted the section from Little River Falls to Eberhart Point. There is a good reason for this. I know of no one who has successfully made this run! If there are any, they are the few in kayaks with skill, experience, adequate support personnel, and enough caution to know when to portage! This, of course, is in high water. In low water there are not enough floatable stretches to bother with. There is never any problem identifying "low" water, but the person who does not know this particular river will be unable to determine "high" water. A few inches can make the difference. One other factor–in case the challenge of the section below the falls overwhelms you–there's another eight foot fall about ½ mile downstream from Little River Falls. And don't forget the hydraulics, which abound, and the sheer volume, weight, and power of the water in this narrow bed that make it almost impossible to dodge the boulders! I recommend that you get your name in the paper for something else rather than as a victim of Little

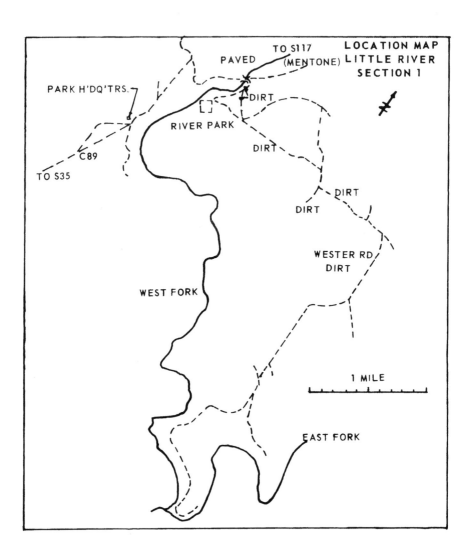

LOCATION MAP
LITTLE RIVER
SECTION 1

TO S117
(MENTONE)
PAVED
DIRT
PARK H'DQ'TRS.
RIVER PARK
DIRT
C89
TO S35
DIRT
DIRT
WESTER RD
DIRT
WEST FORK
1 MILE
EAST FORK

River.

Sections 1 and 2 are usually made as one run because the road to the take-out for Section 1 (Section 2 put-in) is a little hard to negotiate in wet weather due to some deeply rutted areas and a few large mud puddles. I doubt that a passenger car would make it even in dry weather. The combined run, however, is rather long and is about a seven hour trip in low water.

An indication of water level for Sections 1 and 2 (although not too precise) is Little River Falls at Highway 35. If water is flowing over the entire lip of the falls except for the promontory near the left, I would advise your staying off of Section 1 unless you're an expert. If the water is flowing only at the far right and left-hand ends of the fall, then it's a safe level, although it may be a little shallow in places.

Paddling up a cool and shady side stream.

SECTION 1

LITTLE RIVER 8.3 MILES

Lake Lahusage to Dirt Road
Drop: 19.2   Difficulty: 3–4
Topos: Valley Head, Jamestown   Hazards: Up to Class 3 rapids

The put-in is down a steep rocky bank on the left, just below the Lake Lahusage Dam. Parking is limited to the shoulder of the road, but there is plenty of room if you line up. You cannot drive across the dam as the left-hand end of it is partially collapsed. See the general comments for water level indication. The river is about 50 feet wide at the put-in and averages this for the run except where it necks down at the rapids and some shoals.

Most of this run is in a rocky valley. The whole river bed is extremely rocky with flat slabs on the bottom of the pools and boulders on the banks and in the water. Some of the rapids in this stretch are' caused by the river being almost blocked by these boulders.

Down to the camp dam near mile 1, you will find numerous low drops and shoals with marked elevation changes. At the 18 inch drop shown near mile .4, you have an "s" passage through rock ledges with an eight foot passage at the end. Immediately below the dam is a conglomeration of islands, bars, jams, and shoals that you will have to wind your way through.

From this point on there is little I can say about the run. There are shoals, rapids, narrow twisting passages, and drops that are fun in low water and very rough in higher water, but all of this is completely variable over a range of 12 inches of water. In summer when the falls (see the general notes) are low, this is a scenic and fun ride. A few inches of water less, and it's a no-fun walk; six to eight inches *more* water, and you need much more skill to make the run. The drop usually occurs in 12 to 36 inch elevation changes, most of which are graduated over the length of a shoal or rapid, but there are also vertical drops. This section is pretty well choked with islands and rock formations that neck the river down to as small as 10 feet. In the summer you will also have to paddle through passages in shoals where

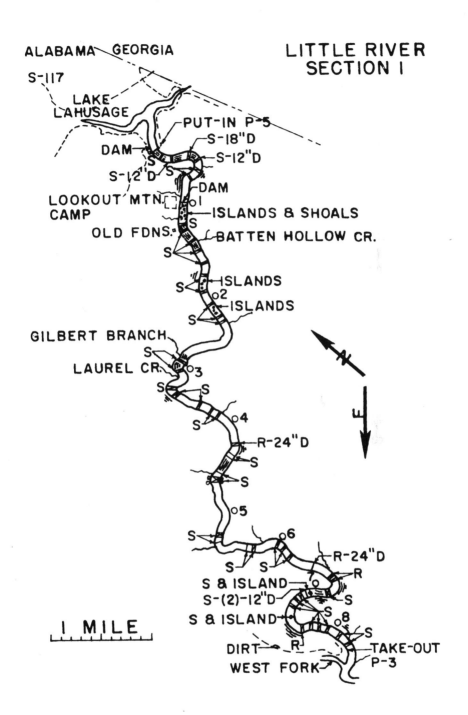

LITTLE RIVER
SECTION I

ALABAMA GEORGIA

S-117

LAKE
LAHUSAGE

PUT-IN P-5
S-18"D
DAM
S-12"D
S-12"D

DAM
LOOKOUT MTN.
CAMP
OLD FDNS.
ISLANDS & SHOALS
BATTEN HOLLOW CR.

ISLANDS
ISLANDS

GILBERT BRANCH
LAUREL CR.

N

E

R-24"D

R-24"D
R
S & ISLAND
S-(2)-12"D
S & ISLAND
DIRT R
WEST FORK
TAKE-OUT
P-3

1 MILE

199

trees and bushes have grown almost all the way across the river on these islands. Added to this are some places that demand tight turns and precise maneuvering to successfully negotiate the rapids. I suggest you scout the rapids first at any location where you can't see a pretty clear path.

The take-out is on the right about 75 yards before the junction of the east and west forks. You can't see it from the river, so you'll have to watch out for the west fork entry and stop just as it comes in sight. The bank is overgrown and about six feet high. The road is about 20 feet off the river. If you park here, try not to block the narrow dirt road. Turn-around space is a bit cramped, but you can do it.

SECTION 2

LITTLE RIVER 6.3 MILES

Dirt Road to State 35
Drop: 6.3   Difficulty: 0–1
Topos: Jamestown, Fort Payne   Hazards: None

This is a much milder, easier stretch than Section 1. See the general comments for water level indication. The river is about 50 feet wide at the put-in and gradually widens to about 75 feet at the take-out. See the take-out information for Section 1 for this put-in.

The topography opens out below the junction of the two forks, just downstream from the put-in, and the river flows through a wider, lower banked, and less rocky valley than the preceding section. This ride will normally present no problem to the average paddler except for a few of the shoals in which standing waves may offer some hazard of swamping. The river is still rock-bottomed and still has numerous rock formations in and along it, but they tend toward horizontal slabs and are generally fewer and less massive than those in Section 1.

You will see several scenic bluffs, but after mile 4.0 the terrain is generally low wooded hills. There are no rapids in this section, and the shoals are moderate. The only shoal you will

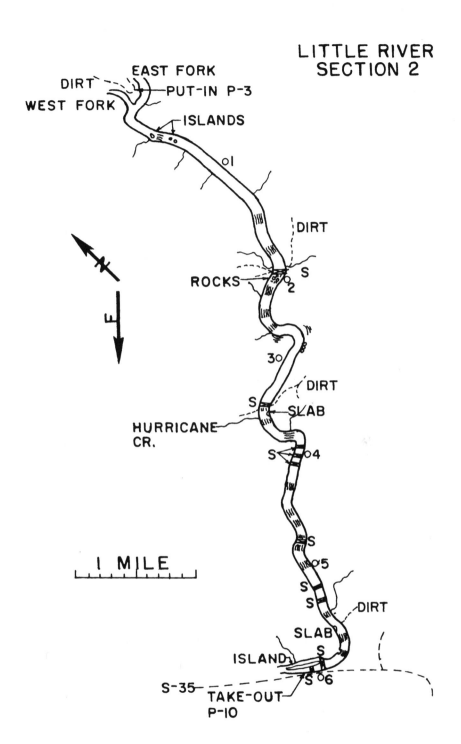

have to watch out for at all is the one at the beginning of the island just before the take-out. This is an inclined, smooth rock face with a standing wave and hydraulic at the bottom that will try to hold your boat.

The take-out is on the left. You'll have to carry about 20 yards up a well-beaten path to a grassy area by the road. There is plenty of room to park here as a small dirt road runs off the highway onto the grassy area. If you wish, you can take-out slightly downstream at an informal-type picnic area on your left that is a little closer to the water.

There's just one point—don't forget that Little River Falls is only a slight distance around the next bend!

SECTION 3

LITTLE RIVER 6.0 MILES

Eberharts Point (chair lift) to Campground
Drop: 30.0   **Difficulty: 3—4**
Topos: Little River   **Hazards: Up to Class 4 rapids**

This is a popular and challenging ride for kayakers and canoeists in higher water and a real fun ride for inner tubes and small rafts in low water. All of the ride is in Little River Canyon which has some magnificent scenery. The river is about 50 feet wide at the put-in and holds this almost to the take-out.

Access to the put-in is via *foot* down a ¼ mile, rutted dirt road that parallels the chair lift. It's not really a bad carry—just all downhill. Parking is at the top on the shoulder of the road. In the past the chair lift operators have sometimes tied the boats to their service car and carried them down, but this is not standard practice.

Water level can be estimated two ways. One is at the stone wall on the river bank behind the chair lift. If the water is about a foot below the top of this wall, it's a good level for *supported* trips by skillful canoeists and kayakers. If the water is very shallow here, walk down to the old dam site in the first bend. If you can *just* float over this in a tandem canoe, then you'll have

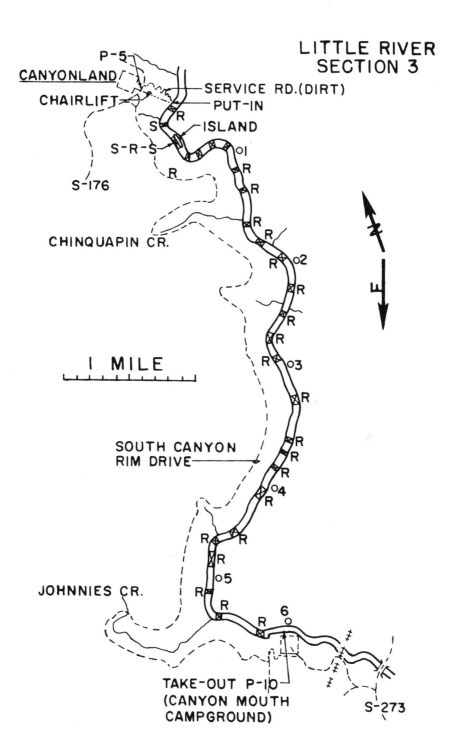

LITTLE RIVER
SECTION 3

P-5

CANYONLAND

CHAIRLIFT

SERVICE RD.(DIRT)

PUT-IN

R

S ISLAND

S-R-S ⊠ ⊠ ○1

R

S-176 R

R

CHINQUAPIN CR.

R

R ○2

R

R

R

1 MILE R ○3

R

R

R

SOUTH CANYON R

RIM DRIVE R

R ○4

R

R R

R

JOHNNIES CR. ○5

R

R

R ○6

TAKE-OUT P-10

(CANYON MOUTH

CAMPGROUND)

S-273

203

a good low water trip, but you'll still need to exercise caution in spots.

DO NOT BOAT THIS STRETCH ALONE! It is dangerous at high water, and once committed to the trip, you're in for the length of it unless you want to walk out the trail that runs along the right-hand shore.

The really rough rapids are pretty well concentrated in the first two miles. For the next mile they are not as bad, and after about mile 3 the pools begin to lengthen out and most of the rapids get milder, with a more gradual drop and smaller rocks. After you pass the rapid at Johnny's Creek, you have pretty smooth sailing to the take-out.

The take-out is very good. It's an easy beach sloping into the river on your right at the campground swimming area. Parking is off the road in parking spaces. You should ask the park manager for permission to park there as a matter of courtesy. Your shuttle road is the South Canyon Rim Drive, which will give you an opportunity to view this part of the canyon from above.

PART THREE
Appendix

BUT JOHN - WHAT HAPPENED TO THE REST
OF THE RIVERS?

The preceding rivers have been presented in detail. But what about all the rest of the floatable rivers and streams in the state? A glance at even an oil company road map is enough to show that no single volume of any manageable size could possibly cover all of them, and when you begin to examine topographic and county maps and see the number of even smaller streams, then the task becomes rather staggering.

Nonetheless, I feel that I should at least mention some of these streams and give some indication of rides that can be taken on them. If there is ever a Volume II of this book, many of these runs will probably be covered in precise and abundant detail. For now, I'll just give a brief description—somewhat of a glorified list.

The floater in the southern parts of the state will obviously find the rivers quite different from most of those in the north central parts of Alabama. The topography is different due to these rivers and streams being in the Coastal Plain area of the state; consequently the drop is less. Although the areas of rapids are far to the north, you will find a few shoals on some of the southern rides, and, surprisingly, most of the rivers have a swift current. In the summer you are likely to encounter greater heat simply as a function of latitude. You are also likely to encounter more snakes, but as a counterbalance you get a greater abundance of flora. Well, different anyhow!

In any event, each ride will offer you something different in the way of scenery and interest, and they are all worth taking.

Just in case some of you are still not happy about my leaving out some of the rivers, I have included a little explanation for a few of them. This is tucked way over in the back because I know perfectly well that my reasons probably won't suit you. If they don't—then go ahead and float the rivers anyway. As long as *you* enjoy it, that's all that counts!

A SMALL EXPLANATION OF THE
APPENDIX

This appendix covers rivers and creeks that I have not run. I have examined every put-in and take-out, however, and have rated them with the various considerations of parking space, turn-around area, distance to the water, easiness of access to the put-in and of access to the water. Hopefully, the information will save you time and trouble in planning your trips.

As in Part II of this book, I've tried to break the rides into about 10 mile lengths with at least fair put-ins and take-outs. As usual this is great in theory and not too wonderful in practice, so it hasn't always worked, and I've wound up with a few short rides, a few long rides, and some poor take-outs here and there. I have included intermediate take-out or put-in points where they exist, and I've described them so you'll know if they're good or bad. This way you do your own ride length, adjusting if you so desire. If I don't have any intermediate take-outs listed, then they're usually not there, although I've doubtless missed a few. Also, as in the rest of the book, I've started at the upper end of a river and worked down it.

All river widths and flows and all conditions at the put-ins were observed during the spring months. The water levels were not at flood stage but they were at normal wet weather heights, so you may find conditions at the put-ins and the river widths and flows somewhat different if you make any of these rides during very dry weather.

Let me repeat that I have not run these stretches covered in the Appendix and have no idea at all of what may lie in between the various put-ins. My opinion is that you will find just swift, flat water for the most part, with a few minor shoals on a few of the streams—but I don't know this for a fact. Let me also add that the ride lengths are estimated distances, and most were estimated off county road maps which, while usually great for roads, are usually not so wonderful in their accurate portrayal of creeks, streams, and rivers.

For many of these runs it will be essential that you have a county road map or a topo map of the area. I think you'll find the county road map most useful. They are available for most counties either free or for $.50. You can get them by writing the County Road Department of each county at the county seat. If they don't have them or you want to get them all from one source, then write the State Highway Department in Montgomery for a list of their county road maps. You'll find that they come in various scales (½ inch to the mile is most useful), and there is a nominal charge that varies according to the size of the map.

A few of these county road maps are pretty lousy, but most of them are accurate and fairly well up to date. About the only place you might get confused is in tree farm areas where the tree farm roads are hard to distinguish from the county dirt roads.

The rivers covered in the following chapters are divided into four large groups with the common denominator that the creeks and rivers of a group all run together at some point. There are also three individual rivers. I have stopped at the Alabama side of the state line in each case.

Remember that all directions given are facing downstream as if you were in a boat. And finally—once more—happy floating!

EXPLANATION OF RIVER CHARTS

I have tried to arrive at an easy-to-read chart that will give you all the information you need on the put-ins, take-outs, etc., on a ride and avoid a lot of repetitive writing. I have broken each point into three sections: information on getting you to or out of the river, information on the parking, and information on the river itself.

The "Miles," "County," and "Intermediate Points," are self-explanatory, so let's start at "Put-In," the part to get you in the water.

Location: The location of the put-in in relation to the bridge.
- A. LH & RH—Left hand and right hand
- B. DS & US—Downstream and upstream
- C. Where there is only a "LH" or "RH," there is no bridge—usually these occur at boat ramps or at roads that don't cross the water.

Bank:
- A. Normally if I have a height such as "2 feet" then the bank is pretty straight down, although you'll usually find an eroded place to make access to the boat easier.
- B. A term like "ramp" is obvious—it's a boat ramp, either paved or dirt but a ramp. If I add "steep," it is, but it's still a ramp.
- C. Beach or sloping—This is generally an almost flat slope into the water. A very easy access. If it's not, I'll say so.

Carry:

Approximately how far in feet you'll have to carry your boat from your vehicle to the water (or vice-versa). Obviously this will vary with how many are parked there.

Access Road:

The location of the access to the water in terms of where you leave the main road to go down to the water. Usually this is the same as the location of the put-in or take-out, but sometimes an access road will go down on one side and cross under the bridge. Often an access road will start up to ¼ mile away from the bridge. Where I say "None" applies to where parking is on the shoulder.

Here's the "Parking" section:

Vehicles:

This is obvious. Again the number depends on how you park. This number also considers the fact that you can cram a lot of cars in a place, but sooner or later you have to be able to get out.

Parking Location:

This is usually near the water, but even when it's not, it's the relationship of the available parking to the bridge.

Type:

A. "Shoulder" means no access road, and you have to park on the shoulder of the road. If I don't indicate otherwise, then the shoulder is wide enough to park on and be completely off the main road.

B. "Pull-off" also means no access road as such but indicates an area other than the shoulder where you can "pull-off" the road into a parking area.

Turn-around:

A. "Drive-around" means you can drive in, then turn around and out. Otherwise you'll usually have to do a little backing and filling to get out.

B. "Limited"—if you park carefully, you can jockey your way around—this is assuming that the maximum number of vehicles are not parked there.

C. "None"—You'll have to back out.

AND—The river itself.

Width:

Estimated, always in feet.

Flow:

"Swift"—doesn't mean much, I know, but it's faster than "Moderate" or "Slow."

The rest of the chart is general. My overall rating considers all the points I brought out in my "Explanation Of The Appendix." The comments part is just that—pertinent remarks that didn't fit anywhere else.

RIVER GROUP NO. 1

EAST AND WEST FORKS OF THE CHOCTAWHATCHEE AND THE CHOCTAWHATCHEE RIVER - GENERAL DALE AND GENEVA COUNTIES

The East and West Forks of the Choctawhatchee River start near Clayton in Barbour County and flow in a southwestwardly direction. They join just north of U. S. 231 near Midland City in Dale County to form the Choctawhatchee River which continues on southwestwardly to the City of Geneva where the Pea River flows into it. About 3½ miles below the junction, the river crosses the Florida line.

The Choctawhatchee and its forks are pretty. The banks are usually sand, and you'll find no swamp along its shores except at one point. There is one ride each on the forks, both of which have their take-outs at the same point on the Choctawhatchee River. There are four rides on the main river itself.

WEST FORK OF THE CHOCTAWHATCHEE RIVER
ALL

S57 TO DIRT ROAD BETWEEN C18 AND S123 ON THE CHOCTAWHATCHEE RIVER

MILES: 9.5   COUNTY: Dale
INTERMEDIATE POINTS: Mile 4 (Dirt Road between
                                                C18 and C59) and
                                                Mile 6 (U. S. 231)
PUT-IN: Location - RHDS   Bank - Sand beach
Carry - 200 feet* Access Road - Good, sand on RHDS of bridge
Parking: Vehicles - 8-10   Location - RHDS*
    Type - Flat, open   Turn-around - Drive around
River: Width - 100 feet   Flow - Swift
General Rating of Put-In: Good
Comments: The put-in is 150 feet DS of the bridge in a wooded
                area. In summer the section would probably be
                shallow. There is a long shoal just below the put-in.
*Another dirt road leads to the put-in beach but is so rutted for the first 30 feet that a passenger car couldn't make it.

211

INTERMEDIATE POINT: (Mile 4)

Location - RHUS   Bank - 4 feet

Carry - 40 feet   Access road - Good, dirt,
1/8 mile off RHUS
end of the bridge

Parking: Vehicles - 10-15   Location - RHUS

     Type - End of road   Turn-around - Good

River: Width - 50-75 feet   Flow - Swift

General Rating of Point as Put-In or Take-Out: Good

Comments: Point is about 150 feet US of bridge, about one mile DS you will see the East Fork coming in. After this junction you are on the Choctawhatchee River.

INTERMEDIATE POINT: (Mile 6, U. S. 231)

Location - LHDS   Bank - Steep, overgrown

Carry - 50 feet   Access Road - Good, dirt,
2/10 mile on LHDS
of end of bridge

Parking: Vehicles - 10   Location - LHDS

     Type - Flat, open   Turn-around - Good

River: Width - 75 feet   Flow - Swift

General Rating of Point as Put-In or Take-Out: Poor

Comments: This is a good point for parking but poor for put-in.

TAKE-OUT: Location - RHDS   Bank - Sand Bar

Carry - 20 feet   Access Road - Pull-off

Parking: Vehicles - 15-20   Location - RHDS

     Type - Flat, open   Turn-around - Good

River: Width - 75-100 feet   Flow - Swift

General Rating of Take-Out: Good

Comments: The take-out is about 50 feet DS of a railroad bridge on the Choctawhatchee River. The road to the take-out is good. An alternate take-out is on the RH 300 feet below the bridge. A road off the main road leads to this shady area. The lower area would make a good camping spot.

EAST FORK OF THE CHOCTAWHATCHEE RIVER
ALL

C67 TO DIRT ROAD BETWEEN C18 AND S123 ON CHOCTAWHATCHEE RIVER

MILES: 9.0   COUNTY: Dale
INTERMEDIATE POINT: Mile 4.5 (C59)
PUT-IN: Location - RHUS   Bank - Sloping
Carry - 40 feet   Access Road - Good, sand, ¼ mile
                              off RHUS of end of bridge,
                              few holes near river.
Parking: Vehicles - 15-20   Location - RHUS
     Type - Flat, open   Turn-around - Good
River: Width - 50 feet   Flow - Swift
General Rating of Put-in: Good
Comments: Access road slopes on into river. This is a pretty
     area and would be a good camping spot.

INTERMEDIATE POINT: (Mile 4.5, C59) Carry - 100 feet
Location - LHUS Bank - 2 feet   Access Road - None
Parking: Vehicles - 1-2   Location - LHUS
     Type - Shoulder   Turn-around - None
River: Width - 50-60 feet   Flow - Swift
General Rating of Point As Put-in or Take-out: Poor
Comments: This is a very picturesque location. The point is
     about 75 feet US of the bridge. From the parking
     area you have to carry across a ditch and through
     bushes to the point. Another road leading to a
     good put-in on the LHDS is 1/8 mile on the left
     end of the bridge but is sometimes chained.

TAKE-OUT: For the final take-out on this ride, see the Mile 6,
     U. S. 231 intermediate point information of the
     West Fork of the Choctawhatchee.

CHOCTAWHATCHEE RIVER
SECTION 1

U. S. 231 TO S92

MILES: 14.75   **COUNTY: Dale**
INTERMEDIATE POINTS: Mile 3.5 (Dirt Road between
                                                  C18 and S123) and
                                                      Mile 4.75 (S123)
PUT-IN: See the Mile 6, U. S. 231 intermediate point information on the West Fork of the Choctawhatchee River
for this put-in.

INTERMEDIATE POINT: (Mile 3.5) See the take-out information for the West Fork of the
Choctawhatchee River for this
first intermediate point.

INTERMEDIATE POINT: **(Mile 4.75, S123)**
Location - RHDS   **Bank - 4 feet**
Carry - 75 feet   **Access Road - Good**
                                            sand, RHDS end of bridge.
                                            Paved as it leaves S123
Parking: Vehicles - 20   **Location - RHDS**
    Type - Flat, open   **Turn-around - Good**
River: Width - 75-100 feet   **Flow - Swift**
General Rating of Point as Put-in or Take-out: Good
Comments: The point is directly under the bridge. The 75 foot
carry is gently sloping.

TAKE-OUT: Location - RHUS   **Bank - Sand beach**
Carry - 40 feet   **Access Road - Good, sand, off**
                                              RH end of bridge.
Parking: Vehicles - 10   **Location - RHUS**
    Type - Flat, open   **Turn-around - Good**
River: Width - 100 feet   **Flow - Swift**
General Rating of Take-out: Good
Comments: Take-out is directly under the bridge. Alternate
parking on LHUS and RHDS but poorer access to
the water.

CHOCTAWHATCHEE RIVER
SECTION 2

S92 TO S167

MILES: 11.5   **COUNTIES:** Dale, Geneva
INTERMEDIATE POINT: Mile 3.4 (U. S. 84)
PUT-IN: See the take-out information for Section 1 for this put-in.

INTERMEDIATE POINT: (Mile 3.5, U. S. 84)
Location - LHDS   Bank - Sand beach
Carry - 30 feet   Access Road - Good, sand, off the LH *upstream* end of bridge approach (goes under bridge).*
Parking: Vehicles - 10-15   Location - LHDS
     Type - Flat, open   Turn-around - Good
River: Width - 150 feet   Flow - Swift
General Rating of Point as Put-in or Take-out: Good
Comments: Alternate point on RHUS reached by good sand road on RHUS end of bridge.
*0.2 mile long bridge approach, LH *upstream* road is a little rough. This would be a good camping area.

TAKE-OUT: Location — RHDS   Bank - Sand beach
Carry - 125 feet*   Access Road - None**
Parking: Vehicles - 2-3   Location - RHDS
     Type - Shoulder   Turn-around - None
River: Width - 100 feet   Flow - Swift
General Rating of Take-out: Poor
Comments: *100 feet to bridge abutment steps, then up steps. Carry is at edge of swampy area.
** A rough, narrow, dirt road leads almost to the water on the LHDS, but it's rougher getting out of the water here. You'll also have to back out 1/10 mile as there is no turn-around at this location.

CHOCTAWHATCHEE RIVER
SECTION 3

S167 TO RECREATIONAL AREA
ON ROAD BETWEEN C41 AND S85

MILES: 13.0   COUNTY: Geneva
INTERMEDIATE POINTS: None*
PUT-IN: See the take-out information for Section 2 for this
      put-in.

TAKE-OUT: Location - LH   Bank - Paved boat ramp
Carry - 10 feet   Access Road - Paved lot at
       end of main road
Parking: Vehicles - 40   Location - End of road
    Type - Paved   Turn-around - Drive around
River: Width - 175 feet   Flow - Swift
General Rating of Put-in: Excellent
Comments: This is a recreational area with picnic tables, etc.
      The parking lot, ramps, and road to the area are all
      paved. This would be a good camping area.
*You will pass under an old steel bridge on a road crossing
between S167 and the town of Bellwood. There is no parking or
put-in at this location.

CHOCTAWHATCHEE RIVER
SECTION 4

RECREATIONAL AREA ON ROAD
BETWEEN C41 AND S85 TO S52

MILES: 8.5   COUNTY: Geneva
INTERMEDIATE POINTS: None
PUT-IN: See the take-out information for Section 3 for this
      put-in.

TAKE-OUT: Location - RHUS
Carry - 100 feet

Bank - 1 foot
Access Road** - Good, paved, then sand.
Location - RHUS
Turn-around - Good
Flow - Slow

Parking: Vehicles - 10-20
    Type - Flat, open
River: Width - 100 feet*
General Rating of Take-out: Good
Comments: *175 feet under bridge.
**Turn US at junction of S52 and S85, go 400 yards on S85, and turn back toward river on a paved road. Follow for 1½ tenths mile, it turns into dirt, follow for 1½ tenths mile more to river.

NOTE: About 1½ miles downstream, the Choctawhatchee is joined by the Pea River. About 3½ miles below that junction, the river crosses the Florida line.

A preview of coming attractions.

RIVER GROUP NO. 2

BIG CREEK, WHITEWATER CREEK

Big Creek forms near Troy in Pike County, flows almost due south, and enters Whitewater Creek about 6½ miles above Elba, Alabama. Whitewater Creek forms near Banks in Pike County, flows south to Coffee County, then turns southwestwardly and runs into the Pea River just above the U. S. 84 crossing in Elba, Alabama.

There is only one short ride on Big Creek, so I suggest that you take it, then continue on down the Whitewater and Pea to U. S. 84. There is another possible put-in on Big Creek at C82, but there is no off-road parking, access to the water is steep and overgrown, and the general area is rather swampy. The Whitewater has two rides, the second one ending at U. S. 84 on the Pea River.

BIG CREEK
ALL

C60 (LEWIS MILL BRIDGE) TO S87

MILES: 4.5	**COUNTY:** Coffee
INTERMEDIATE POINT:	Mile 1.5 (Tims Bridge)
	between C21 and C37
PUT-IN: Location - RHUS	Bank - Sand beach
Carry - 50 feet	Access Road - Good, sand,
	1/10 mile on RHUS
	of bridge.
Parking: Vehicles - 5	Location - RHUS
Type - Flat, open	Turn-around - Good
River: Width - 50 feet	Flow - Moderate
General Rating of Put-in: Good	

Comments: This is in a scenic, wooded area.

INTERMEDIATE POINT:	(Mile 1.5, Tims Bridge)
Location - RHDS	Bank - Bushy slope
Carry - 40 feet	Access Road - RHDS,
	rough, rutted

218

Parking: Vehicles - 3-4   Location - RHDS
    Type - End of road   Turn-around - Limited
River: Width - 50 feet   Flow - Swift
General Rating of Point as Put-in or Take-out: Fair
Comments: Trees overhanging the water here.

TAKE-OUT: Location - LHUS   Bank - 5 feet steep
Carry - 40 feet   Access Road - Pull off
Parking: Vehicles - 3-4   Location - LHDS*
    Type - Grass (line up cars)   Turn-around - None
River: Width - 30 feet   Flow - Swift
General Rating of Take-out: Fair
Comments: *The carry goes under the bridge. No, it's not an
    error about the creek being 30 feet wide here. It's
    strange but true. It's also shallow.
NOTE: If you wish to add 7.5 miles to this ride, continue on
downstream for a mile to Whitewater Creek. Follow Whitewater
for 6.5 miles to the Pea River and see Section 7 of the Pea River
for information on the take-out.

WHITEWATER CREEK
SECTION 1

S167 TO C37

MILES: 11.0   COUNTY: Coffee
INTERMEDIATE POINT: Mile 6.5 (C60)
PUT-IN: Location - RHDS   Bank - Sloping
Carry - 110 feet*   Access Road - None
Parking: Vehicles - 2   Location - None
    Type - Shoulder   Turn-around - None
River: Width - 30 feet   Flow - Fair
General Rating of Put-in: Poor
Comments: The general terrain is swampy and trees overhang
    the creek. The bank slopes into a side channel,
    then you will have to paddle out to the main chan-
    nel on the left. In summer you would probably be
    able to carry the 200 feet out to the main channel.
*10 foot slope at shoulder, then 100 feet to water.

INTERMEDIATE POINT: (Mile 6.5, C60)
Location - LHUS Bank - 4 feet steep
Carry - 20 feet Access Road - Good, dirt,
1½ tenths on LH
end of bridge.
Parking: Vehicles - 10 Location - LHUS
Type - Flat, open Turn-around - Good
River: Width - 50-60 feet Flow - Swift
General Rating of Point as Put-in or Take-out: Good
Comments: An alternate point is on the RHDS. Access road is
200 feet up paved C60 on RH *upstream*, turn on
dirt road back to river and under the bridge to a
sloping bank, 25 foot carry and parking for five
vehicles with limited turn-around.

TAKE-OUT: Location - LHUS Bank - Sand beach
Carry - 20 feet Access Road - Good, dirt,
off LHUS stub road.
Do not block gate on
main road off C37.
Parking: Vehicles - 2-3 Location - LHUS
Type - End of road Turn-around - Fair
River: Width - 50 feet Flow - Swift
General Rating of Take-out: Good
Comments: There are a few shoals just upstream. This area is
not swampy.

WHITEWATER CREEK
SECTION 2

C37 TO U. S. 84 (SECTION 7 OF PEA RIVER)

MILES: 9.5 COUNTY: Coffee
INTERMEDIATE POINT: None
PUT-IN: See the take-out information for Section 1 for this
put-in.
TAKE-OUT: See the take-out information for Section 7 of the
Pea River for this take-out.

PEA RIVER - GENERAL

The Pea River forms near Midway, Alabama, in Bullock County, and flows southwestwardly to Elba where Big Creek joins it. The Pea then turns south to near Samson, Alabama, where it swings first back to the east and on to the north near Geneva in Geneva County. At this point, it joins the Choctawhatchee River. There are 11 rides on the Pea River.

PEA RIVER
SECTION 1

S10 TO C77

MILES: 11.0   **COUNTY:** Pike
INTERMEDIATE POINT: None
PUT-IN: Location - LHDS   Bank - Sand beach
Carry - 30 feet   Access Road - LHDS on stub road off S10 down to beach.
Parking: Vehicles - 4-5   Location - LHDS
   Type - Flat, open   Turn-around - Limited
River: Width - 75 feet   Flow - Swift
General Rating of Put-in: Fair
Comments: The beach is soft sand - be careful. Don't block the road to the beach. You will have to paddle out about 150 feet to the main body of the river. In summer your carry will probably be longer and your paddle shorter. This is a semi-swampy area.

TAKE-OUT: Location - LHDS   Bank - Sand
Carry - 40 feet   Access Road - Pull-off, then sand road down to river. Road is rutted.

Parking: Vehicles - 5* Location - LHDS
    Type - End of road Turn-around - Limited
River: Width - 75-100 feet Flow - Swift
General Rating of Take-out: Good
Comments: This is still in a low area but not as swampy as the put-in. The channel is clear, the banks dry and sandy.

*Park five on sandy area and three at end of road. Alternate take-out on LHUS. Pull-off to access road is steep, but then it levels out and you have a four-foot bank at the river and parking for four or five vehicles with turn-around.

PEA RIVER
SECTION 2

C77 TO C36

MILES: 11.5 COUNTY: Dale
INTERMEDIATE POINT: Mile 6.5 (U. S. 231)
PUT-IN: See the take-out information for Section 1 for this put-in.

INTERMEDIATE POINT: (Mile 6.5, U. S. 231)
Location - LHDS* Bank - 3 feet
Carry - 30 feet Access Road - Rough dirt, on LHDS
    of old bridge. 3 roads.
    Use first one that turns
    and runs parallel to U. S. 231
Parking: Vehicles - 10 Location - LHDS
    Type - Flat, open Turn-around - Good
River: Width - 75 feet Flow - Swift
General Rating of Point as Put-in or Take-out: Good
Comments: *Under bridge. This point is at the old bridge US from a new bridge.

TAKE-OUT: Location - RHDS* Bank - 2 feet
Carry - 150 feet** Access Road - Main road
Parking: Vehicles - 1 Location - RHUS
    Type - Shoulder Turn-around - None

River: Width - 75 feet   Flow - Swift
General Rating of Take-out: Poor
Comments: *90 feet DS of bridge.
**40 feet from river to flat area, 100 feet to bridge abutment,
then up abutment steps to road. This is a new bridge. The old
one is just upstream and is not accessible.

PEA RIVER
SECTION 3

C36 TO S167

MILES: 11.0   COUNTY: Coffee
INTERMEDIATE POINT: Mile 5.0 (C60)
PUT-IN: See the take-out information for Section 2 for this
        put-in.

INTERMEDIATE POINT: (Mile 5.0, C60)
Location - LHDS   Bank - 2 feet
Carry - 50 feet   Access Road - Dirt path off
                                         C60 down to sand beach
                                         below bridge.
Parking: Vehicles - 3-4   Location - LHDS
    Type - Shoulder   Turn-around - None
River: Width - 75 feet   Flow - Swift
General Rating of Point as Put-in or Take-out: Fair
Comments: An alternate point with a sloping sand beach is 150
          feet downstream.

TAKE-OUT: Location - LHUS*   Bank - Sand beach
Carry - 20 feet   Access Road - Good dirt, off
                                         LHUS end of bridge.
Parking: Vehicles - 10-15   Location - LHUS
    Type - Flat, open   Turn-around - Good
River: Width - 50-60 feet   Flow - Swift
General Rating of Take-out: Good
Comments: *Under bridge.
The access road is paved off S167, then turns into dirt.

223

PEA RIVER
SECTION 4

S167 TO WEEKS BRIDGE (Dirt Road
between U. S. 84 and C79)

MILES: 6.25   COUNTY: Coffee
INTERMEDIATE POINT: Mile 4.0 (Roe Bridge)
                                (Dirt Road between
                                    S122 and C79)
PUT-IN: See the take-out information for Section 3 for this
     put-in.

INTERMEDIATE POINT: (Mile 4.0)
Location - LHUS   Bank - Sand beach
Carry - 50 feet   Access Road - Pull-off.
                                     Path leads down
                                          to water.
Parking: Vehicles - 10-15   Location - LHUS
     Type - Flat, open   Turn-around - Good
River: Width - 75 feet   Flow - Swift
General Rating of Point as Put-in or Take-out: Fair
Comments: This is in a wooded area. The dirt road out to this
     point is narrow but good. Possible camping at
     point.

TAKE-OUT: Location - RHUS*   Bank - 2 feet sloping
Carry - 10 feet   Access Road - RHUS off old
              road to under new bridge (old road goes
                                under new bridge).
Parking: Vehicles - 10   Location - RHUS
     Type - Flat, open   Turn-around - Good
River: Width - 75 feet   Flow - Swift
General Rating of Take-out: Good
Comments: *Of new bridge located 50 yards DS from old
     bridge. Possible camping here—it's pretty wooded.
     Watch out for the old bridge—it's a low water type
     without much clearance under it.

PEA RIVER
SECTION 5

WEEKS BRIDGE TO U. S. 84

MILES: 11.0   **COUNTY:** Coffee
INTERMEDIATE POINT: None
PUT-IN: See the take-out information for Section 4 for this put-in.

TAKE-OUT: Location - LHDS   Bank - Boat ramp
Carry - 30 feet   Access Road - LHDS off end of
                           bridge - road is paved.
Parking: Vehicles - 15-20   Location - LHDS
    Type - Flat, open   Turn-around - Good
River: Width - 60 feet   Flow - Swift
General Rating of Take-Out: Good
Comments: This is a City of Geneva recreational area within the city limits. No camping here.

PEA RIVER
SECTION 6

U. S. 84 TO S134

MILES: 16.0   **COUNTY:** Coffee
INTERMEDIATE POINT: Caution - Dam at Mile 6.5
PUT-IN: See the take-out information for Section 5 for this put-in.

INTERMEDIATE POINT: Caution - Dam at Mile 6.5

Although there is a lot of parking and turn-around in this very picturesque spot, access to the water is blocked by the high banks and proximity to the 30-foot high dam. If you make this trip, portage the dam on the sand beaches on your left and be careful—the dam could sneak up on you. There is an island in the middle of the dam, but don't let it tempt you—there's no way onto it from upstream.

TAKE-OUT: Location - RHUS**   Bank - Rutted slope
Carry - 90 feet*   Access Road - Good, sand,
                          1/10 mile on RHUS of bridge, take left fork
                                                    into woods.
Parking: Vehicles - 10-20   Location - RHUS
    Type - Flat, open   Turn-around - Drive-around
River: Width - 75-100 feet   Flow - Swift
General Rating of Take-out: Fair
Comments: This would make a good camping area—it's flat,
          shady, and remote from the road.
*50 feet from parking and 40 feet down slope to river.
**About 100 yards US of bridge.

PEA RIVER
SECTION 7

S134 TO C6

MILES: 5.0   COUNTY: Coffee
INTERMEDIATE POINT: None
PUT-IN: See the take-out information for Section 6 for this
        put-in.

TAKE-OUT: Location - LHUS   Bank - Sloping
Carry - 200 feet   Access Road - Rough, 1/10 mile
                                             off LH end of bridge,
                                             one US and one DS.
Parking: Vehicles - 5   Location - At bridge
    Type - Flat, open   Turn-around - Fair
River: Width - 75-100 feet   Flow - Swift
General Rating of Take-Out: Poor
Comments: The access road has swales in it. You can drive
          down one road, under the bridge, and back up the
          other road.

226

PEA RIVER
SECTION 8

C6 TO DIRT ROAD BETWEEN S153 AND C17

MILES: 12.5   **COUNTIES:** Coffee, Geneva
INTERMEDIATE POINTS: None
PUT-IN: See the take-out information for Section 7 for this put-in.

TAKE-OUT: Location - RHDS   Bank - 15 feet
Carry - 20 feet   Access Road - End of
       main road.
Parking: Vehicles - 6   Location - RHDS
  Type - Flat, open   Turn-around - Good
River: Width - 60 feet   Flow - Swift
General Rating of Take-out: Poor
Comments: Sign at beginning of road says "Bridge Out." It is. Road out is good. This is a very pretty bend in the river but a bad put-in.

PEA RIVER
SECTION 9

DIRT ROAD BETWEEN S153 AND C17 TO C17

MILES: 9.0   **COUNTY:** Geneva
INTERMEDIATE POINT: Mile 3.0 (S52)
PUT-IN: See the take-out information for Section 8 for this put-in.
INTERMEDIATE POINT: (Mile 3.0, S52)
Location - LHUS*   Bank - 10 feet sloping
Carry - 40 feet   Access Road - Good, sand,
       2/10 mile off LHUS
       end of bridge.
Parking: Vehicles - 10   Location - LHUS
  Type - End of road   Turn-around - Limited
River: Width - 100 feet   Flow - Swift
General Rating of Point as Put-in or Take-out: Fair
Comments: *Under bridge.

TAKE-OUT: Location - LHUS*   Bank - Boat ramp
Carry - 20 feet   Access Road - Good, sand,
                                                      2/10 mile off LHUS
                                                             of bridge.
Parking: Vehicles - 30-40   Location - LHUS
     Type - Paved   Turn-around - Drive-around
River: Width - 100 feet   Flow - Swift
General Rating of Take-Out: Excellent
Comments: *50 yards upstream at partially paved recreational
     area.

PEA RIVER
SECTION 10

C17 TO S87

MILES: 14.0   COUNTY: Geneva
INTERMEDIATE POINT: None
PUT-IN: See the take-out information for Section 9 for this
     put-in.

Reward of a winter trip.

TAKE-OUT: Location - LHDS

Carry - 20 feet

Bank - Sand beach*

Access Road - Good, sand

1½ tenths mile on

LHDS end of bridge.

Parking: Vehicles - 5

Type - Flat, open

Location - LHDS

Turn-around - Good

River: Width - 100 feet

Flow - Slow

General Rating of Take-Out: Poor

Comments: This is a swampy area.

*Beach is into side waters. You'll have to paddle out to the main river. In summer you can probably drive farther and have a shorter carry. The Florida line is about 1/10 mile down the road on the RH.

PEA RIVER
SECTION 11

S87 TO S27

MILES: 13.0   COUNTY: Geneva

INTERMEDIATE POINT: None

PUT-IN: See the take-out information for Section 10 for this put-in.

TAKE-OUT: Location - LHUS

Carry - 20 feet

Bank - 5 feet, rough

Access Road - Dirt, rutted,

1/10 mile off LHUS

end of bridge.

Parking: Vehicles - 8

Type - Flat, open

Location - LHUS

Turn-around - Good

River: Width - 100 feet

Flow - Swift

General Rating of Take-out: Poor

Comments: This is a rough, overgrown take-out, but the last one in the state of Alabama.

RIVER GROUP NO. 3

CONECUH RIVER - GENERAL
PIKE, CRENSHAW, COVINGTON, ESCAMBIA COUNTIES

The Conecuh is one of the major rivers of south Alabama. It forms near Saco in Pike County and flows southwestwardly to near River Falls in Covington County, where it is dammed and forms Gantt and Point "A ' Lakes. Patsuliga Creek enters the Conecuh here in Point "A" Lake.

The Conecuh forms part of the boundary between Crenshaw and Covington, Covington and Pike, and Conecuh and Escambia Counties. The Sepulga River joins the Conecuh near the corner of Conecuh and Escambia Counties. Below the Florida line, the Conecuh is known as the Escambia River.

From S223 in Pike County down to about U. S. 331 in Crenshaw County (about 65 river miles), the Conecuh generally flows in a low area with a tendency toward swamp. Unless you like distinctly jungly rides (which I don't), these 65 miles offer little in the way of desirable put-ins. From U. S. 331 on down to the Florida line, the river is very pretty, however, with basically dry, sandy banks at the put-ins and rides much more to my taste.

For those of you who like such things, however, I have included three rides in the upper section, any of which will probably fulfill all your desires to play swamp rat. One thing to bear in mind is that in the dryness of the summer you may find the river very small on these three rides—possibly too small to float. There are 13 rides on the Conecuh River.

CONECUH RIVER
SECTION 1

U. S. 29 TO C28

MILES: 12.5	COUNTY: Pike
INTERMEDIATE POINT:	None
PUT-IN: Location - RHUS	Bank - Grass slope
Carry - 50 feet*	Access Road - None

Parking: Vehicles - 4-5   Location - RHUS
    Type - Shoulder   Turn-around - None
River: Width - 75 feet   Flow - Slow
General Rating of Put-in: Fair

Comments: The general area is low and swampy. The channel is fairly distinct, but there are a lot of trees in the water.

*Carry is up the highway embankment.

TAKE-OUT: Location - RHDS   Bank - 5 feet, sand
Carry - 40 feet   Access Road - None
Parking: Vehicles - 2   Location - RHUS
    Type - Shoulder*   Turn-around - None
River: Width - 60-75 feet   Flow - Moderate
General Rating of Take-out: Poor

Comments: The area is low and swampy. The channel is fairly obvious; some trees overhang the river completely. In wet weather you have about a 50 foot paddle or wade to the main body of the river. In summer you can probably drive almost to the main river.

*Shoulder is not quite wide enough to clear road.

CONECUH RIVER
SECTION 2

C28 TO C6

MILES: 9.5   COUNTY: Pike
INTERMEDIATE POINT: None

PUT-IN: See the take-out information for Section 1 for this put-in.

TAKE-OUT: Location - RHDS   Bank - Sloping
Carry - 10 feet   Access Road - Good, dirt, on RHDS of C6.
Parking: Vehicles - 3   Location - RHDS
    Type - In road   Turn-around - Limited
River: Width - 75 feet   Flow - Swift
General Rating of Take-out: Fair

Comments: This is still in the swampy area. The channel is fairly distinct.

CONECUH RIVER
SECTION 3

C6 TO U. S. 331

MILES: 15.5 **COUNTIES:** Pike, Crenshaw
INTERMEDIATE POINT: None
PUT-IN: See the take-out information for Section 2 for this put-in.
TAKE-OUT: Location - LHUS **Bank** - Sloping
Carry - 10 feet **Access Road** - Good, dirt, 1/10 mile off LHUS end of bridge. Paved where it leaves U. S. 331, has a few ruts.
Parking: Vehicles - 10-15 **Location** - LHUS
Type - Flat, open **Turn-around** - Good
River: Width - 50-75 feet **Flow** - Swift
General Rating of Take-out: Fair
Comments: This is in a generally swampy area. The channel is fairly well defined. You will have a 200 foot paddle from the put-in out to the main channel. In summer you can probably drive closer to main channel. Alternate take-out is on RHUS. The carry here is only 100 feet on the flat, then up a 30 foot slope to U. S. 331. Parking is limited to four vehicles on the shoulder, but the main channel is on the right, so this is closer to the river.

CONECUH RIVER
SECTION 4

U. S. 331 TO DIRT ROAD OFF U. S. 29

MILES: 8.5 **COUNTY:** Crenshaw
INTERMEDIATE POINT: None
PUT-IN: See the take-out information for Section 3 for this put-in.

TAKE-OUT: Location - RH
Carry - 20 feet
Parking: Vehicles - 10-15
    Type - Flat, open (dirt)
River: Width - 75 feet
General Rating of Take-out: Good

Bank - 5 feet sloping
Access Road - Pull-off
Location - RH
Turn-around - Drive around
Flow - Swift

Comments: This is your first ride in the upper section that is not swampy. There is no bridge here, so watch sharply for the take-out as it's hard to see from the river. There is an island just above it, and you'll have to paddle through the trees to the main shore (in summer you probably won't have to do this). The dirt road out to the put-in is good, with a few slightly bumpy areas.

Getting from here to there the hard way—without paddles.

DIRT ROAD OFF U. S. 29 TO DIRT ROAD
OFF C43 AT HEADWATERS OF GANTT LAKE

MILES: 12.0   COUNTIES: Crenshaw, Covington
INTERMEDIATE POINT: Mile 7.5 (C77)
PUT-IN: See the take-out information for Section 4 for this
        put-in.

INTERMEDIATE POINT: (Mile 7.5, C77)
Location - LHUS   Bank - Sloping
Carry - 50-60 feet   Access Road - None
Parking: Vehicles - 2   Location - LHUS
    Type - Shoulder   Turn-around - In Road
River: Width - 100 feet   Flow - Swift
General Rating of Point as Put-in or Take-out: Poor
Comments: This is in a swampy area. The carry is through
        bushes. The channel here is well defined.

TAKE-OUT: Location - LH   Bank - Boat ramp
Carry - 10 feet   Access Road - None
Parking: Vehicles - 10-15   Location - LH
    Type - Flat, open   Turn-around - Good
River: Width - (Lake)   Flow - Slow
General Rating of Take-out: Excellent
Comments: This is in the headwaters of Gantt Lake at a boat
        launch area. This would be a good camping area, or
        you could follow the dirt road downstream to an
        even better area—all shady and dry. The dirt road
        to the take-out is narrow but very picturesque,
        with Spanish moss brushing the top of your vehicle
        as you drive down it. After the dirt road to the
        take-out leaves C43, you'll come to a fork—take
        the left-hand side of it.

NOTE: Unless you want to paddle about 4.5 miles on the lake,
this is the final take-out for the upper part of the Conecuh
River.

Making the maps—somewhere beside a river.

CONECUH RIVER
SECTION 6

DIRT ROAD OFF C43 AT HEADWATERS OF GANTT LAKE TO C43 AT MIDDLE OF GANTT LAKE

MILES: 4.5   COUNTY: Covington
INTERMEDIATE POINT: None
PUT-IN: See the take-out information for Section 5 for this put-in.

TAKE-OUT: Location - LHDS   Bank - Slopes gently
Carry - 40 feet   Access Road - Pull-off
Parking: Vehicles - 10*   Location - LHDS
   Type - Flat, open   Turn-around - Good
River: Width - 150 feet   Flow - Slow
General Rating of Put-in: Good
Comments: This is a dead water paddle in a lake over 1/2 mile wide.

*Take-out is at a store, so get permission to park there. An alternate take-out is to use the bridge itself, as it is very low to the water, or use the shore adjacent to the bridge. The lake necks down here.

CONECUH RIVER
SECTION 7

U. S. 84 TO C42

MILES: 10.5
INTERMEDIATE POINT:
PUT-IN: Location - LH*
Carry - 40 feet

COUNTY: Covington
None (See Note)
Bank - 75 feet**
Access Road - LHUS,
partially paved, then
slopes to sandy area.

Parking: Vehicles - 5
  Type - End of road
River: Width - 125 feet
General Rating of Put-in: Poor
Comments: *Under bridge.

Location - LHUS
Turn-around - Limited
Flow - Swift

**Overgrown bank—poor for a put-in but the best there is at this location.

TAKE-OUT: Location - RHUS
Carry - 50 feet

Bank - Sloping
Access Road - Good, sand
3½ tenths mile off RH
upstream end of bridge
(road goes under bridge).

Parking: Vehicles - 30-40
  Type - Flat, open
River: Width - 75 feet
General Rating of Take-out: Good

Location - RHDS
Turn-around - Good
Flow - Swift

Comments: Another road leads off into the woods here, and you could probably camp there.

NOTE: 4.5 miles downstream from the put-in on Section 7 is an old steel bridge. One glance at it as you float along will tell you why I didn't list it as an intermediate point!

CONECUH RIVER
SECTION 8

C42 TO DIRT ROAD BETWEEN U. S. 29 AND C42

MILES: 17.0   COUNTY: Covington
INTERMEDIATE POINT: None
PUT-IN: See the take-out information for Section 7 for this put-in.
TAKE-OUT: Location - LHUS   Bank - 1 foot*
Carry - 30 feet   Access Road - Good, sand, at end of bridge.

Parking: Vehicles - 5   Location - LHUS
   Type - Flat, open   Turn-around - Limited
General Rating of Take-out: Good
Comments: Main road out to take-out is fair but does have a few bumpy areas and ruts. A passenger car could make it. This take-out is in a wooded area.

*This is a sort of natural boat pier in the bank, about five feet wide and 15 feet long with a sloping bank into the water at the end of it.

CONECUH RIVER
SECTION 9

DIRT ROAD BETWEEN U. S. 29 AND C42 TO U. S. 29

MILES: 15.0   COUNTIES: Covington, Escambia

Sandbar and dark waters on a southern river.

INTERMEDIATE POINT: None
PUT-IN: See the take-out information for Section 8 for this
        put-in.
TAKE-OUT: Location - LHUS*   Bank - 1 foot
Carry - 40 feet   Access Road - Good, sand on
                                    LH upstream of main
                                    bridge (several bridges
                                    here). Road has a few
                                    low places in it.
Parking: Vehicles - 10   Location - LHUS
    Type - Flat, open   Turn-around - Adequate
River: Width - 150 feet   Flow - Swift
General Rating of Take-out: Good
Comments: *Under the bridge. Despite the several bridges here
            and the wet look of the general area, the banks are
            dry and the area is not swampy.

NOTE: You will see the Sepulga River entering on your right on
this ride.

CONECUH RIVER
SECTION 10

U. S. 29 TO ROAD OFF U. S. 29 (RECREATIONAL AREA)

MILES: 7.0   COUNTY: Escambia
INTERMEDIATE POINT: None
PUT-IN: See the take-out information for Section 9 for this
        put-in.

TAKE-OUT: Location - RH   Bank - Paved boat ramp
Carry - 20 feet   Access Road - End of main road.
Parking: Vehicles - 30-40   Location - RH
    Type - Paved lot   Turn-around - Good
River: Width - 150 feet   Flow - Swift
General Rating of Take-out: Excellent
Comments: This is a recreational area with boat ramps and
            other facilities. Main road off U. S. 29, parking,
            and ramps are all paved.

CONECUH RIVER
SECTION 11

ROAD OFF U. S. 29 (RECREATIONAL AREA) TO C4

MILES: 12.5   **COUNTY:** Escambia
INTERMEDIATE POINT: None
PUT-IN: See the take-out information for Section 10 for this
put-in.

TAKE-OUT: Location - LHDS   Bank - Sloping
Carry - 30 feet   Access Road - Good, dirt, off
                                         LHDS end of bridge
                                                approach.
Parking: Vehicles - 4-5   Location - LHDS
    Type - End of road   Turn-around - Limited
River: Width - 150 feet   Flow - Swift
General Rating of Take-out: Good
Comments: The take-out is at the end of an "S" curve. In the
"body" of the "S" (and visible as you drive to the
take-out) is an excellent, shaded, untended campground with tent sites and a spring. The river at the
campground is very wide and scenic, with large
sandbars on the far side. The take-out is around the
bend past the campground and not visible from the
campground. The campground itself is a poor
take-out as the banks are steep and high, but it
would make an excellent end point for a trip down
the Conecuh.

CONECUH RIVER
SECTION 12

C4 TO S41 (RECREATIONAL AREA)

MILES: 15.5   **COUNTY:** Escambia
INTERMEDIATE POINT: None
PUT-IN: See the take-out information for Section 11 for this
put-in.

240

TAKE-OUT: Location - LHDS   Bank - Paved boat ramp
Carry - 40 feet   Access Road*- Good, dirt, then
                                    paved at parking area.
Parking: Vehicles - 30-40   Location - End of road
   Type - Paved   Turn-around - Good
River: Width - 175-200 feet   Flow - Swift
General Rating of Take-out: Good
Comments: *Go to C55 (0.2 miles off LH end of bridge), turn
          upstream on C55, immediately turn toward river
          on a wide dirt road. This will lead you under the
          bridge and will become paved as you go under the
          bridge.

CONECUH RIVER
SECTION 13

S41 TO DIRT ROAD OFF U. S. 31
NEAR POLLARD, ALABAMA

MILES: 10.5   COUNTY: Escambia
INTERMEDIATE POINT: None
PUT-IN: See the take-out information for Section 12 for this
        put-in.
TAKE-OUT: Location - RH   Bank - Paved boat ramp
Carry - 20 feet   Access Road* - Good, sand
Parking: Vehicles - 10   Location - End of road
   Type - Flat, open (dirt)   Turn-around - Drive-around
River: Width - 300 feet   Flow - Swift
General Rating of Take-out: Good
Comments: There is no bridge here, so you'll have to watch
          sharply for the ramp. The area is wooded.
*The road out is good with a few bumps and ruts toward the
river end of it. A passenger car could make it with no trouble.
The road is paved from Pollard, across a railroad track, and for
1/4 mile after you turn right at the St. Peter Baptist Church.
Then just follow the dirt road.

NOTE: This is the lowest point in Alabama on the Conecuh
River. Below this point you're in Florida.

PATSULIGA CREEK - GENERAL
CRENSHAW, COVINGTON COUNTIES

Patsuliga Creek forms near Grady in Montgomery County and flows southwestwardly until it runs into Point "A" Lake on the Conecuh River near Andalusia in Covington County. It forms part of the border between Pike and Crenshaw Counties.

For your information, Patsuliga Creek is pronounced locally as if it were spelled Patsa-laga, with the emphasis on the "laga" part. On a map you'll notice an apparent put-in at U. S. 29 in the city of Luverne, but out in the real world there's no place to put-in there. There are three rides on Patsuliga Creek.

PATSULIGA CREEK
SECTION 1

S106 TO A DIRT ROAD BETWEEN C23 AND C37

MILES: 16.0   **COUNTIES:** Crenshaw, Covington

Emptying a swamped canoe using canoe over canoe rescue technique. Very easy in still water—a lot harder in swift current.

INTERMEDIATE POINT: None
PUT-IN: Location - LHUS Bank - 10 feet sloping
Carry - 50 feet Access Road - LHUS 1/10
mile on LHUS of bridge.

Parking: Vehicles - 5 Location - LHUS
   Type - Flat, open Turn-around - Good
River: Width - 50 feet Flow - Swift
General Rating of Put-in: Fair
Comments: There is a roadside park here. The creek parallels
S107, then turns and goes under the bridge. The
put-in is just as you round the bend and can see the
bridge.

TAKE-OUT: Location - RHUS* Bank - Dirt ramp
Carry - 20 feet Access Road - Good, dirt off
RHUS end of bridge.

Parking: Vehicles - 5 Location - RHUS
   Type - Flat, open Turn-around - Drive-around
River: Width - 75 feet Flow - Swift
General Rating of Take-out: Fair
Comments: The main dirt road is good.
*The take-out is 150 feet upstream of the old bridge and out of
the main current. You'll have to watch for it.

PATSULIGA CREEK
SECTION 2

DIRT ROAD BETWEEN C23 AND C37 TO
DIRT ROAD BETWEEN C59 AND C23

MILES: 8.0 COUNTY: Covington
INTERMEDIATE POINT: None
PUT-IN: See the take-out information for Section 1 for this
put-in.

TAKE-OUT: Location - LHUS Bank - Sloping
Carry - 20 feet Access Road - Good, dirt.
Several lead off upstream
from the main road before
you get to the bridge. All
lead to the take-out.

Parking: Vehicles - 5   Location - LHUS
   Type - Flat, level   Turn-around - Good
River: Width - 100 feet   Flow - Swift
General Rating of Take-out: Good
Comments: This is a local picnic area. The take-out is about 200
feet upstream of the old wooden bridge.

PATSULIGA CREEK
SECTION 3

DIRT ROAD BETWEEN C59 AND C23 TO POINT "A" LAKE
(DIRT ROAD BETWEEN S55 AND U. S. 29) ON
CONECUH RIVER

MILES: 10.5   **COUNTY:** Covington
INTERMEDIATE POINT: Mile 3.5 (C82)
PUT-IN: See the take-out information for Section 2 for this
    put-in.

INTERMEDIATE POINT: Mile 3.5 (C82)
Location - LHDS   Bank - 2 feet*
Carry - 150 feet   Access Road - None
Parking: Vehicles - 1   Location - LHDS
   Type - Shoulder   Turn-around - None
River: Width - 100 feet   Flow - Swift
General Rating of Point as Put-in or Take-out: Poor
Comments: *Overgrown.

TAKE-OUT: Location - LHDS*   Bank - Boat ramp
Carry - 10 feet   Access Road - Main road
Parking: Vehicles - 10   Location - LHDS
   Type - Pull-off   Turn-around - Good
River: Width - In Lake   Flow - Slow
General Rating of Take-out: Good
Comments: This take-out is in Point "A" Lake just above the
    dam.
*You'll go under a new bridge as you enter the lake. Continue
on 1/2 mile to the old "causeway" type road crossing the lake.
This is a local boat launching and fishing area, so almost any-
where along here is a good take-out.

SEPULGA RIVER - GENERAL
CONECUH, ESCAMBIA COUNTIES

The Sepulga River forms near Midway, Alabama, in Monroe County, flows southwestwardly to its crossing by U. S. 84, then turns south until it joins the Conecuh River a few miles above the U. S. 29 crossing of the Conecuh. It forms part of the boundary between Butler and Conecuh Counties in its upper stretches and part of the boundary between Escambia and Conecuh Counties just before flowing into the Conecuh River.

It is extremely difficult to locate two of the possible put-ins just below I-65 due to a lot of intertwining dirt roads that don't show on the county maps, so the rides here start at the U. S. 31 crossing. There are three rides. The last ride is rather long and carries you to the Section 9 take-out on the Conecuh River (U. S. 29). None of the put-ins are swampy.

The thrill of whitewater on an Alabama stream.

SEPULGA RIVER
SECTION 1

U. S. 31 TO U. S. 84

MILES: 8.0   COUNTY: Conecuh
INTERMEDIATE POINT: None
PUT-IN: Location - RHDS   Bank - 5 feet steep
Carry - 150 feet   Access Road - Good, sand on
                                          right-hand end of bridge.
Parking: Vehicles - 15-20   Location - RHDS
   Type - Flat, open   Turn-around - Good
River: Width - 60 feet   Flow - Swift
General Rating of Put-in: Fair

Comments: This put-in is at the *old* bridge. A new bridge is under construction just upstream. The path from parking to put-in has one steep slope on it. An alternate put-in is on the LHDS, but you have a longer carry.

TAKE-OUT: Location - RHDS   Bank - Sand dune, sloping
Carry - 30 feet   Access Road - Fair, 1½
                                        tenths mile on right hand
                                            of bridge. Few bumps,
                                           but a passenger car
                                         would have no trouble.
Parking: Vehicles - 10   Location - RHDS
   Type - Flat, open   Turn-around - Good
River: Width - 75 feet   Flow - Swift
General Rating of Take-out: Good

Comments: This is a very pretty area with white sandbars. You could camp here or in the nearby woods.

SEPULGA RIVER
SECTION 2

U. S. 84 TO DIRT ROAD OFF C43

MILES: 13.5   COUNTY: Conecuh

INTERMEDIATE POINT: None

PUT-IN: See the take-out information for Section 1 for this put-in.

TAKE-OUT: Location - RHUS	Bank - Dirt ramp, steep
Carry - 75 feet	Access Road - Right hand of bridge pull-off.
Parking: Vehicles - 10	Location - RHUS
Type - Flat	Turn-around - Adequate
River: Width - 60 feet	Flow - Swift

General Rating of Take-out: Fair

Comments: The road to the take-out is a good, sand road. Take-out is 30-40 feet upstream of the old steel bridge. This is a wooded area and used as a local picnic spot.

SEPULGA RIVER
SECTION 3

DIRT ROAD OFF C43 TO U. S. 29 ON CONECUH RIVER

MILES: 20.0	**COUNTIES: Conecuh, Escambia**
INTERMEDIATE POINT:	Mile 8 (C42)

PUT-IN: See the take-out information for Section 2 for this put-in.

INTERMEDIATE POINT:	(Mile 8, C42)
Location - C42, at bridge	Bank - 50 feet steep
Carry - 50 feet straight up	Access Road - None
Parking: Vehicles - None	Location —
Type -	Turn-around - None
River: Width - 60 feet	Flow - Swift

General Rating of Point as Put-in or Take-out: Very Poor

Comments: Banks are overgrown in addition to being very steep. Good luck!

TAKE-OUT: See the take-out information for Section 9 of the Conecuh River for this take-out.

BIG ESCAMBIA CREEK - GENERAL
ESCAMBIA COUNTY

Big Escambia Creek forms near Repton in Conecuh County and is known as the Little Escambia River until it crosses into Escambia County. It flows almost due south, gets big enough to float at C40 in Escambia County, then begins a big swing back to the southeast. It flows into the Conecuh River after both the creek and the Conecuh have passed the Florida line. The single river thus formed is then known as the Escambia River.

BIG ESCAMBIA CREEK
SECTION 1

C40 TO C27

MILES: 9.75   **COUNTY: Escambia**

INTERMEDIATE POINT: Mile 6.0 (Dirt Road off C17)
PUT-IN: Location - RHDS   **Bank - Sandbar**
Carry - 20 feet   **Access Road - None - Pull**
                                                   off main road.
Parking: Vehicles - 5   **Location - RHDS**
   Type - Pull-off   **Turn-around - None**
River: Width - 50 feet   **Flow - Swift**
General Rating of Put-in: Good
Comments: The main road out is very good. Be careful of the sand in the parking area—it gets soft if you go a little too far. There are some beautiful white sand dunes on the LHDS reached by a dirt road in that location.

INTERMEDIATE POINT: (Mile 6.0)

Location - LH*   Bank - Sloping

Carry - 20 feet   Access Road - End of dirt
road to river.**

Parking: Vehicles - 3-4   Location - LHUS

   Type - End of road   Turn-around - Limited

River: Width - 50-60 feet   Flow - Swift

General Rating of Point as Put-in or Take-out: Fair

Comments: This point is rather hard to find.

*150 feet US of a set of old wooden bridge pilings. There is no bridge here—just pilings.

**Cross under I-65 on C40, turn south on a paved road parallel to I-65. Follow until it turns into a dirt road; ignore first RH fork, take the next 2 RH forks (the second one has an old overgrown road off to the left), ignore the next "T" on your right. The road stays good but becomes progressively narrower as you approach the creek.

TAKE-OUT: Location - LHUS*   Bank - Sand beach

Carry - 150 feet   Access Road - Sand road from
parking area just
off LH end of bridge.**

Parking: Vehicles - 5-10   Location - LHUS

   Type - Flat, open   Turn-around - Good

River: Width - 50-60 feet   Flow - Swift

General Rating of Take-out: Excellent

Comments: *600 feet upstream on big sandbar.

**C27 is paved to bridge, and the pull-off into the first parking area is paved. A series of small roads lead from here to the actual take-out.

This is a pretty, wooded area. There is some clearing going on nearby, so if you make this trip, you may find yourself taking out in the backyard of a factory or something equally unnecessary to the beauty of the creek!

BIG ESCAMBIA CREEK
SECTION 2

C27 TO U. S. 31

MILES: 14.5   **COUNTY:** Escambia

INTERMEDIATE POINT: None

PUT-IN: See the take-out information for Section 1 for this put-in.

TAKE-OUT: Location - RHUS   **Bank - Slope**

Carry - 20 feet   **Access Road* - Good, dirt off RH end of bridge.**

Parking: Vehicles - 10   **Location - RHUS**

    Type - Flat, open   **Turn-around - Good**

River: Width - 50-75 feet   **Flow - Swift**

General Rating of Take-out: Good

Comments: *Recreational area. Sign is at end of bridge. Road is paved off U. S. 31, then turns into dirt. It is very rutted for a short distance. This take-out is in the city limits of Flomaton, Alabama.

Lunch stop and "bathing suit" trip in the summer.

RIVER GROUP NO. 4

PERDIDO RIVER - GENERAL
BALDWIN COUNTY

The Perdido River flows in a general southerly direction from near Atmore in Escambia County to Perdido Bay, which is located between Mobile, Alabama, and Pensacola, Florida. The river forms the boundary between Alabama and Florida for most of its length. The Perdido generally has sandy banks and flows through a dry area with none of the put-ins being in swampy sections. It is too small and shallow to try to float above the first put-in listed. On all of these runs, your left-hand shore is in Florida, and your right-hand shore is in Alabama.

PERDIDO RIVER
SECTION 1

C61 (DYAS CREEK) TO DIRT ROAD OFF S112

MILES: 24.5   COUNTY: Baldwin

INTERMEDIATE POINT: None

PUT-IN: Location - LHDS   Bank - 10 feet sloping

Carry - 10 feet   Access Road - Good, sand on
left-hand end of bridge.

Parking: Vehicles - 15-20   Location - LHDS

Type - Flat, open   Turn-around - Good

River: Width - 40 feet   Flow - Slow

General Rating of Put-in: Fair

Comments: Put-in is on Dyas Creek. You will have a 1/4 mile paddle down to the Perdido River.

TAKE-OUT: Location - LHDS   Bank - Sand ramp

Carry - 30 feet   Access Road - Good, sand on
left hand end of bridge.

Parking: Vehicles - 5   Location - LHDS

Type - Flat, open   Turn-around - Adequate

River: Width - 100 feet   Flow - Swift

General Rating of Take-out: Good

Comments: This is an old wooden bridge. Good take-outs on
LHUS and RHDS also. Left half of river is shallow—the main channel is 40 feet wide on right.
Wooded area, could camp here. Road to bridge is
good, wide, well-packed.

PERDIDO RIVER
SECTION 2

DIRT ROAD OFF S112 TO S112

MILES: 10.0   COUNTY: Baldwin
INTERMEDIATE POINT: None
PUT-IN: See the take-out information for Section 1 for this
put-in.

TAKE-OUT: Location - LHUS   Bank - 6 feet sloping
Carry - 10 feet   Access Road - Good, sand ½ mile
on left-hand end of
bridge upstream.
Parking: Vehicles - 20-30   Location - LHUS
Type - Open, flat   Turn-around - Good
River: Width - 100 feet   Flow - Swift
General Rating of Take-out: Very Good
Comments: Take-out is 100 yards upstream from S112 bridge.
Parking area is shady, and the general area is
wooded and pretty with white sandbars in the
river. This would be a good camping spot.

PERDIDO RIVER
SECTION 3

S112 TO U. S. 90

MILES: 12.0   COUNTY: Baldwin
INTERMEDIATE POINT: None
PUT-IN: See the take-out information for Section 2 for this
put-in.

TAKE-OUT: Location - RHDS   Bank - Gentle slope
Carry - 80 feet*   Access Road - None
Parking: Vehicles - 3-4   Location - RHDS
   Type - Shoulder   Turn-around - None
River: Width - 100 feet   Flow - Slow
General Rating of Take-out: Poor
Comments: *Carry is 50 feet to base of steps at bridge abut-
ment, then 30 feet up steps. Take-out is in the
upper reaches of Perdido Bay.

NOTE: This is the lowest point on the Perdido. There is another
take-out a few miles downstream off of C91 that offers better
parking and a shorter carry, but it's private; if you want to
take-out there, you would have to get permission from the
residents.

STYX RIVER - GENERAL
BALDWIN COUNTY

The Styx River forms near Bay Minette and flows into
Perdido Bay near Seminole, Alabama, but is not big enough to
float until it approaches I-10. Even at this point it is rather narrow, but it is a pretty river with the typical sandbars and banks
of this section and without any swampy areas at the put-ins.
There is only one good ride on the river.

STYX RIVER
ALL

C64 TO U. S. 90

MILES: 14.0   COUNTY: Baldwin
INTERMEDIATE POINT: Mile 5.0 (C87)
PUT-IN: Location - LHDS   Bank - Sandbar
Carry - 50 feet   Access Road - Good, sand,
      on LH, 100 yards
      upstream of bridge
      (road goes under bridge).

253

Parking: Vehicles - 4-5   Location - LHDS
    Type - Flat, open   Turn-around - Adequate
River: Width - 75 feet   Flow - Swift
General Rating of Put-in: Fair
Comments: The river is shallow for 2/3 of its width. It has a 15 foot main channel on the right. In summer this is probably a *very* shallow area. The general location is pretty.

INTERMEDIATE POINT: (Mile 5.0, C87)
Location - LHDS   Bank - Sandbar
Carry - 150 feet   Access Road - Sand, 1/10 mile off LH, *upstream* end of bridge (road goes under bridge).
Parking: Vehicles - 10-15   Location - LHDS
    Type - Flat, open   Turn-around - Adequate
River: Width - 75 feet   Flow - Moderate
General Rating of Point as Put-in or Take-out: Fair
Comments: The general area is wooded and pretty. The river is shallow.

TAKE-OUT: Location - RHDS   Bank - Sand, ramp*
Carry - 10 feet   Access Road - Good, sand off RH *upstream* end of bridge (road goes under bridge).
Parking: Vehicles - 5-6   Location - RHDS
    Type - Flat, open   Turn-around - Adequate
River: Width - 200 feet   Flow - Slow
General Rating of Take-out: Good
Comments: *This is a public boat tie-up area. The general area is pretty, and you're just entering the upper reaches of Perdido Bay.

NOTE: This trip may be extended 1.5 miles as there is a take-out on C91 further downstream. This is a private area, however, and you will have to get permission to use it.

INDIVIDUAL RIVERS

YELLOW RIVER - GENERAL
COVINGTON COUNTY

The Yellow River forms in northwestern Covington County near Rose Hill and flows in a southwestwardly direction into Florida. Down to and including the U. S. 84 crossing near Babbie, the river is too small to float, but in the next few miles the addition of several large creeks more than doubles its size, and from the first put-in listed on down, it is a fair-sized river. After it crosses the Florida line, this river becomes part of the Florida Canoe Trails system.

YELLOW RIVER
SECTION 1

DIRT ROAD OFF OF A DIRT ROAD
BETWEEN C45 AND U. S. 331 TO S55

MILES: 16.0   **COUNTY:** Covington
INTERMEDIATE POINTS: Mile 2.2, Mile 4.5, Mile 8.5
PUT-IN: Location - RH   Bank - Boat ramp
Carry - 20 feet   Access Road* - Main road
Parking: Vehicles - 10   Location - RH
    Type - Flat, open   Turn-around - Drive around
River: Width - 40-50 feet   Flow - Swift
General Rating of Put-in: Good
Comments: This is a shady, wooded put-in. There is no bridge
         here.
*You will see two dirt roads as you turn off C45. The one to the south takes you to the put-in. The road is good.

INTERMEDIATE POINTS: All three intermediate points are not suitable for use. The one at Mile 4.5 has no parking and rough access to the river. The one at Mile 8.5 has totally overgrown and steep banks.

255

TAKE-OUT: Location - RHUS   Bank - 5 feet
Carry - 40 feet   Access Road - Good, dirt,
       ¼ mile off RHUS
       end of bridge.
Parking: Vehicles - 10-15   Location - RHUS
   Type - Flat, open   Turn-around - Good
River: Width - 60-75 feet   Flow - Swift
General Rating of Take-out: Good
Comments: The main river is on the left-hand end of the bridge. The bridge has a long approach. There are several swales in the access road.

YELLOW RIVER
SECTION 2

S55 TO C4

MILES: 15.0   COUNTY: Covington
INTERMEDIATE POINT: Mile 7.0
PUT-IN: See the take-out information for Section 1 for this put-in.

INTERMEDIATE POINT: This is a dirt road to the river. I have no information on it.

TAKE-OUT: Location - LHDS   Bank - Dirt ramp
Carry - 40 feet   Access Road - Pull-off
Parking: Vehicles - 3-4   Location - LHDS
   Type - Flat, open   Turn-around - Limited
River: Width - 75 feet   Flow - Swift
General Rating of Take-out: Fair
Comments: The next take-out is in Florida and is a part of the Florida Canoe Trails system. This take-out at C4 is next to a house, but the area at the bridge is public access—I think! Better check at the house before shuttling to this point.

LITTLE RIVER - GENERAL
BALDWIN, MONROE COUNTIES

Little River forms near Goodway in Washington County and flows westward into the Alabama River. For part of its length it forms the boundary between Washington and Escambia counties and then the boundary between Washington and Baldwin counties. Little River pretty well lives up to its name—it is little, being too small to float until it reaches the County 1 crossing at the junction of the three counties whose borders it separates. There is only one good ride on the Little River.

LITTLE RIVER
ALL

C1 TO C84 (DIXIE LANDING)

MILES: 12.0   COUNTIES: Baldwin, Monroe
INTERMEDIATE POINT: Mile 7.0 (S59)
PUT-IN: Location - RHUS   Bank - Sand, 4 feet
Carry - 10 feet   Access Road - Good, sand, 1/10 mile off RH upstream end of bridge.
Parking: Vehicles - 10-15   Location - RHUS
    Type - Flat, open   Turn-around - Good
River: Width - 40 feet   Flow - Swift
General Rating of Put-in: Good
Comments: This is a pretty, shaded wooded area with another road leading upstream to a picnic area with tables. The river has white sandbars and is shallow, with a main channel of about 10 feet. In summer this section is likely to be unfloatable.

INTERMEDIATE POINT: (Mile 7.0, S59)
Location - RHUS   Bank - Slight slope
Carry - 20 feet   Access Road - Good, sand, off RH upstream end of bridge.
Parking: Vehicles - 10   Location - RHUS
    Type - Flat, open   Turn-around - Good

Early morning start on the river.

River: Width - 60-70 feet　　　　　　　　**Flow - Swift**
General Rating of Point as Put-in or Take-out: Good
Comments: This is a roadside park, no camping allowed. It's a
　　　　　pretty wooded area. An alternate take-out is on a
　　　　　sandbar 100 yards upstream and reached by a sand
　　　　　road out of the parking area. The river is shallow.
TAKE-OUT: Location - End of road　　　　**Bank - Boat ramp**
Carry - 10 feet　　　　　　　　**Access Road - Main road**
Parking: Vehicles - 5　　　　　**Location - See comments**
　　Type - Flat, open　　　　　**Turn-around - At ramp**
River: Width - 600 feet　　　　　　　　　**Flow - Slow**
General Rating of Take-out: Good

Comments: This is a boat launch area on the Alabama River.
　　　　　Little River comes in a short distance upstream,
　　　　　and you stay on the left of the Alabama to the
　　　　　take-out. Ask where to park so you'll be out of the
　　　　　way of the fishing boat traffic.

ESCATAWPA RIVER - GENERAL
MOBILE COUNTY

The Escatawpa River forms near Yellow Pine, Alabama, in Washington County, and flows generally southward into Mobile County, then turns west into Mississippi. The river is too small for floating (or lacks put-ins) down to C96 in Mobile County.

The two rides here carry you only to the Mississippi line. The put-ins are in dry, sandy places and generally very pretty.

ESCATAWPA RIVER
SECTION 1

C96 TO MASON FERRY ROAD

MILES: 10.0   COUNTY: Mobile
INTERMEDIATE POINT: Mile 4 (Dirt Road off S217 at junction of S217 and C21)
PUT-IN: Location - RHUS   Bank - Sand beach
Carry - 300 feet   Access Road - None
Parking: Vehicles - 2   Location - RHUS
    Type - Shoulder   Turn-around - In road
River: Width - 75 feet   Flow - Swift
General Rating of Put-in: Poor
Comments: This is in a wooded area. The river is very shallow with lots of sandbars—some with trees growing on them. The main channel is on the left. You will have to wade to the main channel.

INTERMEDIATE POINT: (Mile 4)
Location - LHDS   Bank - Sandbar
Carry - 30 feet steep   Access Road - None; pull off by bridge.
Parking: Vehicles - 5-10   Location - LHDS
    Type - Pull-off   Turn-around - In road
River: Width - 75 feet   Flow - Swift
General Rating of Point as Put-in or Take-out: Good
Comments: The river is shallow with big sandbars in the water but has a deeper channel. The dirt road out to this point is good.

TAKE-OUT: Location - LHUS   Bank - Sandbar
Carry - 70 feet   Access Road - None, pull off
                                                    at end of bridge.
Parking: Vehicles - 5   Location - LHUS
    Type - Pull-off   Turn-around - Adequate
River: Width - 60-70 feet   Flow - Swift
General Rating of Take-out: Good

Comments: The take-out is on a big white sandbar on your left, in a curve just as you come in sight of the old wooden bridge. This is a pretty, shady area and would make a good camping area.

ESCATAWPA RIVER
SECTION 2

MASON FERRY ROAD TO U. S. 98

MILES: 13.0   COUNTY: Mobile
INTERMEDIATE POINT: None
PUT-IN: See the take-out information for Section 1 for this put-in.

TAKE-OUT: Location - LHUS   Bank - Dirt ramp, steep
Carry - 40 feet   Access Road - Good, sand, 1/10
                                                    mile on left
                                                    upstream of bridge.
Parking: Vehicles - 10-15   Location - LHUS
    Type - Flat, open   Turn-around - Good
River: Width - 100 feet   Flow - Swift
General Rating of Take-out: Good

Comments: The river forms an "S" here, with the bridge at the downstream end of the "S" and the take-out on the upstream at the beginning of the "S." You cannot see the bridge from the take-out. There are some pretty sandbars here, and the shady parking area would make a good camping spot. The U. S. 98 bridge is in Mississippi, so this is your last take-out in Alabama.

WHY I DIDN'T INCLUDE SOME RIVERS!

I have already explained (twice: in Part I and Part III) why a lot of the smaller rivers and streams are not included in this book. Here's why a few of the major ones, major at least in size, are also missing.

Tennessee River—This river is just too big to paddle. Wind and boat traffic would quickly take all the joy out of it.

Tensaw and Mobile Rivers—The same comments as the Tennessee—just too much boat traffic. These are good rivers to play Huck Finn on, however, until the tide catches you.

Tombigbee—From the Mobile River up to Demopolis, there's too much boat traffic, and the river is too big for my liking. Floaters have a hard time where motor boats are active. Above Demopolis, well, I just didn't get to it.

Alabama, Coosa—Both are too big and too full of dams and lakes. Portions of the Alabama could still be enjoyable, however.

Black Warrior—Just read all the above comments which apply up to about Port Birmingham. The river is fairly well covered down to near this point.

Chattahoochee—Portions of it would be OK—but I didn't get around to it. The rest of it is too dammed and too full of motors.

The Blackwater River—Despite appearing so prominently on road maps, the Blackwater is too small and too shallow for floating until it reaches C91 in Baldwin County. This is a fair put-in, but unfortunately there is no public access take-out below it unless you paddle far down in Perdido Bay (the wide part) or paddle back up the Perdido to the Styx.

FISHING

A person with great experience in selling books has suggested to me that I include some information on fishing the various streams of Alabama. As this person is the publisher of this book, I feel somewhat constrained to do as he says even though I know nothing about fishing.

Alabama streams, creeks, and rivers listed in this book, as well as most of the others in the state that are not listed in this book, do have fish in them. If you're a fisherman and you're smart and lucky, and if you're at the right place at the right time with the right equipment, you'll probably catch them! If you're not all the above, then you'll still enjoy the floating down the river!

About the Author

John Foshee, who began canoeing in the 1960s, has run the gamut from whitewater to downriver racing to wilderness cruising. He is co-founder and past-president of one of the largest and longest lasting canoe clubs in the Southeast and has been an active member in several other canoeing groups. He has taught solo and tandem river canoeing in these groups, for the University of Alabama at Birmingham, and privately.

A photographer, draftsman, log-home builder, and writer, he is the author of numerous outdoor-oriented articles, a "how-to" book *You, Too, Can Canoe,* and the popular guide to the canoeing waters of Alabama, *Alabama Canoe Rides and Float Trips.*